MANHATTAN: Seeds of the Big Apple

GLORIA WALDRON HUKLE

Bloomington, IN Milton Keynes, UK

authorHOUSE

AuthorHouse™
1663 Liberty Drive, Suite 200
Bloomington, IN 47403
www.authorhouse.com
Phone: 1-800-839-8640

AuthorHouse™ UK Ltd.
500 Avebury Boulevard
Central Milton Keynes, MK9 2BE
www.authorhouse.co.uk
Phone: 08001974150

First published by AuthorHouse 6/20/2006

ISBN: 1-4259-4260-1 (sc)
ISBN: 1-4259-4261-X (dj)

Library of Congress Control Number: 2006905321

Printed in the United States of America
Bloomington, Indiana

This book is printed on acid-free paper.

For Julie
Kate and Cassie

Remember the Past, but embrace the Future

PREFACE

The pioneering Dutch of the seventeenth century, who sailed to ancient North American shores and settled within the Dutch West India's colony of New Netherlands, would forever refer to their heart's home as "Fatherland."

Initially, wealthy men such as Amsterdam merchant, Kiliaen Van Rensselear invested heavily in the colonial venture, yet they were never to set foot upon New Netherlands' soil. Instead, the investor or patroon sent managers or agents who acted as overseers for their master's vast bowerie farms, where indentured servants as well as Negro and Native American slaves worked the acreage. Soon, families of both freedmen and indentured servants from many countries were enthusiastically welcomed by the Dutch authorities, and a colorful, multifaceted society like no other was begun.

Many of the Europeans, who established what was to become all of the State of New York, as well as part of the States of New Jersey and Connecticut, were common folk hoping to rise above what they had been in their birth land. Those who met the original settlers—Native Americans known as Esopus, Wickquasseek, Cayuga and Manhattan Island people—came to America with a great desire to renew their lives. History was to prove them far from ordinary.

Although the official religious doctrine of the colony was Calvinist, the Dutch New Netherlands was home to Catholic, Jew, Quaker, and other religious sects as well.

Those living in the colony that were held in bondage served a variety of merchants, clergy and soldiers, many of whom were employees of the great Dutch West India Company, the governing strong arm of the entire Dutch penetration in North America.

This is a story of the struggle of one immigrating family as it mingled amid the searing cultural diversities of their own time. The account is devoted to those whose light burned brightly for a time in America over three hundred years ago, but whose existence has all but been erased from history.

The following pages are a remembrance of all who have ever lived on the land the Algonquin called, Mahikan... Island of Rolling Hills. The Europeans translated it, Manhattan.

ONE

Two years before, if anyone had told her that she would leave her family and travel to the other end of the earth before she was twenty-five, Tennake would have thought that the poor soul had lost all wit. She loved the glorious golden city of Amsterdam, and would call Holland, "Fatherland" until the day she died. However, girlhood dreams did not always set the path of one's future, as she now knew.

The vessel, Princess, sailed upon the vast, glistening waters of late summer. As Tennake struggled for balance, the ship's sway rocked the unborn child within her swollen body. The child pressed gently against her ribs, a subtle reminder that like it or not, many changes would soon come. Leaning back against the man to whom she was joined in holy matrimony less than a year before, she felt his protective arm around her as his caressing long fingers firmly encompassed all of her right hand. Her pleasure could not be measured as she turned to look up into his face.

"The worst is behind us," he reassured her, his eyes remaining focused ahead upon the distant shoreline.

"Behind us," she whispered to the sea, wondering how her beloved came to be known as Resolved. 'Twas a fitting name to be given him, she bemused.

Could his mother have known the man from the babe that grew within her womb, or did she look into the small peeping eyes of her infant son and thereupon know his destiny? Did she then apply to Resolved a title, which would be a prophecy? Or, did the child grow into a man who had blossomed in his mother's heart, thus fulfilling the prophecy long before the birth?

She felt her belly. Would her child inherit the mystic charm of his father? If this babe be a boy, would he, too, speak words of persuasion leading yet another from her father's table? And, what if the child be a daughter? In what far corner of the world would she give birth to her babe? Such were her thoughts as she closed her eyes recalling their first meeting.

What maid would not enjoy his countenance? She chided herself for her lack of modesty in wondering how many maids before her had welcomed the attentions of her new husband while he was without a wife.

How many had felt his long amber whiskers against the softness of their face or the lips of his firm mouth upon their own? Who among them would not follow him if asked; but it was hard to believe that this staunch Hollander had chosen the slight daughter of a minister. A murmur of excitement interrupted her quiet thinking.

"Me sees the land! Look Tenny!" Resolved shouted.

Tennake cupped her eyes shading the imposing glare of the sun, but although earlier several ship masts seemed to appear along the horizon, she still barely saw the line of the land that they were to call home, the place that had been promised as a wondrous Garden of Eden.

Resolved called her Tenny from the first, yet was careful to address her as Tennake, her true Christian name, in front of her parents. In the privacy of their bedchamber he whispered, "little songbird," though to all other ears she was addressed as Mistress Waldron or Wife. Today he had undoubtedly forgotten himself completely.

A few moments passed and then she saw the distant shoreline. Shipmates were bursting into uncontrollable laughter at the sight of the grand windmill; and as the points of Fort New Amsterdam came into view everyone aboard were overcome with jubilation. Clutching one another, men and women alike were shedding tears against a backdrop of boisterous crewmen. After eight long, frightening weeks of suffering the foul odor of their own flesh and soiled clothing, fighting disease and death, they now rejoiced that their trail of horror had come to an end.

Tennake wondered what were the thoughts of her husband. His narrowed, brown eyes glowed with such intensity of purpose; as though he was Moses caught up in complete rapture before the burning bush. Did he think of his older brother, Joseph Michael, who lay buried within this foreign island's soil? According to correspondence her husband had received from his sister-in-law six months ago, the widow had remarried and relocated to Kent Island, a few days walking journey from the Manhattans. Resolved was eager to find her and anxious to see that his brother's children and their mother were well cared for.

Suddenly, thoughts of family dimmed as she was summoned in spirit toward the fragrant sea air, an agreeable clarity that she could not recall nor identify from any of her past memories. Once more she breathed deeply, thus taking into her soul all that her senses could absorb, allowing the distant island to call to her, as did the sirens of old to lost sailors. Although frightened, in some strange way she was already a willing captive of this exotic land. They had arrived in America at the Dutch West India Company's colony called, New Netherlands.

During the journey, she had heard the stories of fierce wild men that lived upon the island of the Manhattans and within the sweet woodlands, but now she pushed away her misgivings. She longed for an hour in a room alone with a solid floor beneath her feet, a place where she might cleanse herself and hang a new herbal sweet bag about her neck.

Foolish prideful thoughts, she chided herself once again as her husband's three children ran toward them. Moving as quickly as her enlarged, awkward body allowed, she caught the smallest, three year old Aeltie, whose silky, golden braids danced around her shoulders.

Young Will had also sprung forward in pursuit of his youngest sister, though still protectively holding onto the hand of yet another most unwilling maid, his sister Rebecca, a sturdy, rosy-cheek six-year-old who greatly resembled her father. Tennake had given her holy oath that these children would be cared for as though they were of her own body, a task she has learned during the past weeks that shall not be easily accomplished.

With a sigh of relief, she saw that Resolved's young brother, Joseph Adam, had also noticed the rambunctious children and quickly scooped up Rebecca, her white cap flying away before she could catch it. Observing her new family, Tennake silently recalled how she had been noticed so many months before. She had been introduced to her husband at a funeral feast that they both attended. The week following the funeral, father had brought this man to their home and quietly explained that Resolved's wife, the former Rebecca Hendricks, had been taken to God Almighty at the early age of twenty-eight, leaving him a widower with three small children.

Resolved Waldron was a man well past forty, of some position having served as a soldier and then a surveyor for the Dutch West India Company of Holland. He had lived in the Company's colony in Brazil with his wife and children, but returned to his homeland after the Portuguese had taken the colony away from Holland. Despite this, he had planned to return to the Fatherland because his wife was ailing and he had hoped that the climate of their birth land would provide a cure. Sadly, the climate had not improved her health, and she died two days after their ship had come into the harbor at Amsterdam.

After the death of his wife, he entered into a printing trade partnership in the city of Amsterdam with his younger brother, Joseph Adam, working almost exclusively for the Dutch West India Company.

Tennake's father, Barent Nagel, a devout Calvinist minister, had seen a great light flowing within this widower from the very first. He was impressed with this big man who had fearlessly traveled to many ports and was held in the highest esteem with his company. Resolved Waldron was also a solid worshipping member of their church, a steadfast Calvinist, which as far as any good Dutch knew was the only true faith.

Tennake understood that it would not be unusual for an aging father with an unmarried daughter to place a keen eye upon such a man, yet a concerned parent must move expediently since most widowers were pressed to remarry quickly, usually within a matter of weeks. Love might come later if the marriage was agreeable, but the necessity of obligations was the rule. Resolved Waldron needed a young, strong woman to be the mother of his children, one who would bear him more healthy babes.

Her parents had been fortunate to have found themselves blessed with a harmonious marriage, and wishing the same for all their children, had smiled upon the widower. Tennake's mother expressed pity for the babes who were cared for by Mistress Till, a stern, bitter, little strip of a woman, a teacher with a harsh tongue and no heart, whose husband had died from a fever years before. Tennake assumed that her Mother jested when she considered whether the husband had died from a fever or the woman had poisoned him.

Tennake's father led all his flock both in his home and his church in the love of the Almighty with fortitude. His one great domestic desire was to see his last unmarried daughter speak her vows before he departed this world. She was his seventh daughter, twenty-three years of age and unmarried.

Dominie Nagel was in the habit of praying zealously to end daughter number seven's unfortunate state of solitude, often glancing at her with sad anxious eyes, which caused Tennake to move restlessly in her chair. Her maidenhood was more than he could take to eternity, and Tennake was never allowed to forget that she was growing older by the hour. Unresolved business was what her sisters called her. It seemed that to find her a husband was the campaign of her entire family. Of course, after the initial meeting, her father invited Resolved to the house often, but at first her heart did not sing with the prospect of this man as suitor. Although he had a fine countenance, forty-three seemed a lifetime older than she.

Having experienced all that he had before her, what would Resolved Waldron have left to share with an inexperienced young bride who knew little of the world and nothing of child rearing? She had expressed her concern to her mother, who thought her a silly shallow girl to speak thus. Her mother found his advanced years appealing, certainly an advantage to a sheltered young woman, which her daughter had been. Far better to marry an experienced man of the world than an inexperienced boy, her mother had jested, advising her not to put her nose up in the air.

Mother reminded her that most of her sisters and her brother had been born to her and her husband after he was more than forty years. "Think more of your Christian duty and be grateful for this blessing of a holy God, who has given you this opportunity to mother these orphans," her mother admonished.

All that was left to a young maid after a suitor had been accepted by her parents was that she respected their choice. Still, until the sacred vow was spoken there was always hope, Tennake had confided to her dearest friend, Cornelia.

Often, Resolved would bring along his younger brother, Joseph to dine at the home of her parents. Despite her family's concern, Tennake still thought herself in the blush of youth and, in the beginning preferred the younger brother to the older widower, for Joseph had never taken a wife. He was without the burden of three young children clinging to his limbs. However, Joseph was a dreamer, whilst if he did have a thought to pursue a wife, it could not be her because he quickly understood that Resolved was the suitor and had chosen Tennake Nagel to suit him.

Upon the third or fourth visit to her father's house, Tennake began to be glad of heart that Resolved had taken a liking to her. She had grown bored with the gentle, soft-spoken younger Waldron, who nearly always buried his nose in one of her father's divinity books in his library after the meal had been eaten.

In contrast, the widower always had an amusing tale to tell, a story from his colorful past to be enjoyed with the wine and the cheese after the cloth had been removed from the table. When Resolved Waldron sat down to dine, none in attendance could be sorrowful, for the room rolled with laughter.

The man had a thousand stories to tell of great manor houses and his work upon vast sugar plantations in Brazil, as well as bloody battles fought long ago beside the great hero Peter Stuyvesant. His adventures left the women wincing and then applauding the valor of their countryman.

It was after one such meal that the expected jovial discourse became an unexpected announcement of change. Her family had gathered together to celebrate her father's birthday and sat contentedly awaiting another of the widower's robust tales; but, instead, Resolved had grown somber.

He disclosed that he was to sail within six months to New Netherlands in America, the Dutch colony that was owned and operated by the merchant's Dutch West India Company. He would take his children, his brother Joseph, and hopefully a wife to this new land.

In front of everyone, Resolved had looked directly into her eyes, and boldly straight into her heart.

"If you agree, Tennake, I would take you for my wife," he said.

All were silent while twenty pairs of eyes awaited the correct response with her answer. The unmarried seventh daughter would provide the best of all the tales that had been told over the last weeks. And it was spoken more swiftly than she would have believed that she could speak.

Yes, she would become his wife.

Resolved told them that the offer had come directly from a high official in the Dutch West India Company. No one found this surprising because many colonists who had been in Brazil were now being encouraged to colonize the sparsely populated Company lands. It was extremely difficult to find Hollanders to relocate to the colonies and the Company needed the talented experience of men such as the Waldron's in New Netherlands.

He and his brother had been well educated and spoke English as well as Dutch and some Latin. English would be especially appreciated since the colony's five thousand inhabitants were bordered by over thirty thousand English colonists on both the north, the New England colony, and the south, the English Virginia colony.

This voyage to New Netherlands was to be a true family venture: an aging adventurer who would seize a second chance with gratitude, and a new adventure for Joseph who was promised plenty of printing work. Resolved had assured Joseph that he would soon need the help of an indentured man since he could no longer be his brother's partner.

As for Tennake, she was to be a new addition to this body of Waldrons.

Tennake could not imagine her new brother-in-law wanting to leave the beauty and gracious society of Amsterdam to build a life in the harsh unknown wilds. In truth, she herself had no desire to leave Holland, but her duty stood clearly in front of her. At her age, how many more proposals of marriage would there be? Most probably this was her last offer.

Resolved had declared his intent to wed her, but she sensed that Joseph was not in favor of the marriage. She could not understand this at all because she had showed him every courtesy and kindness.

But Joseph enjoyed taunting her when out of earshot of the others. One afternoon he caught her alone in the garden where he read her a passage out of one of his own books that he had brought along to share with her father.

Smiling sweetly he read the words of the Englishman, Robert Herrick, translating the verse into the Dutch as he went along.

Gather ye rosebuds while ye may;
Old Time is still a-flying
And this same flower that smiles today
Tomorrow will be dying...

On the last verse Joseph's voice rose ever so slightly.

Then be not coy, but use your time;
And while ye may, to marry:
For having lost but once your prime,
You may forever tarry.

She had refused to allow Joseph to lord over her and quickly caught her wit, replying demurely that she wondered to whose prime he did indeed refer. With her head held high she walked away from her future kinsman and rejoined her husband. It was the last time Joseph made any attempt to mock her.

She would go to America, but oh, how she would miss the brilliantly colored tulips that waved gently against the tall lush green grasses that grew so peacefully outside of her father's home.

The Dutch had long been the masters of all maritime commerce of the world, and her father's house enjoyed the good fortune that had been provided to Holland's citizens during these prosperous times. The Nagel family was not considered people of great wealth, but their great wooden carved Kas held shelves stacked high with goods reflecting an abundance that was unknown in other seventeenth century countries. There was no wharf in the entire world that was too small for Dutch ships to venture into so that they might serve the Dutch merchant.

Tennake had never thought of leaving the Fatherland. She had always thought that when she married it would be to a neighboring member of the church. She had planned to grow old in Amsterdam side by side with her friends, sharing the delights of their children and grandchildren, and then a long way down this familiar road would come her death in Christ. She would be buried in the sacred ground of their cemetery, lying peacefully beside her husband, mother, and father.

Why could her last proposal not be one that stayed in Holland? The only answer was as her mother had told her. It was the Lord Almighty's will.

Though she dreaded the day of departure, she looked forward to her wedding with great expectations, for her love for the widower continued to grow and he seemed to find her very pleasing. Still, her uncle, Thomas Cole told stories of life in the Virginia wilderness that came to her as she slept and often she awakened with her nightdress soaked through.

Uncle Thomas was not a blood kinsman, but a dear friend of her father whom Tennake had addressed as uncle since her childhood. The restless son of generations of poor English farmers, Thomas went to North America as a bondman when he was not yet twenty. He had long dreamed of becoming a king in a new land where, as the advertisements said, the gold was to be picked up from the streets.

He signed himself over to the Virginia Company, but upon arriving in the New World he found no gold, but plenty of work twelve hours a day, six days a week for seven years until his debt for his ship's passage had been paid.

When his seven years of service had been completed, he was offered a position working for meager wages on a tobacco plantation which was owned by a physician and located two miles away from a small village called Henricus, forty miles from the Jamestown settlement. With this opportunity to work for the physician and save for a small piece of land to be his own kingdom, Thomas Cole thought that his life would finally turn around.

The village overlooked the great James River, where because of the healthy air, the English had built a hospital with over forty beds where they nourished the sick and sea-weary back to health after enduring the voyage.

Uncle Thomas had declared that if a man was fortunate enough to survive the voyage from England to the Virginia colony in those times, he could not count his blessings until he had lived through a seasoning, as was called going through the first time of suffering from the summer fever of the New World.

After living near Henricus for two years, tragedy struck that community when every man, woman and child was massacred by heathen. Fortunately, Thomas and the colonists living on the outlying farms had escaped.

Later, when the neighboring farmers had discovered the slain inhabitants of Henricus, the grotesquely mutilated bodies were a horror beyond all civilized imagination. Twenty-nine year old Thomas had been one of those who buried the remains of his friends, and the terrible memory of their tortured remains haunted him for the rest of his life.

As anxious as he had been to arrive in North America, he was more eager to depart the place. He left that hollow of destruction and returned to safe, prosperous Holland along with his Dutch wife, a girl whom he had married the year before the massacre. Her family had been runaways from the settlement of Christina of the New Netherlands colony.

Although Tennake knew it was useless to convey her fears to her father, she had done so, whereupon he had assured her that these were old tales. As he soothingly patted her hand, Barent Nagel told her that the present New Amsterdam could not be compared to that pitiful English village that had existed some thirty-five years before. "Nay, nay, you will be under the safe protection of your good husband while traveling to the Dutch colony. It is a powerful civilized place supported by the great West India Company. Thousands of settlers live there."

In the city of New Amsterdam there were over fifteen hundred residents, all protected by a strong fortress which was manned by hundreds of soldiers under the command of Peter Stuyvesant who had personally requested Mr. Waldron to join him in command.

Dominie Nagel had prayed about all of this and when he questioned the safety of the colony, he was told that the wild men of the forest had a covenant of trade with the Dutch that had existed for many years and there was peace between them. Assured of his daughter's safety, he saw the marriage as an opportunity for a bright future as mistress of the house of a fine Christian man who firmly believed in his company's motto, "Unity makes Strength."

The day that Tennake took her vow of marriage, she stood before God and man without reservation. She looked at her new husband through eyes of love, happily experiencing the passion of the marriage bed from the first night, rather than enduring a union of convenience which was made by so many girls, including some of her well-meaning sisters.

The date of their wedding held great significance as they were wed on May 10th, which was also her husband's birthday. He spoke most sweetly to his young bride on their wedding night while he stroked her softly, bidding her not to fear his caress. He teased her that she was a birthday gift from Almighty God. His ardor was most unrelenting, his love so powerfully given that soon into the marriage she had found herself with child.

Shortly after, they took passage upon the Princess, and Tennake Waldron felt her heart pressed between two rocks, the larger side of which she felt would always remain in Holland with her mother and father, her handsome brother Johannes, and her flighty sisters.

Oh, Mother, she had thought as tears filled her eyes the night before they were to board the ship. Will I ever see thy sweet face again? She would never again lovingly stroke the veins of her mother's capable hands or feel the warmth of her strong, yet tender embrace. How she would miss her father's three-hour sermons, lessons in faith that she and her sisters complained of secretly.

The morning of departure they had all gone to the place called Criers Tower in Amsterdam–Resolved and his brother Joseph, Resolved's children, her mother and father, four of her sisters and her brother. Dearest to her, next to her family, was her friend since the cradle, Cornelia Cole, who now walked with her arm in arm. Tennake was glad that Cornelia, as usual, chattered constantly without allowing her a word in-between, for that was the way Tennake wished to remember the one who had shared her girlhood giggles, secrets, and hopes.

The oarsmen accompanying three small rowing boats pulled the vessels securely to the little wharf. While she waited, her husband and his brother helped little Aeltie, Rebecca, and young Will into one of the small boats. Two other families were also making the voyage to the New World. The appointed time had come.

Tennake turned to be embraced one last time by her father, who whispered final words of love and courage in her ear. She took hold of her mother, who held her head high.

"Courage," her mother said. "Always remember who you are."

Tennake did not miss the expression of loving loss in her mother's eyes, though her lips were curved upward toward the heavens as she released her daughter and returned to the waiting supportive arms of her own aging mate.

She recalled the lonesome despair that descended upon her as she looked back toward the cluster of her four sisters.

Finally, when Resolved gently lifted her into his boat, she could not hold back her tears although she had vowed that she would not show her family a sad remorseful face at last glance. As their small boat was rowed away toward the Princess, she felt about her the strong arms of the man who must now replace father, mother, brother, and friend.

She did not turn around although she could hear the cries of her family on the shore behind her. She never saw the shore disappear; yet she felt the distance. Soon they had boarded the giant vessel that would be their home for many weeks. As the wind filled the sails she was all too swiftly carried away from everything she had ever known.

During the voyage, over seventy passengers ate and slept side by side, many falling ill—some dying—as had Marie Van Tassel whose body was then thrown into the sea, leaving her bereaved husband and two young babes to go on alone to their new life in the wilderness. After Marie's death, Tennake dreamed of the body sinking to the depths of the blackest part of the sea, where it became food for the fearful creatures that lurked below the rocks.

Five other souls had gone to the Lord that way, including Adam Dackaert's two-year old child. The babe's mother could be heard wailing pitifully for two weeks after, and the pain of her loss clung to all of them. A retired Captain returning home to New Amsterdam made an effort to cheer everyone during the voyage by offering optimistic tales of adventure.

In an endeavor to keep their minds from the devil's play, he told them of the Englishman, Hendrick Hudson, who, in 1609, sponsored by their good Dutch monies, had sailed his vessel named, "Half-Moon," along with a crew of eighteen to the land they were all to call their homeland.

Likewise, Captain Bergen enthralled them with the story of the renowned Dutch explorer, Adraen Block, who, sent by a group of merchants from their own magnificent city of Amsterdam, made two voyages to New Netherlands. On his second trip, his vessel called, "Tiger" was burned in the harbor, thus forcing them all to stay for the winter, which they had survived only by the grace of God and the help of good natives.

In the spring the crew built another vessel, which they called, "Restless." When they arrived back in Holland, these men extolled the glory of a wonderful new land that overflowed with beaver, lumber, and vast areas, which abounded with friendly savages that called themselves, Manhattans. In 1621, the Dutch West India Company was formed for the good and prosperity of trade with this new land.

As Tennake stared upon the new lands of which Captain Bergen had spoken, sixteen-year old Elizabeth Beekman, who was traveling with her brother, John, came and stood by her side. She put her arm affectionately about Aeltie as the child looked up at her and smiled. Tennake knew the Beekmans would not be staying in New Amsterdam, but would continue by sloop up the North River to the distant post of Beaverwyck where they would join their eldest brother who had gone over three years earlier. Little Aeltie had taken Elizabeth's hand and Tennake realized how sad she would be to see her go.

"'Tis a sight for sore eyes. Is it not?" Elizabeth asked.

"Thank God that we are alive to see it," Tennake replied.

Elizabeth nodded.

"Will your eldest brother come to meet you in New Amsterdam?" Tennake asked.

"Nay, he stays in Beaverwyck village in the north of the colony, but we shall go to him as soon as is possible.

"But happy am I for this day, and I will thank God not to see another hammock strung for the rest of my life, though you be the fortunate one nestled safely in your settle bed every night," Elizabeth jested.

Tennake rolled her eyes. "I should count my blessings methinks." She folded her hands about her belly.

Her friend laughed and wandered off to her brother.

Tennake could now plainly see the twin-peaked church roof that reached toward the heavens from within the protection of the planked walls of the Fort, as well as a row of little yellow brick houses peeking out of the center of a thick forest.

Half-naked savages rowed through crystal clear waters toward their ship in strange low vessels, and Tennake marveled at the vast schools of fish that swam curiously nearby the ship. While she recalled the dirty murky waters of Holland, Resolved leaned toward her and whispered, "The heathen vessels are called dugouts."

Soon their ship anchored and they gradually made their way in the little ship-to-shore craft, Pinnance toward the small wharf called Schreiger's Hook. As the oarsmen rowed, everyone was comforted by the sight of colorful sails of blue and white stripes adorning several Dutch ships that passed by, for although it was a far cry from the "forest of masts" in the Amsterdam harbor, their souls awakened as they viewed this familiar display of their Fatherland's maritime banners.

Later, Tennake wrote to Cornelia:

"From first sight of land, till the last night of the last dream, my dear friend, I shall recall my feelings upon viewing those glorious sails blowing so proudly upon our arrival. 'Tis no longer a dream, Cornelia—we have arrived, and it appears that God Almighty has made his choice. We have not been swallowed up by the devil seas!"

TWO

Resolved anxiously led his family around the disembarking crowd of new colonists and onward through a cluster of forty or more seasoned settlers who had come down to the wharf to greet the arrival of the vessel, "Princess." He would learn that bidding welcome to a ship from home was a common pastime for the citizens of the city of New Amsterdam.

Judith Stuyvesant, wife of the honorable Peter Stuyvesant, rarely missed this occasion to dress in her grandest attire while she presented herself to be viewed by the newcomers as "Mistress of the Island of Manhattans." Women passengers craned their necks in order that they might be able to get a good look at their fashionable royal, as well as scrutinize the plain female folk waiting apprehensively by the shore for letters from family that may have just arrived.

While his brother eagerly searched the crowd for the face that was the last connecting link in the chain of their journey, Resolved strained his eyes past Mistress Stuyvesant's lace-trimmed, black silk gown, which was appropriately drawn back exposing a red silk petticoat underneath. He smiled broadly as he glanced over the equally vivid colorful silks that adorned the three young dark African girls who stood in attendance beside their mistress.

"Do you see Augustine, Joseph?" he shouted.

"Do not fear big brother," Joseph shouted back over the noise of the crowd. "Augustine will find us for he wrote that he would meet us upon arrival; and praise God, we have done so. Have you not defended his loyal attributes a thousand times?"

"Yes, I have. I would do so again, though it would be my misfortune that my old friend would fail me this one time."

"Your fears outweigh your faith."

"Ah, methinks to see him. Yes, there!" Resolved pointed.

Joseph was laughing. "God give us strength! Look at him!"

Relieved, Resolved turned toward his wife, pulling at her sleeve while motioning toward a finely dressed, prosperous looking gentleman, wearing gray plush breeches, colorful red waistcoat, and large broad-rimmed hat decorated with pheasant's feathers. Flanked by several Negroes, the affluently attired colonist waved wildly, urging Resolved forward.

"Augustine Herrman looks to be doing well, for his belly has grown as fat as his purse methinks," Resolved observed amusingly as he eagerly acknowledged his friend's greeting.

"He is dressed high and mighty," Joseph replied. "And, look at the fine Negro who waits on him. The girl is a striking wench, is she not?"

"He is grand, and she is indeed a young bloom."

"Sixteen, be she that," Joseph mused.

Resolved noted the sheepish look upon his brother's face. "Joseph, have you only noticed the wench?"

"I am not blind, but I take no pleasure in the countenance of the great black man that is with her."

Tennake could not hear the discourse between her husband and his brother as they rushed to meet the man whom she assumed was none other than Mr. Herrman. She was having a difficult time trying to keep her husband clearly in sight while at the same moment keeping an astute eye upon young wandering Will.

However, she did note with interest the mysterious dark people that accompanied several of these American colonists.

She had rarely seen any of their kind before, but perceived these people to be African Negroes who were often used as slaves in the colonies. She had listened with fascination to the many stories that her husband had related of his life in Brazil, but nothing seemed to stir her soul, as did the stories that Resolved told of the Africans.

Years before, in her native Holland, she saw an African man as he walked beside his master on a street in old Amsterdam. She recalled that he was as finely dressed as his master. Everyone knew that there was little call for the service of Negro slaves in her homeland because Holland was a nation of merchants, bankers, craftsmen, clergy, and adventurous mariners.

If servitude was required upon their large dairy farms, a bound man or two might be found there. Other higher bound labor positions were eagerly sought after and filled by fourteen-year-old apprentices, sons of wealthier citizens who apprenticed them to become merchants or bankers. The middle class sent their sons to be trained in the trades where they would also learn to read, correctly wield their pens and cipher.

Tennake also observed the black-skinned maids clad in red silk while recalling her beloved father's opinion on the subject of enslavement.

She remembered the discourse that had transpired between him, Resolved, and herself one Sunday afternoon, as her suitor spoke of this form of Negro labor, which he had observed while employed at the plantation in Brazil.

Her father, who was against any form of bondage, passionately felt that it was a sin to take a man from his family, lock him into chains and make him a slave. Tennake could still hear his exact words:

"Though they be heathen without benefit of baptism, they still be men."

The Dominie had persisted, insisting that it was against God's holy will to steal—an offence, which in all civilized understanding would be considered crime.

Resolved had grimaced, but her father went further.

"'Tis a sad sack that is filled with hopeless tears. Only the most fortunate of the Africans taken may see freedom in their old age if they have been good loyal servants to their masters. But as we both know, these servants are not eligible for their freedom until twenty years of service have been given to their lords and most shall never see that glorious day."

Her father had then proposed a question to Resolved. "If a Dutchman steals a cow or another man's boat, do we not fine him or banish the thief for the offense? Does this thief not have to make amends to God and his fellow citizen? He is fortunate not to have his right hand burned, whereupon he then would lose the good use of it to make his living and be forced into the street to beg his bread.

"Yet, consider that men of God who profess to love the Lord God Almighty steal other men and then profit from their transgression as though their goods were a shipment of spice. I grieve and sorrow for them, for God and all his angels and saints will judge their souls for partaking of this devil's trade."

Tennake had shifted her weight uncomfortably.

Resolved took a harder view of the matter, though he did not argue with the father of the woman he would soon marry. He had agreed that it may not be the way of the righteous, but did not consider the keeping of a slave a sin unless the master treated his servants badly, without justice. Who could blame the master of a great plantation if he looked to the Negro workers since it was difficult to obtain help from Europe, especially Holland, where times were so good, and it took fifty to one hundred workers to operate a good size farm in the colonies.

Her father began to shake his head dolefully when Resolved supported the plantation owner by insisting that slaves of one country or another had been used for over a thousand years and were but a reasonable supply of labor for the success of a plantation. He related that he had known many overseers on the sugar plantations in Brazil who would prefer to leave the Africans in Africa since it had been his observation that the Negro is wild and troublesome to train.

"It is more desirable to have a worker who speaks our language and knows our customs than for an overseer to struggle to communicate the simplest command to a wild savage," Resolved had commented.

Tennake took a deep breath. She would now live among these savages from Africa and the wild men born upon this soil, which surrounded her. She pulled Rebecca and Aeltie closer, silently asking God for courage.

Resolved greeted Augustine Herrman with such a warm robust embrace that the man's grand hat fell from his head. Time apart had not diminished the regard the two held for one another. Tennake knew that Augustine Herrman was possibly the only other soul in the world, other than kin, that her husband considered a loyal friend. Mr. Herrman was the same age as her husband with long, dark brown, wavy hair that framed a round, plump face. He had a chin, followed by a second chin that melted into his neck; and Tennake smiled as she noted that both Mr. Herrman and her husband had more hair that grew upon these chins than they had growing atop their smooth heads.

The seasoned settler that had greeted them was barely over five feet tall with a thick middle attesting to just how very seasoned he had become. Tennake judged from his appearance that he had not for some time enjoyed the robust activity of those great adventures her husband raved about. But his portly manner was deceiving since he could not have been a slothful man having accomplished so much during his years.

She had been told he was a uniquely talented fellow, proving himself a fine illustrator, a surveyor, and a trusted agent for the Dutch West India Company. He also had an eye for the right investments, owning several houses in New Amsterdam and a large warehouse that he presently rented to the Dutch West India Company for storage of the tobacco they grew.

The one accomplishment that the Waldron brothers admired most about Mr. Herrman was how quickly he had become a wealthy man in this colony. Though he had inherited property from an uncle, he had more than tripled his inheritance. It was this man who had sung the song of prosperity and opportunity and had beckoned all of them to his, "land of milk and honey," or more appropriately Resolved had mused, "The land of beaver and wampum."

"New Netherlands is the most favorable place to obtain the golden life that has been lost in Brazil," Augustine had written to her husband nearly two years ago.

"The golden life," she thought sourly as she looked toward the dark young girl standing impatiently next to the merry-faced, round man. If her father could look upon this place, he would call it Sodom before he would call this cluster of barbarians after his own fine Amsterdam.

The three middle-aged men embraced with the vigor of reunited tribesmen from the Old Testament, yet Tennake thought that their eyes sparkled as though they were boys once again.

She heard Mr. Herrman bark a sharp order toward his slaves to fetch the Waldron trunk.

"We have very little to be carried," Tennake ventured modestly to Mr. Herrman.

"You will find only two trunks and our settle bed that is filled," Resolved added.

Tennake watched as the slaves ran to fetch all her worldly goods. It was a disappointment to be allowed so little to begin a new life: a few pieces of clothing, and her most precious commodity, cloth to make new garments, as the making of any fabric was strictly forbidden in the colony. She hoped that their glass panes had survived the journey.

She had also managed to squeeze into her trunk a few household items: a copper pot, six pewter plates, six spoons, and gratefully, the large bowl with the Haarlem border that had been her mother's. Of course, they had also brought along their good Dutch Bible which was safely placed in its own carved oak chest. The birth and baptisms of Resolved's children had been recorded within the Book and soon, Tennake thought lovingly; a new name would be added.

When their children married, their marriages would be recorded, and then the birth of their own children. Upon Resolved's death, the Bible would be willed to his eldest son, William, or if William died, the next eldest son, should Tennake be fortunate enough to bear sons for her husband. This was their custom for many generations.

Unmindful of proper introductions, their new neighbor abruptly whirled around to salute her. His smooth full hand clasped her own in a firm welcome, and though Tennake had been surprised by Mr. Herrman's direct manner, she could not find any offense to be taken with his hearty warmth. Though concerned that Mr. Herrman obviously believed in partaking of the devil's trade, she had begun to find him all too hilarious of nature to dislike. As he introduced himself and bent to bow, the feathers atop his grand hat brushed her lips and she nearly laughed aloud.

"A fine morning to you, Mistress Waldron, I am Augustine Herrman," he announced boldly.

"I am most pleased to meet you at long last," Tennake replied.

Without releasing his captive's hand, he looked into her eyes and with what Tennake took for much mischief declared; "I would have known Resolved Waldron's wife anywhere."

"How so?" Tennake asked curiously.

Leaning forward, Augustine whispered, "You are the only woman within my sight that I can compare to the delightful songbird. Your husband tells me that he married the most beautiful of all the songbirds, an angel to mother his orphan children."

Tennake's eyes grew wide with horror, while her cheeks could not have been so flushed since her wedding day.

Her husband had been near enough to hear his friend's teasing comment, which he knew to be of the deepest complimentary nature, though sometimes his old colleague could have an adverse affect upon women. Perhaps, Resolved thought while frowning, this was why the man had never been able to induce a maid to take the sacred vow with him.

"Augustine, Augustine, I can see that you have not mended your bothersome ways with our women!" Resolved chided amicably.

After finally releasing Tennake's hand, Augustine threw his own into the air. "Do I not speak a truth?"

Joseph could endure the scene no longer and burst into laughter. "Better to watch the hawk when near the songbird," he whispered to his older brother.

Resolved put his arm around his wife protectively. "My wife is the daughter of the godly Barent Nagel," he said proudly.

"I meant you no insult, Mistress," Augustine replied soberly.

"No insult has been taken," Tennake replied. "On the contrary, I am so happy that we have a good friend such as you here in the wilderness." She could see that Mr. Herrman wished only to please her. It was not Mr. Herrman with whom she was annoyed, but rather that her husband had written his friend something that she felt was to be for her ears only.

Amid this nest of swarming heathen, the indiscretion was but a small matter. Other concerns had come into her head and she wished only to appear gracious to this flamboyant gentleman while making a first favorable impression.

She had noticed the grand Mistress Stuyvesant looking her way and she shifted her weight uncomfortably, remembering how dirty and unseemly she and her family must appear. How could she show herself as a fine asset to the Director's wife when the smell of her own enlarged body was offensive even to herself? There was not a sweet bag in the entire world that would mask the foulness.

She felt more like a little brown sparrow than a melodious songbird. Tennake looked down at Rebecca and Aeltie.

"My husband's daughters," she said to Mr. Herrman. The girls quickly curtsied as young Will ran toward them.

"Hold yourself, son!" Resolved shouted briskly to his eldest child.

"My husband tells me that you will recall young William, here," Tennake said softly.

"I remember both William and this pretty Rebecca, although this little one I know not," Augustine said as he bent down to cup Aeltie's chin with his hand.

"This be my Aeltie," Resolved said. "My Rebecca went to the Lord Almighty soon after Aeltie was born."

Augustine stood up and looked kindly at Tennake. "I recall you writing thus, but God has been good to you, Resolved. I wish you God's blessings upon your marriage and good delivery of your child."

Tennake blushed. "Thank you," she whispered.

Looking over Tennake's head toward the commotion of the crowd, Augustine Herrman saw another New Amsterdam citizen that he wanted to introduce to the newcomers. "Samuel, over here!" he shouted above the boisterous gathering.

A man with a kindly, serious countenance appearing to be well into his fifties approached them.

"Allow me to introduce Dominie Samuel Drisius, who will be one of your neighbors. He owns a property only two houses from my own which is located within the same block where you shall be living." The tall, broad-shouldered man bowed his head.

"Samuel, this is Mr. Waldron and Mistress, who have just arrived with their children," Augustine said politely.

"It is most good to meet you," Resolved said.

"I am honored," the Dominie said gently.

"I, too, am honored," Tennake ventured shyly. "My father is Dominie Barent Nagel of Amsterdam. Do you know him?"

"I have heard his name, Mistress, though I have never had the honor of making his acquaintance personally."

"Please excuse us, as we are not presentable to make your fine acquaintance," Resolved said. "But, I will consider myself fortunate that Jesus has been merciful and sent our family a gift in the way of a pious good neighbor that may keep us all to the straight path."

"The Waldron's house is presently under construction and is only two doors from my own," Augustine added quickly.

"Yes, I know, Augustine, and I hope that we shall be good neighbors for many years, should this please Our Lord God," Dominie Drisius said.

"Let us then proceed forth," Augustine said, happy that the introductions were concluded.

Dominie Drisius walked beside Tennake. "I have seen the fine strong house that has been constructed for your family, Mistress. I watch the bricklayers lay the brick for the front of the dwelling as I pass them each day on my way to St. Nicholas church."

Tennake sighed. "I am so happy to be in a good Calvinist colony and I look forward to being of service to the church women."

The Dominie looked down at the tiny frame of his companion. His brow wrinkled with concern. "There are some matters that you should know regarding our fair colony, Mistress. Although it is true that the colony is officially Calvinist and our faith is strictly observed by our Director who strongly encourages his flock to attend service and support the church, we have people of other faiths in New Amsterdam as well.

"It is the will of our leaders in Holland that we offer a tolerant patience for those of other faiths in the colony. Alongside of good Calvinists, we also have Catholics, Jews, Puritans, Lutherans, and also a group of Anabaptists. These have been forbidden by our

Director, the goodly Peter Stuyvesant, to hold open meetings or to build a church; but we are sure that they continue to practice their religion in secret. As long as they make no effort to gather or form a church, we turn a deaf ear upon their customs. I myself pray for their souls every day.

"Alas, if the Company has chosen to throw open the doors of her house to every country in the world in order that we may fatten the settlement of this land, then we must expect an ingathering of heretics. But, fear not, Mistress, for you are a part of the one true faith which is housed within the one true religion and these heretics are under control. I have no doubt you will make many fine staunch Calvinist friends here."

"I do not concern myself with what does not concern my family, and I shall look away from the heretics," Tennake said quietly.

Upon listening to this serious and a bit uncomfortable discourse between the two, Augustine became concerned. He had only wished that his dear old friend's young wife hear glad tidings on her very first day in his city, because a happy wife brings contented joy to her man. He wished joy and contentment for Resolved as he had excellent plans for him. He had simply wanted to make the daughter of a Christian minister feel at home by his introduction.

Samuel was a good man, he thought to himself, but his gloom always left the maids shaking worse than a Quaker. God help him! There had been times when he wished that the Company would send a merry minister, if there were such a man.

"Come, Samuel, let us share good news with this mistress," Augustine said jovially. "We have a fine church here in New Amsterdam and plenty of our own with whom we might worship. Forget the heretics and let us dwell upon the good that has been accomplished within these last years.

"Very soon, Everet Duyckinck, who is an expert craftsman, will be setting in the new windows in God's house. They shall be magnificent and will make St. Nicholas as fine as any church in Europe!"

The Dominie, obviously impressed with Augustine's optimism, softened his furrowed brow much to Augustine's relief.

"The windows will be grand to be sure, Augustine, but there might be one or two churches in Europe that may compare."

Augustine wouldn't let the matter rest. "Nay, pay no heed to Samuel's humility," he told Tennake, "I tell you that Duyckinck's work will be the crowning glory to our fine church, for he will be burning into the glass of each pane the coat of arms of some of the most prominent members of this church, thus staining the glass for eternity with the most beautiful colors."

"To whose glory?" the Dominie murmured again turning a serious face toward the sky.

"Trust me, Mistress," Augustine added to Tennake, "there will not be a soul that comes to worship in St. Nicholas that does not know he is in a civilized Christian colony!"

Tennake's eyes widened. "I will be most desirous to see them," she said.

"As will I," Joseph said as he walked beside young Will.

Augustine chucked. "You should have seen this sorry town when our good Director arrived seven years ago! Of course, they sent him over to clean her up and so he has done. There was not even the smallest hint of a church when he arrived, and then he had to trick a good lot or our fattest merchants into putting up their money to build one.

"He waited until they were all happy with their fill of wine at a wedding feast before he asked them to make their pledge for construction. You can imagine their surprise the next morning! However, in time they rejoiced, for a colony with a prosperous church at its head does show our community to be a solid and permanent settlement."

Resolved smiled and looked over at his brother.

Augustine, seeking new grounds for conversation, asked Tennake,

"Mistress, have I mentioned that accommodations await you and your family at my home?"

"'Tis good to hear thus," Resolved said, poking his brother.

Augustine explained, "I fear that your house will not be completed for another two or three weeks, but I am sure that you will be comfortable in my own house."

Pigs, ducks, chickens, and goats roamed noisily everywhere. Tenny held her skirt high to avoid the filth of the dirt attaching to her hem, instructing Rebecca to do the same. Will ran ahead of his family looking much like a frisky colt, paying little attention to his mother's warning regarding the mud and animal waste to be found in his path.

"Do you like your ride?" Tennake called up to Aeltie who was straddled upon her father's shoulders. The child giggled and nodded in affirmation.

After eight weeks at sea, the noise of the wagons and carts that passed by seemed unusually loud to Tennake. Listening to fragments of their unusual talk was also unsettling. Where did all these colonists come from? The tiny settlement in the wilderness that looked so Dutch sounded more to her like the roar of the whole world.

"Your new home will never be dull, Mistress," Augustine said. "In our small town you can hear eighteen different tongues spoken all at the same time. I have come to call such music, 'The National Melody of New Amsterdam'."

As the group passed the Fort, Resolved addressed Augustine, "Is this the great Fort of which you boasted in your letters, Augustine? Are these the very same walls that protect the grandest church in all North America?"

The words had barely left Resolved's lips when a group of company soldiers erupted from the front gate of the Fort spouting every curse word known to the Dutch. Several pigs had been rooting at the bottom side of the east wall, tearing away part of the base of the structure and flinging stones in many directions. The soldiers posed a hilarious sight as they threw rocks, sticks, and their own swords at the squealing, frightened animals.

Mr. Herrman, out of breath from the pace, stopped in his tracks.

"Well, my friend," Augustine gasped as he wiped the sweat from his brow, "you have just witnessed one of our public problems that I am sure you, Resolved, will put to the right as soon as you take the oath of office."

Joseph could not stop laughing as he watched the pack of pigs run in every direction. The children were also delighted by such a funny sight.

"Ah, big brother," Joseph said excitedly, "you knew you were ordered to the New World to contain the pigs, though methinks that you thought they were two-legged swine. I see now that your first mission will be one of the utmost valor and importance! Perhaps I shall be summoned by the high and mighty Stuyvesant to print an accounting of the scrimmage and post it all around the town."

"You are twisting my meaning," Augustine protested.

"I only meant that the owners of these pigs refuse to pen their animals. Both are a constant source of trouble. Peter Stuyvesant does not wish to pay his soldiers to chase pigs or to repair walls, though our soldiers have done so on many occasions. Better to have our new Assistant Sheriff fine the disobedient owners and not take monies away from our pot for such foolish pursuit."

Joseph glanced at two limp human bodies in the street. "More pigs for you to corral," he whispered to Resolved. Tennake covered her mouth as she passed the men lying in a pool of their own vomit. She had noted with disgust that it seemed every other dwelling on the street was a brew house that flowed with the curse of all mankind and robbed good men and women of their dignity.

"We are near to reaching my house," Augustine said sympathetically. "I hope that you will forgive me for your discomfort, Mistress.

"Your husband wrote me that you were expecting a child and I had planned to have my wagon at the wharf to receive you. Unfortunately I had to lend my horse, Harry, to a neighbor who found it necessary to ride out to his bowerie yesterday and he has not yet returned. I was certain that he would be back, and therefore I made no other arrangement.

"Our roads being what they are, we have little need of fine carriages. However, Mistress Baker owns a fine carriage and the only finer one is owned by the Director himself. Methinks that I should have a boat, since most of our travel is done by way of the river, but of course a boat would have done us no service today."

Tennake smiled at the heartfelt concern of her host. "I am happy to walk, Mr. Herrman. It feels good to stride at length."

"My wife is no bigger than a flea on a dog, but she is a strong flea!" Resolved said affectionately.

As they continued up the gentle slope of De Herre Street, they paused once again to rest in front of Colonel Phillip Pieterson Schuyler's grand yellow brick house, one of the largest dwellings on the Broadway. Nearby, several rough looking men clad only in breeches were deeply engaged in conversation with three native Indians.

"Alas, they do smell bad," Tennake whispered to her husband. She thought the European men looked as savage as the Indians.

Aeltie mimicked her older sister and held her nose as they proceeded past the group. "It is the bear grease," the Dominie said quietly.

"Bear grease?" Tennake asked.

"Yes, the Indians liberally apply the grease to their bodies in the summer months to dissuade the bite of the vile insects that we have here in our great woods. During this season, however, they use it less generously than in the winter months when it also warms their skin. The white fur traders, whom you see yonder, have adopted the custom themselves," the Dominie said.

"Many of the white fur traders have taken native wives," Augustine added. "When they roll around on their mats together, they take no offense as the odor finds a perfect harmony."

"Oh, they smell as badly as cow dung!" Rebecca called out.

"Quiet, Rebecca!" Tennake whispered sharply.

"You will find much that is both pleasant and unpleasant here, Rebecca," the Dominie said. For the better part though, this land is full of God's abundance; and most importantly, child, you must remember that the great bear, the tiny insect, as well as the heathen, though they may be savage and troublesome, were created by our Almighty Lord God.

"We have a responsibility to these creatures that live along with us in this Garden of Eden. I would instruct you to recall that just as there were temptations of evil in the first garden, so there are temptations in the beauty of this New World. We must show a good example. Do you understand child?"

"Yes, I love Jesus," Rebecca said shyly.

"Good, then you will be safe," the Dominie said gently. "Now, I must leave you to call upon Mistress Harrow. I'll be praying with her and her neighbor women who are lying in with her this afternoon. Her child is soon to come and the midwife has been summoned."

As the minister proceeded down Heere Dwars Street and disappeared around the corner, Augustine cleared his throat, nervously. "I did not jest when I wrote to you that this is the land of milk and honey. Do you know that one of the last Company ships that we sent back to Holland last season held over seven thousand beaver skins and over six hundred otter skins which were taken from the great northern woods of our colony? We also sent mink and wildcat pelts.

"I would dare to say that the shops of Europe have not seen that much fur in all their history! We fill one ship upon another with our colony wood. Deer are so plentiful that they make a pest of themselves in our gardens, while the rivers here are clear and produce so much good edible fish that a man will never starve in the New Netherlands."

Resolved stood with his arms folded listening to Augustine's account of the condition of the land where the Waldrons were about to make their home. "The canvas that you paint should be framed in gold, Augustine," he said smiling.

"Trust me; in only a short time you shall see that my illustration has been accurate."

Finally, upon reaching Mr. Herrman's house, Tennake was breathless not only from the steep walk up the hill, but also from the sight of such a grand place; for although the house was not as large as Mr. Schuyler's, it was indeed stirring to the senses.

It was one-and-a-half stories high with three twelve- upon-twelve paned windows in the front surrounded by soft light blue shutters which set off the structure magnificently. Tennake knew that only a man of great importance could afford a house with so many panes of costly imported glass. The front of Augustine's house faced De Herre Street and was constructed of fine yellow brick that had also been imported from Holland. The roof was covered with red tiles.

Resolved and his family followed their host as they mounted eight finely carved wooden stoop steps. At the top landing, bench seats had been built framing the entranceway.

One could see the owner's appreciation of the splendor of Dutch color by the large oak front door, beautifully painted with a design of red tulips and a pair of white doves. A vine of delicate green leafing encompassed the door's artful arrangement. The background for this unusual scene was the same delightful blue as were the shutters.

They were greeted by a short, well-dressed male Negro servant with hair as white as snow.

"Alas, Jacob, I have finally returned with our collected weary guests," Augustine declared to his servant.

The old Negro smiled widely thus displaying a mouth mostly devoid of teeth. "Good day to you, Master," Jacob returned politely. "Good day," Jacob repeated to each person as they entered through the doorway.

Everyone removed their shoes, placing them neatly in rows by the side of the doorway before they entered further into the room where the wide planked floor shone smoothly from years of scrubbing, and had been sprinkled with a small amount of white sand, as was the custom of Dutch housekeeping.

Once inside, Augustine turned around to face everyone. "This is my house servant, Jacob. He has been in New Netherlands for over thirty years and is one of our original Negroes who were sent here by the Company to build our Fort. In those days, I have been told, he was as strong as a pair of oxen."

Augustine swirled past Jacob and threw his feathered hat upon the nearby large wooden table covered by a plush tapestry carpet. His elderly servant, ignoring the perpetual gaze of the children, quickly retrieved his master's belongings.

As Tennake looked around the impressive room she could see that the first floor was comprised of two large square rooms. The walls of the room she had entered were white and the room was at least twenty feet long by fifteen feet wide.

There was a table, four upholstered chairs, and a large Dutch tiled fireplace with calico fabric hanging from the mantelpiece. She could see the reflection of her face in the copper pots, which hung within the hearth, and quickly noticed the doors that led to a Dutch bedstead built into the wall.

Alongside the bedstead was a magnificent highly- rubbed carved oak Kas, more eloquent than her father's. Painted canvas portraits of brilliant landscapes, colonists, as well as natives, were draped everywhere. Two arms-length iron forks suitable for roasting apples and such hung upon another wall, as well as four Dutch Delft plates that ornamented the wall above the mantle.

The door to the second room was open and Tennake could see a freestanding bedstead surrounded with deeply colored red silk and a handsome writing desk upon which were piled several books.

Within moments, four Negro servants arrived and upon Augustine's direction carried the newcomers' chests and settle bed up to the loft.

"Sarah, come meet our guests," Augustine called as a comely young Negro girl dressed in black linen, with a sweet bag tied with blue silk ribbon around her slender neck, descended the narrow steps of the upper floor from behind the fireplace.

Having performed their duties, the three Negro men also returned from the upper floor. The powerful looking Negro slave bowed to Mr. Herrman. Without speaking he then left the house, while Jacob called out an apparent order to the two young boys that followed the larger man.

"Sarah, this is Master Resolved Waldron and his wife, and Master Joseph Waldron. You will assist the Mistress with her needs. Do you understand?" Augustine asked?

"Yes, Master," the girl replied seemingly unaffected by his businesslike tone of voice.

"Good," Augustine replied, once again assuming his usual merry demeanor.

Sarah smiled warmly at Aeltie who had begun to suck her thumb. "If Mistress wishes I will take the children out back for their fill of cornbread cakes and cream."

The thought of fresh cream and cakes delighted Rebecca, who had complained of hunger constantly aboard the ship. All the passengers were considerably thinner than when they first embarked upon their journey, and Tennake had begun to fear especially for her Rebecca's health.

Will wrinkled up his nose and asked curiously, "What is cornbread cake?"

Tennake was surprised to hear the slave woman speak in perfect Dutch. She would be grateful to have leave of the children, for a sallow sick feeling had come over her and she was forced to take a seat upon one of Augustine's stools.

Sarah quickly crossed to her side and poured a glass of cool water from the pitcher on the table.

"Are you better, wife?" Resolved asked anxiously.

"Yes, do not give me a concern," Tennake replied, having refreshed herself with a few swallows of fresh water. She smiled encouragingly at her husband but she was thinking of home, missing her mother and father—and surprisingly, her bossy sisters, too. She had especially wanted her oldest sister, Catherine, to be at her side when she gave birth to her infant; but instead of Catherine, and familiar friendly gossips holding her hand compassionately, she suspected it would be the black hands of a stranger that pulled the babe forth.

In Holland, relatives and friends filled the house at the baptism festivities, which were held within ten days of the birth of the child. She had loved fondling her new nieces and nephews, praising God along with the child's parents as well as her mother for the safe delivery of every child.

Although women of her family were especially fruitful and fortunately none died in childbirth, Tennake still feared her delivery. Only last year their neighbors, the Van Horns, had lost two of their four daughters during child birthing. Perhaps she, too, would die, and without even the proper prayers of good women beside her. Suddenly Tennake felt terribly alone. Who would be the loving aunt or grandmother to her babe?

She looked at young Sarah who stood next to the three anxious children and was obviously awaiting her command. Her own father's sentiments came back to her. Tennake did not wish to be Sarah's mistress, but it seemed that she had no choice in this new duty. "Methinks that I am well enough, Sarah. Take the young ones to eat," she directed shyly.

"We have plenty upon which to feast," Augustine added, nodding toward Sarah who had already taken Aeltie's hand while the two older children followed her out the door.

Augustine offered Tennake his freestanding bed in order that she might rest. At first, she felt guilty putting the man out of his own bed; but her whole body ached and the thought of a soft feather bed was too much to resist. If, on her first night in this place, she were to be murdered by savages in that bed, then she would die a happy death.

That evening the Waldron family gathered with Mr. Herrman for a welcome feast of baked apples, roasted pig, and oysters that Sarah had gathered from the shore. The seafood was so large that each oyster was cut into three pieces. Sarah also served sweet potatoes, a rare native dish that tasted delicious to the newcomers and yellow flat bread that was made out of a plant that was grown there, called maize.

Later, they were joined by neighbors Gerrit Hendrickson and his wife Ann, a tall redheaded woman with very white skin who was near the age of thirty. They had no children, although during the evening Ann told Tennake that they had been married eleven years.

The two women quickly discovered that they had more in common than their Dutch ancestry. Ann had come to the colony ten years earlier as a bride. Her husband was considerably older than she, and, like her new neighbor she was the daughter of a minister. Mistress Hendrickson had not returned to the Fatherland in all those years, but Gerrit said that they would return the next year for a visit. He had said the same the year before.

Anxious to hear news of home, Ann found the details of Tennake's courtship and family to be music to her ears. Tennake told this stranger of the frightening dreams which had plagued her following Marie Van Tassel's death at sea, of her deep sadness in leaving Holland, and her joy the day she became Resolved's wife.

"'Tis a difficult land, Tennake," Ann said kindly. "Within the protection of our Fort New Amsterdam, under the watchful eye of our soldiers, we are kept from harm, but those living out on the wilderness bowerie farms are not as fortunate. The savages have taken to their bloody ways once again, attacking many farms around the Manhattans.

"I tell you this not to frighten you, but to make you cautious for your safety and that of your husband's children. Hold them fast, lest they wander out beyond the wall of planks that stretches across our island. The wall is close by and children have a way of mischief. God only knows that a young boy such as Will can find the unknown wilderness beyond the wall an adventure too difficult to resist!"

Tennake spoke softly to her new friend. "Before I close my eyes at night, I pray to the Almighty Lord that I might be a good mother to Will and his sisters. Rebecca especially requires my patience. The little one is no trouble, but I have torn my hair and held my hand steady from the want of striking the mouth of Rebecca who recalls her dead mother and is bitter of me. Will, God love him, is usually a good boy although sometimes he does not listen and goes where he would please."

Ann wrinkled her brow. "Does their father object to you making a proper discipline?" she asked.

"No," Tennake replied.

"Methinks that you should not spare the rod, and do not mistake a firm hand for a lack of kindness or tenderness toward them," Ann counseled. "Though I have not myself been delivered of a child, I am sure that a proper discipline is best. And now that you have come here you must be ever more the mindful of them."

"My mother thought the same, though I am at wit's end as to how to do my duty," Tennake paused, asking no further advice. Perhaps she had confided too much during a first encounter.

Later, when the Hendricksons departed, Tennake followed Augustine, Resolved, and Joseph down to the foot of the high stoop that they might say a proper goodbye. Gerrit and Ann lived alongside of the Broadway, on the other side of the Company orchard, a short walk away.

That evening after all had retired, a gentle breeze moved through New Amsterdam, spreading the sweet lingering fragrance of ripened apples.

Darkness covered the little city in the wilderness.

THREE

Tennake Waldron awakened on her first morning in her new land to the raucous sound of clucking chickens, barking geese, and the distant laughter of children. Still lingering in the comforts of Mr. Herrman's soft bed of feathers, lost between the safe pleasantness of her dreams of home, with great reluctance she opened her eyes and heard a voice whisper:

"Good morn, Mistress."

Turning, Tennake was startled to see the young Negro, Sarah, standing by the window, her comely, smooth dark skin illuminated by the brilliant morning sunlight.

She studied her for a moment before throwing aside the coverlet, and silently prayed that the girl would not see her anxiety. She found it extremely odd that the slave woman would invade her mistress' bedchamber. To be sure, this Sarah was stealing her small precious moment of solitude that she had longed for so dearly all these past weeks. Tennake felt violated, she wanted to scream, *Go away and leave me in peace!*

But, now fully awake she recalled her duties. "Where are the children?" she asked. Her abrupt words broke the silence harshly, but Tennake cared not. She was a desperate child in a foreign land. She wanted to return home.

"I was instructed to leave you rest, Mistress, whilst you must not fret for I took good care of all for you," Sarah stammered.

"You tended the children?" Tennake asked curiously.

"Yes, Mistress. They have each put two bowls of corn and cream into their bellies. I did as my master bid."

She stared past Sarah hardly believing that such a sharp response came from her own lips, but justified that her new position as mistress certainly must warrant an authoritative tone.

"Mr. Herrman is in the house, then?" she asked somewhat relieved.

"Master Herrman is not at home, Mistress," Sarah answered quietly. "I speak of Jacob, who is with your young ones out back of the house. When Master Herrman is away, Jacob is master in this house, and I do his bidding."

"Is my husband hereabouts?" Her heart was beginning to pound. What sort of household was this that she had come into?

"No, Mistress," Sarah replied thoughtfully, "he be gone long ago."

"Master Joseph?"

"I don't know where he be going, but he left before the hens opened their eyes," Sarah responded absently, smoothing her starched white apron.

Tennake thought that she glimpsed amusement in the servant's dark eyes.

"Would you need anything, Mistress?" Sarah asked softly.

"No," she replied firmly, still attempting to appear in control. She had been given to understand that the Negroes were difficult to train in their duties, most not capable of learning the simplest prayer, but Sarah spoke Dutch perfectly. This confused her, for Tennake had the preconceived notion that these colonial Negroes were able to speak only a gibberish, part African and part Dutch, and were as savage as the Indians of the wilderness.

Tennake looked over at Sarah waiting patiently by the foot of the bed. She had already decided that the slave who had been forced upon her was far from a savage.

"I have everything that I require. I will dress now, Sarah." She could smell the aroma of fresh bread coming from the hearth in the first room. *I must be sensible,* she thought. *Resolved would not leave us in peril.*

"I depart you then, Mistress," Sarah said.

Tennake watched her until she was out of sight. Snarling at a servant like a beast was not going to bring her any grace, she thought. *I fret foolishly, for surely Mr. Herrman knows his own household.* She had awakened with a foul disposition and was angrier with herself than Sarah, for she had slept far too long. Her mother would not think of letting a daughter of Barent Nagel do such? What would her mother think to see her girl sleeping in a feather bed, whilst a Negro servant woman awaited her beck and call? Would she laugh or scold? Tennake frowned. *My first day in this place, and if my lazy self be known, I will be the talk in every woman's kitchen in town,* she decided.

She picked up the white earthenware pitcher from the table and poured water into the bowl beside it. Quickly she splashed her face, neck and hands, and then knotted her braid upon the top of her head, attaching her white cap over all. She put on a clean white, lace trimmed apron over her dress. Tennake was confident that women gossiped the same in every land, though at the moment she was confident of little else.

Upon entering the first room, she was wondering where Resolved had gone in such a hurry this morning. Although indeed fretful for having been left alone, she hoped that he was meeting with His Honor, Peter Stuyvesant, regarding his new position as Assistant Sheriff. She knew they would make good use of the annual salary promised—two hundred guilders.

Her husband had told her that the Director had hired eight others who would rotate shifts to keep the peace and run the government of New Amsterdam and the surrounding lands. She also knew that Resolved was anxious to see the new pulpit, which was destined to be placed in the church at the Fort in a wild North Country place called Beaverwyck. The pulpit was rumored to be more elaborately carved than the pulpit at St. Nicholas church here in New Amsterdam. Tennake recalled months before, that a Mr. Van Slyk who resided in Beaverwyck had written her father a letter asking for his assistance in locating someone to help the local Dominie transport this precious cargo. Her father was overjoyed to write back to the deacon that he would proudly recommend his future son-in-law for this task.

Resolved had been most excited to accept this duty. Last night, Mr. Herrman said that the pulpit had arrived six days ago. Resolved wanted to make the journey to Kent as soon as possible and see to his deceased brother's family; but now it seemed that such a journey would be impossible because the pulpit had arrived earlier than expected.

She pulled herself up straight. *I will take care of anything else that needs to be attended to,* she thought.

A good resolution, and none too soon as the children noisily burst into the room with Jacob trailing them as quickly as his stiff legs would carry him.

"You have good healthy children, Mistress," Jacob said breathlessly.

Tennake smiled. "They are all of that," she said, glancing toward Rebecca. "Watch where you're going. Methinks that you are all more trouble than the hogs pulling down the Company Fort!" she scolded.

"William and Rebecca wished to go to play in the field out there in the front of the house," Jacob warned. "Whilst I told them the field sometimes became part of our common highway, a desperate road, Mistress." He frowned.

Tennake could tell from the sheepish look upon William's face that the old Negro had been trying to dissuade him from venturing out into peril.

She looked out the doorway at the highway, a dirty patch some twenty feet wide filled with ruts and calamity. Persons of all sorts were passing by, some with carts pulled by oxen, others with horse-drawn wagons, all seeming to stream past the front of Mr. Herrman's house from the direction of the wall.

"The gate is open, and the farmers come to trade. The Fair is to begin soon," Jacob said, noting his Mistress curiously.

"Kermis is today?" Tennake asked brightly.

"Yes, Mistress."

Aeltie had begun to sob. Poor little Aeltie is too little to play the games and too big to be a babe. Tennake pulled the child into her arms and hugged her.

"God's love, go out, the both of you, and leave Aeltie to me," she said to William and Rebecca. But mind that you do not go far away from the house.

"Stay away from the road, whilst methinks that I had better not find either of you near to that wall of planks down yonder, or I will beat you myself with the closest stick I can lay my hands upon."

Jacob dutifully followed the two out the door, his playful charges nearly knocking Sarah over as she came through the entranceway with a basket brimming full of ripened apples. As fruit rolled along the floor, Tennake looked at her servant and sighed.

"They are most always good children," she said. She did not wish the Negro girl to think that these young ones were uncivilized. Most certainly Mr. Herrman's servant already thought her a lazy mother. Tennake feared she had made a bad start in this new land.

Sarah nodded indifferently as she chased the apples.

Tennake pulled Aeltie to her and kissed the little girl's forehead.

"Aeltie, you—not the bigger ones—will be baking with me today, and then we will see what we need to go to the Kermis. You would like to go to the Fair, would you not?" she soothed.

Aeltie nodded, her eyes widening, the tears stopped. She put her small arms around Tennake and pressed her soft, wet, tiny lips to her face. "Good," Tennake said smiling. There was a wondrous sweetness about this child.

Still holding Aeltie in her arms, Tennake stepped out onto the stoop of the house. She was anxious to explore now that sleep had refreshed her. She looked to the left of Mr. Herrman's property and up the broad highway where she could barely see the flat grassy bowling Green that lay in front of the Fort.

Her men would spend plenty of time up there, she thought. Resolved and his brother loved the game of bowls, as did most Dutchmen.

It seemed to her that they preferred to play at bowls rather than take in the charm of the most comely beauty, though they protested this declaration adamantly through fits of laughter. However, no denial would convince her to the contrary, for she knew that there was not one of them that did not yearn to bowl, brew, and boast. The order in which a Dutchman practiced his vices only depended upon how the wind blew that day.

It was another beautiful day, and Tennake wished that she would have the brave heart of a man and could freely wander the streets of their new homeland as did the men. How lovely it would be to jump out of bed and run from the house, the children, and all duty.

But, she would be happy with her lot in life because she was certain that a virtuous woman would go straight to heaven upon her death. The men may have their rewards in the here and now, but women would share theirs for all eternity.

She looked across the highway at the Company farm that swarmed with Negroes harvesting the apples. She would plant a good vegetable garden herself next spring. Eventually she would also like to have a few of those fruit trees, though she knew it would be years before their trees would yield a single apple.

Mr. Herrman had told them that the apple crops were hardy because the Company orchard was part of an established plantation that had been well developed over the last eight years, again the doing of their present Director who took great pride in the vast farm. Half the farm was devoted to raising tobacco crops; the other half produced vegetables and fruit.

Everyone thought Mr. Stuyvesant would be content to spend all his hours as a farmer were he not their leader for he loved this land dearly. He had already established a good plantation for himself near the village of New Haarlem where over sixty of his slaves tended to his crops.

Tennake walked down the steps of the stoop to the edge of the highway, passing the children who were seated upon the ground already having made friends with two other little girls, acting as though they had known them all of their young lives.

Aeltie struggled to be released. In the blink of an eye she ran over to them, forgetting the promise that she could help with the baking.

As Tennake looked to the north, she could see the planked wall; more importantly, she could see the front of their future home. A few feet more and they would be sleeping in the wilderness, she thought.

She turned when she heard Resolved's voice. "Ah, here is my good wife. Awake at last." There was merriment in his voice.

Augustine walked beside Resolved. "Hold on, my friend. Do not rebuke your good wife; the rest has done her justice."

"A flower that does blossom," Resolved said mirthfully in agreement.

"I know that I am bold to say so, but one as sweet as Sarah's cookies," Augustine added.

Tennake flushed. It was clear that these two were enjoying the moment, even if she were not. "Yes, look how rosy her cheeks have become," noted Resolved. "Your suggestion to leave her to bed this morning was a good one, Augustine."

Tennake was next to tears. When she had her husband alone she would want to speak sharply to him, though her mother had taught her that to remain silent was always golden for a wife; yet she could not let this jesting pass. *It is good that husbands cannot see the thoughts in their wives' minds,* she thought.

A third man appeared at the door. He was white-haired, tall and thin.

"Good, you have caught up to us, John," Augustine said. "This is Dominie Johannes Megapolensis."

"I am happy to meet you," Tennake replied.

"The Dominie will accompany us as we guide the pulpit to its new home later this week. Come John, have some of Sarah's delicious cookies."

The Dominie turned toward Tennake. "Welcome to the New Netherlands. A good Dutch woman is always appreciated here."

"Thank you for your kind words," Tennake said softly.

"The Dominie has been many weeks with the farmers along the South River settlements, returning to New Amsterdam just this morning from Pavonia." Augustine stuffed a fresh cookie into his mouth.

Sarah put a pitcher of hot apple cider onto the table and pulled out another batch of cookies from the back of the side oven.

The Dominie explained, "I am very pleased that word came to me whilst I was in the territory. As soon as I learned that the ship carrying the new pulpit sat in sight of St. Nicholas, I could not wait another hour to begin my journey here."

"Will you minister to our needs here also," Tennake asked, thinking it strange that two Dominies would make themselves available to one settlement.

"No, Mistress," the minister said smiling. "I am duty bound to those good souls of the North Country."

"Your interest is understandable," Resolved said.

"I should say so," Augustine added looking at Tennake. "This man served the north community of this colony for over fifteen years as a missionary to the Indians of Rensselearwyck. He is the founder of our Church at Beaverwyck."

"I am honored to meet you," Tennake replied.

"Please, Augustine, do not go on so," the Dominie replied humbly.

Resolved laughed. "Our gracious host is accustomed to praising his guests."

The Dominie reached for another cookie.

"The pulpit is what is worth your praise, not I. It is most beautiful, worthy of the finest church in all of the Fatherland. In truth, it is far more valuable than the twenty-five beaver skins that we paid for it," he said.

"True," Augustine replied.

"I am extremely blessed to have been called to God's duty," the minister mused quietly.

Augustine thought how fortunate the colony was to have the service of such a man.

"Thank God that you were blessed to live through all that you have, since first you came here," he said.

Tennake looked over at Sarah, while she ate her cookies. "Sarah, your cookies are most delicious," she complimented. She had begun to soften toward Sarah for she could see the Negro was a capable servant, held with high regard by her master. She was ashamed that her tongue had wagged so unkindly toward the girl.

Augustine smiled. "Sarah's cookies are most unique, another wondrous discovery here in our colony one might say. They are a combination of ingredients from a Lenape woman. Methinks that they never tasted so good in Fatherland! Sarah and our neighbor, Ann, made the cookies originally from the Indian cakes, though the cookies are really Sarah's secret," Augustine looked proudly at his servant.

Sarah departed the room knowing that her master always spoke the truth. Although she had never been to "Fatherland," she was confident that she was a good Dutch baker.

Augustine observed Sarah's satisfied expression and whispered to the others seated around his table, "It pleases me to compliment her."

"A word of praise will go a long way with our servants, far better than a beating," the Dominie acknowledged.

After a moment, Resolved began to plan the order of business.

"The first order of our business is to secure a sloop and then hoist the pulpit down from the ship to the sloop so that it will be ready for transporting as soon as possible."

"I have already written to the Captain of the Van Rensselear sloop regarding this," Augustine replied.

"We will speak of the installation of the pulpit into the blockhouse church whilst we journey up the North River to Beaverwyck," the Dominie added.

Tennake fidgeted in her chair. She did not like to hear of her husband going into this fierce wilderness land, and she liked even less being left alone in this place so soon after having arrived. However, she would sever her best arm before she would let any of them know how terrified she would be.

She pulled herself straight, remembering what she had been taught: that it was the duty of every woman at the table to create a calm pleasant discourse. She observed Mr. Herrman and smiled pleasantly.

"I was grateful that your old Negro took care of the children earlier this morn, though I am sure that the entire block could hear them playing ball. I hope that I did not hold your slave from his duties elsewhere."

"Do not fear such things, Mistress, for it is Jacob's duty to keep a watchful eye upon the young ones; and methinks that he did not find his duty too distasteful. Jacob is an excellent ball player, better at bowls, though he be a better carpenter. No one is mindful of the noise in New Amsterdam and the clatter is a plentiful commodity on the Broadway."

"You have been so good to us, Mr. Herrman, and I thank you heartily," Tennake said earnestly.

"Mistress, would you not call me by my given name, Augustine?"

"If you wish."

"I do, for I feel that I am among good friends."

"Then I should wish that you call me by my given name, also," she replied.

"Henceforth, I will call you Tennake and you shall call me Augustine," he said jovially.

"I enjoyed watching the children run about this morning," recalled Tennake. "I had no fear they would fall into the sea. It was a long voyage for all, but especially confining for the children. In truth, I am happy for Jacob's servitude."

"Jacob is no longer a slave, but a freedman to whom I pay twelve guilders per year for his good services."

Tennake was startled. "I did hear my good father speak of such freed Negroes."

"Oh yes, it is quite customary here to free a good loyal Negro after a lifetime of service," Augustine explained.

Resolved seemed puzzled. "I did not know that you owned a slave who had given a lifetime of service, Augustine; nor did I remember that you held any slaves in your keeping."

Augustine laughed as he poured himself another glass of the warm apple cider.

"I acquired Jacob from Stuyvesant as payment for the rent of my warehouse space that he was using for his tobacco. Try as I might, I was unable to wrestle a stiver that he owed me. Finally, I suggested to him that we settle upon Jacob as payment.

"I had admired pieces of furniture that the old Negro had made for Mistress Stuyvesant; and at the time, I had only a bed that I had ordered from Holland and a few stools to fill my grand house, so I had good use for a fine carpenter. I am sure that Stuyvesant's wife was sorry to see Jacob leave their service, whilst hardheaded Pete seemed to like the barter of my warehouse space for his old Negro. So, it was done."

"A wise bargain struck," Resolved said thoughtfully.

Augustine continued. "When I acquired Jacob, Stuyvesant had generously given freedom to another of his old slaves, but that Negro had a family there on the Stuyvesant plantation who was not given their freedom. So, of course, the old man kept to his kin, for how could he have gone off into the wilderness alone, praising the Almighty God for his good fortune whilst he left his children behind?

"Of course, Pete Stuyvesant knew he would not. The old Negro remained there on the Director's property until his death."

"We are all free in death," the Dominie said softly.

"Yes, of course," Augustine said. "But, as for Jacob, I cleverly made barter with him; one that I knew would put fire into the breast of his master who was so willing to cheat me in our business dealings. After Jacob had been with me for a few weeks I asked him if he would like his freedom. He answered that he would, but he was alone, and too old to go out to the wilderness to tend to a piece of land, adding that he had never taken a wife, nor had children.

"I said to him, 'Build me a fine Kas and a table with four great upholstered chairs to surround it. If all does please me, I will give you freedman papers, and you will be welcome to stay as a freed man in my house forever.'"

Augustine rubbed his hand lovingly over the great table.

"So it was done. And since I have given the old man his freedom, he has shown his gratitude over and over to me by caring for my house as if he were master. He has also carved me the fine writing chest in the bedchamber, which so pleased me that I gave him an extra stiver.

"If I could find a proper wife to share all of my good fortune with, I would have nothing left to pray to God for," Augustine laughed, appealing to Tennake who was fascinated by the tale.

"Augustine, watch what you wish for, or it may happen that the good Lord grants what you desire!" Resolved warned, humorously.

Tennake ran her hand over the upholstery of her chair. "Your furniture is most fine," she said. "The Kas truly is the most beautiful one that I have ever laid my eyes upon."

"Perhaps you can persuade your husband to have one made for you. I have told Jacob that he may accept the work if he be offered it, though he may only do so after his duties have been completed in my house," Augustine stipulated.

"Have your servants been in your household a long time?" Tennake asked.

"Sarah was born to slaves owned by my family. Samuel comes from Africa, although he spent five years on a sugar plantation in Jamaica before arriving in our New Netherlands. I paid a good price for that one I can tell you!" Augustine said emphatically.

"He looks to be as strong as an ox," Resolved said.

"Works like ten," Augustine replied. "Samuel works much of the time in my warehouse near Van Keulen's Hook, though he often drives wagon for me too."

"He is good with the animals then?" Resolved asked.

"I trust him with my finest mount. Yes, I would never part with Samuel. The man cannot be more than thirty year of age, so I should have many more good years from him."

Resolved stood to his feet. "I would like to have a closer look at our town's wall,"

"So you shall," Augustine said.

"And I must depart for I have much to do today," Dominie Megapolensis interjected.

"We thank you for your good company, John," Augustine assured him.

"It was good to meet you, Mistress Waldron," the Dominie said as he left.

Augustine looked seriously at Resolved. "It is fortunate that Dominie Megapolensis commands such a position of respect in this colony. If our glorious Director General saw fit, he would confiscate that wondrous pulpit and place ours in St. Nicholas, sending the lesser of the two on to Beaverwyck.

"Nary has a ship come into the harbor carrying merchandise that he does not consider to be his own booty, and when he lays his eyes upon our pulpit, he will much prefer to keep it here. But, the Dominie's position is strong and Stuyvesant would not dare to aggravate the high council in Holland any further."

"Yes, he is a hard man to battle," Resolved agreed.

"Then we both understand the sport of our Director; however, the scale still dips favorably, for the man has done much good here, although we do not call him hardheaded for no reason. Pete's laws can be painful.

"You will learn that his way is the only way in New Netherlands, which is why I was so pleased to give Jacob his papers. The Director continues with his policy of complete submission of the people to his supreme official will, in all matters, but I still got me rent!" Augustine boasted.

"That you did, and His Honor's goat, as well, I'll wager," Resolved laughed.

Augustine nodded. "I am of the opinion that our leader comes down too hard upon his children. I blame our lack of good settlers on his harsh policies here. We are too few here, my friend. The English outnumber us in America by five to one. It is not wise under those circumstances for a leader to offer insults, floggings, and fines to a man whose religious convictions differ. Such treatment does not encourage colonists. Methinks he should be gentler."

"Though I cannot completely agree with you, I understand what you are saying," Resolved replied.

"Well, we shall take our leave, Tennake," said Augustine, "and I will return your husband as soon as he has had his fill of inspecting our plank wall."

"I shall not be long, wife," Resolved said with a smile.

As Tennake watched them leave, she feared that she had been far too outspoken in her questions to her kind host regarding his servants. She should learn to keep her mouth closed and not allow her curiosity to run away with her tongue. She had embarrassed herself again, whilst she had learned little about Sarah. Who had been the girl's mother and father? It was not Jacob as she had first assumed.

Tennake knew that her father would have thought of Augustine Herrman as a fallen man, but if he believed this slave owner to be damned, then what would his thoughts be for the colony's Director who owned twenty times more Negroes, she wondered.

Perhaps her father, not having owned servants or slaves himself, was unable to judge these men properly as he did not understand about what he had no firsthand knowledge. Surely these slaves in the Herrman house were treated fairly. Did one not owe his freedom to Augustine?

Tennake shook herself. These were not proper thoughts or concerns of a woman, so why did such thoughts fill her mind? What should it matter to her if a slave be happy or unhappy in duty?

Sarah had told her that her master traveled greatly as ambassador for the Director, and that while Augustine was away she and Jacob lived peaceably in this wondrous house and cared for it as though they owned it. To Tennake's mind that could be troublesome. It seemed strange, allowing two Negroes the privilege of such independence.

Sarah said she cooked, shined the pots, and sewed her master's shirts and breeches, all as Tennake did for her husband. The only task that she had been forbidden was to touch the master's clock, for Jacob alone was the keeper of the time in the master's house.

Tennake wondered who was any more the slave, Sarah, or she. Was a Dutchman's proper wife any less servile to her husband than the Negro slave or a bound woman to her own master? The bound woman would be set free in four or five years, whilst a wife was wife forever.

After only a few short months of marriage, she had learned that all married women had a life that must be filled with fortitude and patience in their own master's world. Although it helped greatly if a wife loved her husband with all her heart as she loved hers, still she would go where Resolved wished her to go, and remain where he wished her to be.

She walked down the street to her house. Resolved and Joseph had paid six-hundred-fifty guilders for the property, having sent the money months before they arrived.

The front of the house was constructed of yellow brick imported from Holland. Of course, the house was still partly under construction and, as she neared, the freshness of the virgin wood filled her nostrils.

As she stood admiring her new home, she watched with amazement as Samuel and Jacob removed from an ox-drawn cart, the most beautiful carved wood table she had ever seen. To her further wonder, the two black men began to mount the steps of her stoop with the table, struggling under the weight of it.

Augustine came running down the street with Resolved. "Wife! What do you do here?" Resolved called.

"I look!" Tennake replied, laughing.

Augustine turned to Resolved and sighed. "You hear the woman. She looks.

"The chairs are not completed as yet I am afraid, but there will be two to begin with. God's blessings upon your marriage, Mistress Waldron," Augustine stammered.

Tears came into Tennake's eyes. "'Tis for us?" she asked, looking at Resolved.

"Yes, wife, it is a generous gift from our good neighbor."

"You do too much for us," she said, tears misting in her eyes.

She followed Jacob through the doorway and ran her hand appreciatively over the smooth, newly finished wood; and when she looked up she could not miss the proud expression upon the elder manservant's face. Tennake suddenly realized that Jacob had created another masterpiece.

"The table is most fine, Jacob," she whispered as she turned to leave her house. Though she hated to depart, duty called. The children awaited her to go to Kermis. As she hastened back she asked God's forgiveness for her lack of kindness toward others, especially Sarah.

FOUR

Joseph had barely slept three hours his first night in the colony. Fearing that his restlessness would awaken the entire household, he had quietly slipped out of Augustine's house into the predawn darkness before any of the servants had risen. He, like everyone else, was overjoyed to experience the treasure of solitude, if only for an hour or so. How good it was to walk freely, his feet balanced in harmony with solid ground, while the sweetness of the distant wild forest filled his nostrils.

Near the town's center, he found the Bowling Green where he laid on his back facing the vastness of the sky, not minding the cold wetness of the morning dew on the grass, for it was a familiarity in this strange land that made him feel all the more right and secure. His only intruders during exploration were two scratching, scraggly dogs who sniffed the field, but came no closer than twenty feet and then went away.

Later, when the sun began to rise, the door to Pieterson's Tavern opened and a bucket of slop, the leftover remains of several of yesterday's meals, was flung into the street officially heralding a new day. The commotion had broken the calm and jolted Joseph upright when suddenly, out of the luminescent dusk came five very large pigs, which rampaged around the corner of Prince Street precisely in the direction of the breakfast provided so generously by Pieterson. Joseph smiled; *but those hogs should be in pens,* he thought.

Having pulled himself to his feet, he ventured within the walls of the Fort. He identified himself to the two sentries on duty, and then proceeded into the church of St. Nicholas where he gave personal thanks to the Almighty God for his family's safe arrival.

His prayers completed, he left the containment of the Fort and walked down Dwars Street passing many dwellings that stood beside ample garden plots holding an abundance of produce, which had not yet been harvested. *A man's wife would surely have to sew her husband's mouth shut before he would go hungry within the plentiful bounty of this fair town,* he mused.

After retracing his earlier steps, Joseph finally came to stand before the brick structure that would soon be his alone, both to live and work in until he could secure a good apprentice. His head filled with a hundred ideas while his heart burst with enthusiastic desire to begin his new life. He would place his small press in the light of the front room, near to a great hearth that would also offer him light during the long winter months, allowing him to work late into the night. He most enjoyed working at night when the hostilities of the day had calmed and his thoughts came easily. The rear room would provide sleeping quarters and storage, as well as a place for a future apprentice to roll out his pallet.

Joseph required little for himself, coming to this new land with the clothing on his back, his press, a bed, and one small trunk full of his beloved books. Meager as these belongings were, it had cost him double the ship's fare to bring what he deemed absolutely necessary, though he had no regrets for the spent money, for the guilders saw to his own private accommodations. He knew it would be good to live in his own small sanctuary and not within his brother's household as Resolved had first implored him to do.

He loved them all, but alone was where he wished to be. He also knew that it was best that some distance be placed between himself and his brother's wife. Resolved had been the fortunate one in gathering up such a strong young woman so soon after the bereavement of his wife Rebecca; while he on the other hand had been unable to find a first wife.

Now, having grown to know his sister-in-law better, he regretted his cruel taunting of Tennake, which had been unforgivable, and yet somehow she had forgiven him. *I should do as Resolved suggests and find a good wife. Do I need a first wife?*

Eight weeks of a voyage that demanded being so close to Resolved's family had taught him the precious value of a quiet thought. Although he admired the youthful beauty and pious diligence of his brother's wife, he was most happy with the liberty of his own life.

He surveyed his house one last time before returning to the disquieting confusion in the household of their host. Turning away, he looked up and saw his young niece, Rebecca, standing sheepishly beside the well.

"Why do you stand there, Sweet Pea? Are you awaiting me?" Joseph called over to her.

"We are late for K E R M I S..." Rebecca sang out to him, musically creating a childlike song.

Ah, Rebecca. She was a persistent one, always pushing for victory, a battleship with the face of an angel. Still, how he adored the child. He did not know why he favored her so. Perhaps it was something that was hidden behind those steadfast, seemingly innocent brown eyes, a wisdom that he recognized from his memory of his own beloved mother. *Yes, that was it. It was her stubborn Dutch independent spirit that blazed forth and warmed his bachelor's heart. No doubt, the Dutch in us is the better part of us all,* he thought to himself.

While he and his brother had been the product of an English father and Dutch mother, they had been raised in Holland, and were none other than thoroughly Dutch, and that idea had been implanted into them in every way by the woman who gave them life. For a moment he was saddened as he thought of the old days. He recalled his mother's quiet tenderness and his eldest brother's foul mood whenever she forced him and Resolved to allow her youngest to follow them to the games. He had not seen his eldest brother since his boyhood and had never met the woman that Joseph Michael had married, nor had he come to know any of their children. Joseph felt no pain for Joseph Michael's loss as he could barely remember him; although his poor mother had never known the babes that her firstborn had sired either. This was a hurt that she had taken to her grave.

Perhaps, Joseph thought, had Resolved's first wife lived a healthy, good long life, he, too, would never have come back home to Holland and Resolved might still be in Brazil with his wife and the children. However, he would never have had the joy of their kinship had his brother's first wife not taken an early path to the Lord God.

Joseph smiled as he watched his niece trying to control her childish impatience with him; a bold sight she was, standing there with her small hands folded.

"Uncle, come on," Rebecca pleaded.

"Am I late, little flower?" Joseph asked coyly. Rebecca took his hand abruptly, pulling him toward the house, imploring him to have done with his morning meal.

As the two approached Augustine Herrman's house, Jacob was sweeping the stoop, but stopped to let them pass.

"Good Morning to you, Sir," he said.

"Good Morning to you also, Jacob. My niece tells me I am in great trouble having missed the morning meal."

"No trouble, Sir," Jacob said.

"Sarah," Jacob called up the steps, "Master Waldron will be having his morning meal now."

Joseph peeked through the open doorway. "A cake or two left for me?" he asked politely. Sarah was already putting a bowl of corn on the table along with bread to be dunked into some sweet milk, while his sister-in-law hastened the process by pouring a large glass of apple cider. "There be plenty for you," Sarah said.

"Sit you down and eat," Tennake added.

He had just swallowed his last bite of flat bread when Resolved and Augustine returned from exploring the orchard of the Company farm.

"Uncle's finished," Rebecca pronounced handing his bowl to Sarah.

Rebecca's father looked at her sternly. "You children should give your uncle some peace."

Joseph immediately rallied to the defense of his niece. "Nay, do not be so harsh with the girl. Rebecca is just in her feelings. I am the one to be blamed. I have held up the family from an early start to Kermis. I am truly sorry."

"You held up nothing brother, though had you returned, you might have come along with us to see the orchard. 'Tis a grand farm to behold."

"Is your belly full, Joseph?" Tennake asked.

"Yes, me belly is full, and whenever my brother is ready we may depart for the fair."

Tennake and Sarah gathered the reed baskets hanging on the wooden sidewall peg, and the two began to traverse the wide Broadway along with the men and the three children.

They were a boisterous clan that flowed and circulated together like the blood of one body along the road. The men laughed as they watched Tennake being pulled along by her husband's two young daughters, while William, who was exasperated because they did not move quickly enough to Kermis to please him, ran ahead.

Will was the only one of the three children who knew what the excitement was all about; he remembered attending the annual fairs of Holland before leaving for the colony in Brazil. He was most anxious to see the prized cattle and the horses.

But even more than the animals, he desired to go back to the wharf, which would be gaily decorated in ribbons and flowers. It would be the most interesting place to be, for as many as fifty vessels would be surrounding the little city on the island this day, and for many days to follow. Farmers and merchants from settlements all over the colony had converged upon New Amsterdam for the opportunity to sell or trade their goods in an open market atmosphere.

Resolved watched his son running ahead of them. "You know where Will shall be for the better part of this day, do you not?" he said to Joseph.

"That I do."

"Where would that be?" Augustine asked curiously.

"Will holds to the water," Resolved replied smiling.

"The boy wishes to be taken into service upon a ship?" Augustine asked.

"He has a mind for it, but I have a mind for another trade for him."

Joseph shook his head. "Brother, I wish you well! How many times did you have to speak to Will on the voyage for disturbing Captain Vermilye? A child of nine or ten can be very annoying to a man whilst he performs his duty, but sometimes I thought the captain seemed glad for the exuberant company of his young passenger. He told me that the boy reminded him of his own young son, Peter, whom he sorely misses.

"His boy also loves the sea, but the captain did not want him to miss the opportunity of his schooling in New Amsterdam, and therefore kept him home with his wife. In another two years he will apprentice him to ship," Joseph explained.

"Our colony is fortunate to have a schoolmaster," declared Resolved. "I want to make arrangements for Will and Rebecca to go to school."

"As soon as is possible my friend," Augustine replied.

"So you do intend that the children have lessons?"

"I would have it no other way," Resolved declared.

"This is good to hear," Joseph sighed. "Dismayed was I when I discovered upon first meeting my nephew and niece that they could not read or even write their names."

Resolved halted his stride up the hill and stood in front of Bicker's Tavern with a look of dismay upon his broad-bearded face.

"Joseph, what was I to do when in Brazil we had no schoolmaster!" He flung his hands into the air in despair.

"Praise God that one is to be had in this colony, or I fear they would be no better off than the savages," Joseph concluded.

"Do not argue, all will be well," Augustine said diplomatically.

Tennake, with Sarah running behind her, had been swept away by the lure of the merchant's booty. During the ten days of the Kermis, people from surrounding farms could buy and sell their goods at the fair. Housewife madness flourished in New Amsterdam.

Joseph recalled his morning walk when he had noticed the harvested vegetable plots. "Methinks that this season's harvest must have been a good one," he said to Augustine.

"Yes," Augustine replied, "fortunately the disputes with the wild men were not within the town and thereabouts during our growing time. The Indians did not disturb our crops, and so they were allowed to grow abundantly."

They passed a group of Lenape Indian fur traders and several Dutchmen arguing in the Lenape's native tongue of Munsee. Augustine nodded toward the Indians. "They've come a far distance, probably a hundred English miles to the northwest."

"Why do they come from so far away?" Resolved asked.

"To sell the fur that was trapped in the wilds where the great woods are so thick with trees a squirrel could travel the entire distance and never touch the ground below. Beaver have left the Island of Manhattan forever, I fear," Augustine said sadly.

"I have seen plenty of game," Joseph interrupted. "Just this morn I saw a herd of deer upon the Green, and later a flock of wild turkeys."

"But I have not seen many beaver for over ten years," Augustine asserted. "Our Lenape Indian friends know that we must have them, so they have moved their hunting grounds to accommodate us. They hunt the pelts and we buy them. This move has given them much grief as now they seek game in the land of other tribes.

"I wager the Lenape took those pelts from animals in Mohawk country and they risk their lives if caught. I fear we have spoiled the neighboring savages with our fine trade goods because the wild men can no longer do without our pots; and most sadly, we must have their furs. So the circle continues, though these Lenape are but small players in comparison to the great Iroquois."

"What will happen to our New Netherlands when there are no more beaver to be had?" Joseph asked.

Augustine laughed. "You are new to this land, my friend. There will be beaver pelts within the distant woods for a thousand years; and after that, who should care? We will all have gone to our rewards."

Resolved and Joseph both laughed.

"I do pity these Lenape though," Augustine continued.

"Why so, Augustine?" Resolved asked. "Do these heathen not receive a fair price for their furs?"

"Fair, of course, though I cannot speak for a trade the English or Swede might make. Still, 'tis sad. This was thought to be their land when the sailors of the Half-Moon first set foot upon the soil. The natives called it 'Lenapehoking,' which in our language means, 'Land of People.' Forty years ago there were thousands of them who lived in this place as they had done since the first sun, but now there are but a few hundred left here. Most have died from the terrible sickness we have brought to them. Many of them have moved away from this, the home of their ancestors. They feared that if they stayed their children would also die from white man disease."

Resolved wrinkled his brow thoughtfully. "I saw much of the same kind of death with the Indians in Brazil."

Augustine nodded a greeting toward two commonly dressed men as they passed. "Their invasion into Iroquois territory seeking beaver to satisfy the Dutch markets, has brought many wars between the tribes which have not been good for us. This situation grieves us because since 1647, we have had a treaty of trade with the Iroquois Federation and it is best that we take their powerful side in this matter, which of course, leaves our humble native neighbors in a precarious position."

Resolved turned to look at the traders once again. "Ah, well," he said, "this may not be the land of milk and honey that you promised me, Augustine, but it is much more agreeable than Brazil, where the insects drain your blood, the sun burns off your skin and what is left of the body suffers the deadly fevers."

"In truth, Resolved, I stand by what I told you as you will see when you acknowledge how few stivers will purchase plenty from these Indians. Glad we were that many of these natives have risked being near to us to make a living, for we could not do without them bringing us fruit, fish, deer meat, wild birds, and baskets that their women weave. All this trouble for very little in payment."

"Tennake," Augustine called out, "save your coin for the fabric and your copper pots."

"I doubt that my wife heard you," Resolved said.

"I will have Jacob carve your wife some wooden spoons and bowls from the hard shell of the gourds. No need to waste your money." Augustine walked over to Tennake and whispered in her ear.

As they approached the Green outside the Fort, Peter Stuyvesant was among the more than a hundred colonists. He stood high up in his wagon, fervently engaged in oration.

"What goes there?" Joseph asked.

Augustine sighed. "You might as well all know about this now as later. Good old Pete has gathered over three hundred able-bodied men for the fight against the Swedes. This is why there were so many Dutch ships in harbor upon your arrival. The rest will arrive in our town within two days and all will embark upon this mission after the last day of Kermis."

"Why did you keep this from me?" Resolved shouted.

"Do not shout at me, Resolved. You will frighten your woman. We will speak of this later. Why ruin her good merriment at Kermis? Your comely young wife yonder need not know today what course she will travel tomorrow."

Resolved looked over at his wife who was running her hand lovingly over a piece of lace. "You will tell us tonight," he said to Augustine.

"Yes, Resolved. Fear not, I have arranged all," Augustine said quietly.

"Augustine is right, brother, let us enjoy the festival," Joseph urged.

Someone in the crowd caught Augustine's attention. "Ah, there is Thomas Laurens." He called out, "Thomas, I am here. Come and meet one of our newest Dutch families just arrived from Holland on the Princess." His friend was watching a game of dice near the wall of the Fort.

"Thomas Laurens, I would wish for you to meet Resolved Waldron and also Joseph Waldron, his brother."

"How did your voyage fare?" Mr. Laurens asked politely in broken Dutch.

"'Twas good," Resolved replied briefly in Dutch.

"Thomas, you may speak to Resolved in English. He speaks the language well."

Resolved looked at the ground, but said nothing to the contrary.

"Yes, Waldron is an English name. Please, do excuse me, Mr. Waldron. I was just going over to the Green since our Director will soon have said all that there is to say of the no-good Swedes; and, God willing, we can get on with the skittles games,"

Mr. Laurens added, "It was a pleasure to have met you, Waldron; and good to meet you, as well, Joseph Waldron."

Resolved and Joseph both nodded, the latter brother managing a smile as the Englishman made his way away from them through the crowd.

"What is your displeasure with Thomas?" Augustine asked Resolved.

"Never trust the English," Resolved stated flatly. "They are a sleeping enemy. My own father was an Englishman, as you know, Augustine, and I could never be close to the man, never understood him either. He could barely wield his pen, drank foolishly, and beat our good mother when the mood struck him. I could not abide him, for he was a brutal man and I left home for the military as soon as I was fourteen.

"When he died, he left our mother not a crust of bread. If I have learned anything in this lifetime, it is that one cannot trust an Englishman!" Resolved said bitterly.

"Well, my friend, there are many English who would say the same of the Dutch, and many Dutch that would say you are English yourself and no Dutchman," Augustine replied.

"God help the one who calls me such!" Resolved replied.

Tennake had strolled back to her husband to proudly display her valued purchases, while Sarah had taken the three children down toward the wharf. Hearing the tail end of the discourse between the two men, she feared an argument was on the horizon.

Augustine raised his voice. "We have a policy here in this colony, Resolved. As long as the Englishman keeps the law of the colony, which you shall be sworn shortly to uphold, he will live in peace and be as good as any Dutch."

I shall hold fast to the laws," Resolved snapped. "I am always a diplomat, and you know that I shall honor my oath to the Company with my life, but do not expect me to invite English to a meal at my table, Augustine. Nay, never ask that of me!"

Tennake gripped the handle of her basket tightly. She well knew how her husband felt about the English. He had told her of his suffering under the wrathful hand of his drunken father; and many times her fingers had tenderly caressed the deep scar across his right shoulder, a prize won from an English sword while in battle. As for herself, she had no quarrel with any Englishman; and in fact, she had found a good loving uncle in Thomas Cole.

"Why would he come to this, a Dutch colony?" Tennake quietly asked Augustine. "Would not an Englishman live better in the Virginia colony, with his own kind? Considering all the terrible war between our two countries, if I were English I would not come to live among the enemy."

Augustine softened his manner. "Not all English are the enemy. Perhaps you would come to New Netherlands if you were English but also a Catholic, for an English Catholic is a rare breed of Englishman. Of course, a Dutch Calvinist coupled with an English Catholic is a rarer breed still and does beget, some would say, a strange fellowship," Augustine smiled knowingly at Resolved.

"An English Catholic!" Resolved roared. "My sore bones, but this colony is an interesting porridge!

"It is no wonder that the Dominie has so joyously taken the Waldrons to heart like a rooster looking for a good hen. The man yearns for some good pure blood in his colony!"

"Say what you will, Resolved. Thomas is a good man and a better friend than many a Dutchman hereabouts."

Resolved took a step backward. "Augustine, my apology to you. I did not mean you any hurt. I should not speak against your comrade; but in all the years that you have known me I have never offered any pretense of my affections for the English."

Joseph listened to the one and then the other. He had decided that it was best to remain out of the center of their disagreement. Privately, he wished only peace and prosperity for all. A man has a place in the world that is arranged by God alone and war should be fought between kings.

Choice of one's religion was another matter. There was but one God, the Lord God Almighty whose son, Jesus Christ, had come down from the heavens to save us all from damnation.

The four stood for a while watching several soldiers challenge the Indians to a game of axe throw. Although the games were friendly, they made a thunderous clamor as several had too much to drink.

Joseph turned to Augustine. "Is not the sale of beer and rum to these savages strictly forbidden?" he asked.

"It is forbidden as well as a serious crime."

"Were I already sworn in, I would fill our jail with the lot of them!" Resolved said.

Augustine chuckled tightly, "Yes and a stiff fine for the Tavern Keeper, as well, for you do not wish to see the trouble that these Indians can cause when they have filled their belly with too much rum."

"Have arrangements been made for us to go to Beaverwyck with the pulpit?" Resolved asked.

Joseph looked curiously at Augustine.

"You do not mention that I, too, shall go with you and my brother?" he questioned Augustine.

"I have more important duty for you, Joseph, but we shall discuss that later," Augustine replied.

Resolved shrugged his shoulders. His face was red with annoyance, but he would keep his patience if it killed him. He had always trusted Augustine, and could not afford to change his allegiance now.

Augustine appeared thoughtful. "We should leave the port as soon as possible with the pulpit because I would like to see it swiftly installed in Dominic Schacts' church up there. The Captain does dislike keeping his sloop in these waters. He fears a burning," Augustine said.

"Then let us leave as quickly as we can," Resolved quickly agreed.

Soon they all returned home together. Tennake was excited and pleased with her purchases of the day—black fabric, lace, and two copper pots. She and the children were exhausted, and were in their beds asleep long before the night had fully closed in upon them.

To insure that she did not hear their discussion, Resolved, Joseph, and Augustine went out and sat on the grass under the stars.

"I am deeply sorry that you came to New Netherlands at such a time; but, be assured that I only knew of this misfortune after your ship had already taken sail," Augustine apologized.

Resolved turned toward his friend. "This I can understand, but please, tell us of the trouble."

Augustine looked out over the still Broadway. "We will tolerate no more Swedish grief. There are seven Dutch warships only hours from here. We have been ordered by Amsterdam to attack New Sweden, retake Fort Casimir and drive those Swedes from the South River once and for all! I have been told that our flagship, Scales, is loaded with thirty-five cannon and is flanked by six warships.

"By weeks end there will be over seven hundred men, a mixture of Dutch soldiers and Dutchmen from our colony assembled here who will be ready to make sail," Augustine lapsed into silence, staring into the sky.

Resolved tugged nervously at his long beard while Augustine continued.

"Every man between the age of sixteen and sixty, except for the Jews and the Negroes, has been called, though we have been excused in order that we see the pulpit safely north."

Shaken by Augustine's words, Resolved roared, "We should be with our fellow colonists to fight the Swedes or we will look like a bunch of blatting lambs afraid to do battle!"

"Friend, remember who sleeps in the house, and keep your voice quieted. Believe me; no one will 'blat,' for everyone knows that the church business that we must attend drives us into dangerous territory."

"I shall fight for both of us," Joseph said bravely.

Augustine was alarmed. "No, Joseph. You shall not go to fight Swedes, nor travel to the North Country. You have been chosen to remain in New Amsterdam to keep watch over the women and children who will be left behind here. Before I hear your rebuke, know that the straw was drawn fairly. Since you were not able to draw the straw, I stood in for you. Yours was the short straw," Augustine said sympathetically.

"How was I so fortunate?" Joseph asked cynically.

"It is done. You were not the only man who drew a short straw. I shall be leaving you with Jacob and Samuel. Jacob can shoot a pistol better than I. And I pity the savage who would come between you and Samuel."

"Joseph, you will have my pistol," Resolved said soberly.

"I fear that our trouble does not lie only with the Swede," Augustine said. "Resolved, if our Director had not been ordered to do so, I am confident that he would never leave his town, but his duty calls him. This trouble that I speak of comes of stupidity."

"How so?" Joseph asked.

"For years Pete Stuyvesant has treated the savages with diplomacy whenever possible, walking upon the shells of an egg with the wild man. Now, his every effort has been washed away with one small amount of foolishness. Old Silver Leg is sometimes a man hard to take, though I must admit that he has been a far better administrator than the mad man the Company sent here before," Augustine reflected.

"Augustine," Resolved said sternly, "You are floating down the river without an oar. You speak in riddles."

Augustine sat up. "My apology. The stupid incident happened some weeks ago, and the fool's name is Van Dyck. In July, he shot and killed an Indian woman, whom he later claimed was stealing a peach from his orchard. I feel, as did many others, that if Van Dyck would have been flogged and returned to Holland on the next available ship, we would have had a better chance of avoiding the violence of tribal retribution.

"Instead, the council decided to imprison him until this business with the Swedes is resolved. He now sits in our jail whilst our Mohawk friends tell us that the Munsee Confederacy is calling their warriors together!"

"But what of these Indians that we saw in the town today?" Joseph inquired.

"They were Lenape and not of the same family. However, keep in mind as they trade here today, tomorrow they may be back with their brethren to cut your throat," Augustine warned.

Holding his head in trembling hands, Resolved said, "I should not have brought my family to this place."

"I would have cautioned you had I been able," Augustine said gently.

"For the trouble he has caused, Van Dyck should have been hanged," Resolved stated.

Augustine was thoughtful.

"Before Stuyvesant came to the colony, there was much bloodshed, but we have been peaceful for nearly five years and although I don't see the way of it, many Dutchmen have married Indian women. If Van Dyck felt that a crime was committed, he should have turned the woman over to the authorities to administer justice. He must have lost his mind and saw only his dead boy's face.

"You see, Van Dyck lost his wife and child years ago in an Indian raid upon his farm; he must have justified his deed as personal retribution. But I do feel the same as you. Van Dyck should have been arrested long ago. Many of our people have suffered at the hands of the heathen yet have obeyed the laws, keeping their hate within themselves."

Resolved stood up. He was full of anguish. "How can I leave my wife and go north now?"

Augustine put his hand on Resolved's shoulder. "You know that answer better than I. We have all committed ourselves to our duties. I promise that you will be back here in less than one week's time."

Augustine turned toward the house, Resolved following. His brother lingered behind on the grass.

Joseph sat quietly thinking that although he was not a fighting man, he was not a coward. In truth, he hated violence, did not own a sword, and until last spring when it was decided that he would come to the New World, he had not fired a pistol.

Thanks to his brother's instruction, if battle came, Joseph would be prepared to fight.

FIVE

For two days Resolved reviewed his circumstances again and again until in the weary end, his prayers brought him to terms with the fact that he had no other choice but to honor his commitment to God and country.

Peter Stuyvesant had sailed for Fort Casimir along with his seven hundred men, leaving a sparsely armed town with a few soldiers and a handful of Jews and Company slaves to defend more than five hundred women and children from possible Indian attack.

Resolved's family would be among that vulnerable number. Although he loathe to be leaving his family, his duty was clear and he would depart tomorrow for the North Country. He wondered if the Swedish leader in Casimir, John Rising, had any idea of the coming attack.

Resolved watched his wife hold her apron right against herself, playfully but proudly displaying her unborn child. He smiled broadly and waved to her, thinking how well his courageous bride had assumed her duties as a colonial wife. She had hardly unpacked their trunks when she was faced with his imminent departure; and admirably, she assured him that all would be well. Surprisingly, there had been no tears, but instead she bravely bade him to think not of her welfare, but only of his safe return.

When he looked deeply into her round blue eyes, Resolved knew he had found in his wife's heart a greater treasure than all the gold left behind in Brazil. Although he had loved and meant no disrespect to the memory of his first wife, he believed that he loved Tennake more.

He was sorry that he could not recall the sparkle in his first wife's eyes, though he remembered them to be the color of the ferns of the glades. When he recalled Rebecca, he saw a frail and sickly woman, whose once warm hands had turned cold; and he knew he had not held them as often as he should have.

As a young man he was eager to respond to the call of battle and spent most of his free hours playing at bowls and dice or consuming rum. He had not even been nearby when she gave birth to any of their three children. He sighed deeply. He had promised the Almighty Lord and himself that should he take a second wife, he would not fall into the trap of turning a fresh, comely woman into a withering vine.

He recalled Tenny's father reading to him one eve from the book of Proverbs. The Scripture said, in Proverbs 20:29, "The glory of young men is their strength, but the beauty of old men is their gray hair." Though not a deeply religious man, Resolved had especially enjoyed this verse as he believed it held a solid message. He would take care to use the wisdom gained from his life lest he die a broken man.

Despite all that had happened in Brazil, Resolved had kept his faith in the opportunity offered by the colonies. He still believed that here a man of common means could aspire to greatness, though not without risk. Brazil had been such a risk, one that had cost him a wife.

A chill ran down his back and his chest tightened. *Tennake is a stronger woman,* he told himself.

What remained was for him to make a success of their lives in North America, where time had built a new stairway and the relentless desire for yonder and better had become the framework of a new home in a new land. Once again he silently swore an oath to the Almighty that he would not fail.

The prior morning at the weekly meeting at City Hall, Resolved had taken his sacred public oath to uphold the laws of New Netherlands. Thus, his second step toward his reconstruction had been achieved. Later, after the ceremony, Joseph had expressed his surprise upon discovering the government's policy in New Amsterdam:

Except for matters of great importance, which were decided upon by the Directors in Holland, the city in the wilderness was totally self-governed since the year 1653, when a charter from Holland had arrived allowing for free elections of officials. However, it was clear that His Honor, Peter Stuyvesant, had the first and the last word on all matters in the colony.

City Hall had many more in attendance than usual at this particular weekly meeting. Resolved and his brother had soon met all the Burgomasters and Schepens and the Director, as well as most of the town officials who saw the need to rid this land of the Swedes or absorb them into the Dutch colony.

When the Swedish leader, Rising, came back to America from Sweden the previous spring with another three hundred settlers, their only recourse, lacking Holland's aid, was to take up arms against them. The Dutch had enough to contend with between Indians and their English neighbors and would be fools to allow the Swede foothold.

Resolved had been sworn in as Night Sheriff of New Amsterdam and Deputy to Nicasius de Sille, Sheriff of the Colony, without the official selection by the town's officials. He had been greatly insulted when one of the Schepens voiced his opposition to "half a Dutchman, half an Englishman" holding public office.

Upon listening to this argument, Stuyvesant banged his wooden leg upon the plank flooring, quickly silencing the Schepen. His Honor pointed out that Waldron was his personal selection based upon a fine record of service to Holland and the recommendations of Mr. de Sille and Mr. Herrman. There was a moment of silence and then the discussion returned to Rising.

All being settled, Mr. de Sille informed Resolved that he would police the town from nine in the evening until four the next morning, and his neatly folded blue and orange uniform awaited him on the table. The Director smiled benevolently as Mr. de Sille further instructed Resolved that if he found a tavern open after the official closing time of nine P.M., he had authority direct from the Honorable Colonial Director to stiffly fine the proprietor as well as the attending patrons.

Privately, Augustine told Resolved that Peter Stuyvesant saw a strong stiff fine as the remedy to most of his troubles and expected his law officers to fill the colonial pots. Fines were also established for anyone drinking on the Sabbath Day or selling liquor to the Indians at any time.

Resolved assured everyone that the laws would be upheld to the letter. After he and Joseph had been excused from the Swedish expedition, the Director informed him his new duties in the town would commence upon his return from installing the pulpit in the church at Beaverwyck. Then, in noble fashion, Stuyvesant had bowed and waved them away.

This morning Resolved carried a mixed bag of emotions upon his shoulders as he observed Tennake. Worry pressed hard against his chest as she called out to him from the far side of the garden:

"There is enough food left in Augustine's garden to feed the whole of Peter Stuyvesant's army."

Resolved smiled at her, remembering how their grand leader had teased his wife when she met him at the Kermis Fair. The Director had come upon her and curiously asked her name, which she said was Mistress Waldron, wife of Resolved Waldron, come fresh from the Princess. She then introduced his two daughters, who had been pleased to be allowed to touch His Honor's wooden leg.

How impressed Tenny had been with the great Peter, Resolved mused. She thought him fine to speak to a common newcomer, and remarked that he appeared quite pleasant and jovial to her, the Director laughing out loud when Rebecca had politely told his greatness that the silver bands adorning his wooden leg were very pretty.

Aeltie, on the other hand, was more impressed with the little wooden man that was made to dance merrily on the strings held by the "puppeteer."

Tenny had apologized for Rebecca's boldness and Aeltie's indifference, insisting later that the Director had been as kind as any father would be, saying that he understood the temperament of the young ones as he had many of his own.

Resolved had laughed, telling his bride that she brought out a tenderness in their leader that few had been privileged to see. She had received his undivided attention, whilst his officials must wait days to gain his ear for a moment.

"Wife, 'tis good news, for now I can get to business without fearing that our brave men will starve upon returning. I will be cutting firewood with Samuel by the side of our house should you need me."

Resolved forced a smile as he watched his beloved disappear into the Herrman's house with a full, heavy basket of vegetables. He would work with his brother Joseph and Augustine's Negro today, cutting wood for the winter season, which was nearing quickly. He hoped that a good section of his ground would be cleared by the end of autumn so that a garden could be sowed early next spring.

Captain Vermilye had offered his son Jeremiah's help when not in school, and Augustine insisted upon sending his Samuel to cut through the massive tree trunks. Come planting season in late April, they would burn the tree stumps and the branches and sow the corn and beans around the stumps in the rich earth which would be mixed with the burned ash.

When Resolved arrived at his property, Samuel was already at work with his axe beside Joseph. "You have me for the remainder of the day, Brother," he called out to Joseph.

"Is all well at the wharf?" Joseph called back to him.

"Yes, tomorrow I make way to Beaverwyck, and glad I will be to get there and back again. Because of these troubled times, I tried to dissuade Elizabeth, who wants to be with her eldest brother, from making the journey; but there was no reasoning with her so she and Adrian will travel with us."

Joseph nodded nervously.

"God willing we will have cleared this field by the first of November. Augustine tells me that we should beware of the winters here, as they will give us much more snow than we knew in Fatherland. But we may purchase dried fish and venison from the Indians to staple us through the hard season, that is, if they have not cut out our hearts first."

"Joseph," Resolved sighed, "the good Lord Almighty will protect us. We have our cow that was given to us by the Company, and Tenny purchased six hens and two fine roosters at Kermis. We will have no blade taken to our throats, and the work will get done."

"Always the strong one," Joseph replied.

"For now, we have the help of Augustine's Negro and our strong arms, and I will return within a week's time and then we will put our backs to it. You will see."

Resolved picked up the axe and was about to join Samuel in the cutting when he saw one of the soldiers from the Fort approaching, waving vigorously.

"I have a message from Dominie Megapolensis for Resolved Waldron and I was told that I would find him at the house nearest to Mr. Herrman's."

"I am Resolved Waldron. Slow down, man, and catch your breath."

"The Dominie wishes that you come to St. Nicholas in all haste."

Resolved dropped his axe. "Tell him that I will come momentarily."

The young man departed in the direction of the Fort.

"What other plague awaits us?" Resolved asked, grimacing.

"As you yourself said, Almighty God will protect us," Joseph replied, swinging his axe at a large defiant trunk.

As Resolved passed Augustine's house he stopped long enough to tell Tennake that he would be at St. Nicholas, and that she should send Captain Vermilye's boy, Jeremiah, to Joseph at their property.

He proceeded directly to the church, following the nearly deserted streets of the city. But upon reaching the Fort he was surprised to find twenty Negro men reinforcing the front bastions without any apparent supervision except for one old man acting as overseer. When Resolved reached St. Nicholas, he found both Dominie Drisius and Dominie Megapolensis engaged in serious discourse with two other savages.

"I'm so happy that you have come," Dominie Drisius said beckoning him forward.

"It doth seem that I have been in every corner of the city today; but please excuse my delay."

"I have been unable to find Augustine," the minister announced with a trace of anxiety.

For a moment, Resolved was taken aback. "My friend was forced unexpectedly to New Haarlem to look over a new barn being built on one of his lots; but he assured us that he will return before dark tonight, since the distance is approximately the same as from old Amsterdam to Haarlem," Resolved replied.

"Yes, it is so," Dominie Drisius said.

"Well, then," Dominie Megapolensis said with relief, "we will leave it to you to be the bearer of the news at hand and we shall concern ourselves no further as to his whereabouts."

"Meanwhile, these two have brought us grave information," Dominie Drisius said, motioning his hand toward the Indians standing nearby.

"They are Mohawk, very old friends of mine from Rensselearwyck," Dominie Megapolensis added kindly.

"How did these Indians know where to find you?" Resolved asked curiously.

Both Dominies were somber as Dominie Megapolensis replied, "As well as you may trust in God above, my friend, you must believe that the Mohawk always know of my whereabouts. In this land they are the keepers of the eastern gate of their great Iroquois Nation and it is their sacred duty to know who arrives and who departs the territory."

One of the Mohawk Indians began to speak to Dominie Megapolensis who listened closely, then replied in the language foreign to Resolved.

"Two Rivers reports to me that last night two yachts were burned as they were moored at the North River near Fort Orange; and he believes that the Munsee, who are members of the Esopus tribe, committed the crime, although no one saw the criminals."

Dominie Drisius frowned. "I doubt that they would be Esopus because they rarely will travel that far north of the Walkill River."

The Indians became agitated.

"They say that the farms of three Walloon families were also burned just six English miles south of Beaverwyck, and insist that the deed was done by the Esopus," Dominie Megapolensis said as he tried to calm the natives.

"Do you think they speak the truth?" Resolved asked with heartfelt concern.

"I believe the yachts were burned and many good people have died upon their farms," Dominie Megapolensis replied cautiously.

"But one cannot be certain who committed the crimes," warned Dominie Drisius. "Although it matters not. We must all be on the alert."

"Have there been any other attacks against the Fort or Beaverwyck?" Resolved queried.

"No," said Dominie Drisius, "although this is not unusual because the savages will most often pick one settlement at a time, or a yacht such as we see here, and then vanish into the night."

Dominie Megapolensis looked at the Mohawk attentively. "I believe that these two are sincere and have come to warn us, a brotherly show of their good will. They want to escort us to Fort Orange tomorrow. Two Rivers tells me that he has sixteen braves and ten canoes camped a short way up the river. He is offering to accompany us. I feel we should accept their proposal."

Resolved did not know how to respond to any of this, and although he was a sworn deputy, his superior, De Sille, was at sail with Stuyvesant. Since he was not experienced with these heathen in New Netherlands, he decided that he would abide by Dominie Megapolensis' decision and, right or wrong, he would accept the consequences for his choice. After all, who better to trust for his wisdom and judgment than this man who had lived among the savages for fifteen years?

"We cannot blame the Esopus for crimes without further investigation," Dominie Megapolensis said. "For all we know, the fires could have been set by drunken Dutchmen. I have seen this bad business before."

"And it could well be the work of the Mohawk or the English," Dominie Drisius added sardonically.

"Be English or Dutch, we live with deceit," Dominie Megapolensis returned quickly. "Some English would murder an Indian and blame a Dutchman."

Dominie Drisius registered exasperation. "In due time our civilized English friends who are surrounding us today may prove to be a worse enemy than the violent savage."

Resolved nodded in agreement. "My sentiments are not so far away from yours. I have heard that in the English colony they already publish pamphlets warning their people to beware of the murderous Dutch who would cut off an English maid's head while in repose. They play boldly at their games, these English!"

"True, it is most difficult to know who one may trust, but my heart tells me now to lower our shields and accept Two Rivers' offer," Dominie Megapolensis replied softly.

"Then I will agree," responded Resolved, "but I will keep my hand upon my sword and stand beside you courageously."

Dominie Megapolensis smiled slightly. "It is most unfortunate that you come to the New Netherlands at a time like this."

"Nay, do not concern yourself for me. I have faced death in battle many times, although I confess that it has been some time since I have bloodied my sword."

"We keep our faith in the good of the Almighty, our Protector," Dominie Drisius declared stoutly.

Resolved stood with his hand upon his sword as he looked into the eyes of the Mohawk brave called Two Rivers. He spoke without a trace of reservation or fear. "Dominie Drisius, please convey my words to the savage that we will be pleased to accept his escort."

The Dominie translated as instructed and Resolved turned to the two ministers. "I have some experience with the Indians of Brazil; however, the Portuguese had the natives fairly well in hand when we Dutch took over the place. Brazil's natives differ from these that I have seen here because they are not a fearsome aggressive race of people, and many are now Christian, converted by Jesuits long ago. Methinks I prefer the Catholic savages of Brazil to these heathen," Resolved said.

"I see," Dominie Megapolensis said, although sarcasm was in his tone.

Resolved's confidence was returning. He was far from a novice in military affairs and he had never run from a decision. "I had more trouble with the Africans while in Brazil than I did with the native Indians. Those old Afrikaners were wild lions when first brought in, I can tell you," he recalled.

The tall aged Dominie sighed deeply. "Only time will show you God's plan whilst you are in this country, Mr. Waldron. I know little of Brazil; whilst in New Netherlands our savages are against one another consistently, and many tribes are far from peaceable. Unfortunately, our previous Director Keift believed negotiation or diplomacy was unnecessary in obtaining the cooperation of the natives. He was more of a savage than any of the tribal people and caused us all great harm by brutally murdering hundreds of them, many innocent children. He maliciously used the war between the Mohawk and the Wappinger.

"Although in prior years we had been on peaceful terms and traded with the Wappingers, Keift ordered his soldiers to kill all the natives in their tribe when they came to us for protection from the Mohawk. The bloody fate of the Wappinger brought a time of blackness and shame upon us all.

"There has been bad blood between the Iroquois Federation and the Munsee Federation for years and so I understand that my Mohawk friends would have us believe their enemies guilty of crimes against us. However, I have known Two Rivers for over ten years, and we must accept his promise of safety, for anything else would be a great insult."

"Dominie Megapolensis, I thank you for your advice," Resolved said.

Resolved knew of the stories of the previous Director, a poor excuse for a Dutch commander, because the tales of violence in New Netherlands had traveled as far away as Brazil and Jamaica. Although Director Keift knew the official policy of remaining neutral in the wars between the tribes, the empty-headed commander had chosen to hunt the Indians down like beasts and drag them back to Fort New Amsterdam where his soldiers laughed while they publicly tortured them to death.

Such inhumane treatment had ignited Indian raids all around the city and had Keift been in power now, Resolved, although he believed in authority and would administer proper punishment when called for, would have no part in cruelty. He and his family would have never come to America had Keift still been at the helm.

"It is unfortunate our people were made to suffer for the actions of one dishonorable man," Resolved commented after a moment of reflective thought.

Dominie Drisius looked sadly at Resolved. "God willing, we will not know such shame again."

Their meeting concluded, Resolved bade good day to the clergymen and took his leave from the church. The wind had begun to blow, causing the more fragile autumn leaves to break away from their branches.

Resolved walked beside the cemetery of St. Nicholas where the yard was filled with many headstones of those who, lifted from the burden of this life, now rested in well-deserved peace. He suddenly stopped to observe Augustine's Negro girl, Sarah, alone in the middle of the graves, kneeling with hands folded tightly in fervent prayer. Resolved stared at her.

What was she doing so far away from the house? Did they bury the Negroes in the same ground as the whites in New Amsterdam? No, this could not be, for in all the colonies there was a separate plot for them.

He called out to her, but she bolted, disappearing into the streets of the city. Resolved walked to the stone where she had knelt. It read simply, Annetie Herrman, Rest in God's Peace.

SIX

Barely a week had passed since arriving on the Island of Manhattan; and already Tennake pondered her quick acceptance of a man who carried with him such a hard, sorrowful past, and a history, which had bequeathed three children in need of a mother's love and care.

They now sat patiently at the table, awaiting their breakfast. Bustling about, placing bowls before them, Tennake sighed, knowing that there really had been no decision process, as such. As her sister once humorously counseled, a maiden's heart and her mind live quite separately.

Tennake took down each child's spoon from the wall rack, understanding that in all the months prior, she was not thinking at all. It seemed that there was much wisdom given in jest, for it happened that Resolved held her close and she felt only the quickened beat of her heart. Indeed, heart and mind were oceans apart.

The child within her kicked sharply while a distinctively crisp, early autumn breeze blew through the open shutters. She paused for a moment to watch a handful of the Director General's African slaves who were harvesting apples within the Dutch West India Company orchard across the street. Loneliness engulfed her while she ran her hands over her swollen belly, but her child kicked once more signaling her that this was not a time for girlish pondering of vows.

She reached for the water pitcher, dampened the apron around her middle, and wiped her brow. She must remember her promise to her husband: remain calm, and show her family a staunch face.

She saw that young Will was staring at her. Innocently, he accorded his new mother his complete trust, but he and his sisters sensed her fear. She knew that her restlessness made their father's absence all the more difficult.

Sarah hummed a tune which Tennake did not recognize and the gentleness of her soft voice comforted her greatly.

"Are you not well, Mother?" Will asked.

"Nay, Will, I am good. I am only a trifle bad-spirited this morning. I am missing your father, be I truthful. But, soon he will be to home and you will not have such a weak partner in the games."

Until nine in the evening the night before, she and Resolved's eldest consoled each other with a game of Tick Tack; and although exhausted when she retired, no rest was to be found within the folds of her soft feather bed. Intermittently, Tennake worried and prayed while listening to the curious strange clamor of the night creatures that roamed outside the house.

In God's good care, she believed that Resolved and his party had arrived Beaverwyck. In God's good care, they would return to this foreign outpost, for surely it had lost its original exotic appeal and now seemed to be next door to the gates of hell.

Will smiled. "Methinks that you could best me in the game if you would," Tennake relaxed. "You came by the win honestly."

Now her thoughts turned anxiously toward her host's elderly manservant. Jacob hoped to rid them all of the monotony of sharing another evening meal of corn porridge and shortly after dawn had walked to the center of the town to purchase fish for their supper. Tennake was doubtful that any would be brought home because the neighboring Indians who might make a trade for their catch had deserted New Amsterdam yesterday.

Rumor was that Mr. Peter's bowerie farm, which lay two miles north of New Amsterdam's planked wall, had been burned to the ground by hostiles. Sadly, he would return home from the Casimir expedition with Peter Stuyvesant's soldiers to find only ashes where his farm had been. No one had escaped the attack and his wife and two daughters had been taken captive.

Despite all calamities, Jacob went marketing. Tennake assumed that since Augustine Herrman's slave had lived in New Amsterdam twenty years, and she was a newcomer, certainly the old Negro knew best. But her heart stirred when Sarah reported that the merchants' wives had boarded up their shops. They had heard the news from a farm woman who along with her nephew had miraculously made her way safely back to New Amsterdam. New Amsterdam was not penetrable yet no one wished to keep their establishments open, making themselves and their babes more vulnerable to hostiles in the absence of their men folk.

Shutters and doors had been bolted by the women in hopes that Director Stuyvesant, their right and honorable colonial leader, after delivering their men folk back safely, would, come judgment day, rot in hell for placing them in such peril in his safe city.

Undaunted by talk of marauding savages from the north, Sarah remained quite at ease in her master's house, saying that later that day she would bake the remainder of the pumpkin squash with wild mint leaves and her freshly churned butter.

Sarah assured Tennake that the women closing their husband's shops were the result of foolish hysteria. The Indians would never dare to attack New Amsterdam; and their husbands would be angry upon return when they learned of the losses brought upon them by such foolishness. Tennake took heart. In truth, what else could she do?

If only Jacob would bring fish back. Perhaps a good meal would help cast out some of the demons.

In the meanwhile, she and Sarah made do serving a breakfast of corn and cream and the remainder of the cheese. After they had all eaten, Tennake removed the soiled white linen cloth from the table, and brushed clean the red and blue woolen rug that remained, covering the square wooden surface. As was her daily practice since the first day on the ship while sailing to the New Netherlands colony, she read aloud to the children from Resolved's great Dutch Bible.

Verses had barely left her lips when the atmosphere of her safe house erupted, and she and those in her charge were struck by the thunder of barbaric human screams. They were shrill frightening whistle-like sounds, a thousand beast-like voices spilling out into one blood curdling cry.

Rebecca bolted around the table to her side, the child overturning her stool in her haste. She clutched at her stepmother's sleeve in terror.

Sarah ran to the window.

"What is it?" Tennake asked. She could feel herself shaking.

"'Tis the wild men," Sarah shrieked in astonishment. "We are being attacked, Mistress! They have come into our city!"

Tennake joined the dark woman and the two put their faces close to the thick glass, straining to see through the panes toward the Company farm across the Broadway. As the horrified women watched, a hundred or more screaming savages streamed through the Company's apple orchard. A large flock of wild blackbirds blustering in panic rose into the sky and created an enormous cloud that seemed to encompass the whole of the Dutch West India settlement.

Tennake could never have dreamed such a sight. Their attackers were armed with crude weapons and were following others with muskets in hand. They forged across the great Broadway which led to the heart of the small city, their smooth, naked, painted bodies thrusting onward toward the town Green where only days before colonists and natives had played games together during Kermis fair.

While Will wedged himself between the women, Sarah uttered, "These are not our island natives. They come from afar."

"They are so many," Will whispered. "Methinks there are hundreds." One could see that the number of intruders coming forth from the orchard seemed endless and Tennake's heart began to freeze. She knew that she must act quickly.

Urging Sarah away from the window, she prayed silently for strength, and then directed, "We cannot allow fear to be our master, woman." She was surprised at the assertiveness of her own voice. Sarah nodded, gasping for air in an attempt to control her wits.

Rebecca was wailing loudly and ran to Tennake once again throwing her arms about her large middle, burying her face in her stepmother's apron.

"I do not want to die. I am afraid!"

"You are not going to die," Tennake replied sternly. "You must be brave, Rebecca. Be brave for your little sister. Look, look at Aeltie. The poor little babe."

Sarah searched the kitchen for a weapon. "You children come with Sarah," the Negro ordered nervously. "We will go to the loft and hide ourselves and trick those wild men. We will stay safe because I have a special charm bag around my neck. Do you all see this?" She pulled the pouch filled with herbs away from her breast.

Three-year-old Aeltie curiously tugged at the long white ribbon attached to the small cloth bag around the slave's neck. "Come children, follow me," Sarah repeated.

Will surveyed his stepmother doubtfully while she worked to pry free Rebecca's clinging fingers. Once the task was accomplished, Tennake's trembling voice issued one final instruction, "Will, take Rebecca with you."

The boy did as asked and grasping his sister's hand quickly followed Sarah, who carried Aeltie up the narrow loft stairs around the side of the hearth. "You come, Mother," Aeltie pleaded from over Sarah's shoulder.

"To be sure, little sparrow, I will come soon," Tennake reassured her softly. After they had gone, she looked around the room for a weapon of her own with which she could defend her family.

"What can I do? Dear Lord of the heavens above, guide my steps." At once her eyes rested upon the Holy Book that lay upon the table. Tennake scooped up the Bible into her arms and darted up the steps to the loft where William now held his hand tightly over Rebecca's mouth in an effort to quiet her sobs.

He watched curiously as Tennake put the great Waldron Bible under her skirt, seating herself upon its thick leather cover. His staunch new mother reached for Sarah. "You and Aeltie come closer."

When Rebecca's sobs had dissipated, Will removed his hand. They all sat breathlessly still for a few moments. Then it was Sarah who began to weep.

"The time of our death has come, Mistress," she whispered to Tennake. With resignation, she laid her head next to Tennake's bosom, quietly saying her Christian prayers and forgetting her magical pouch entirely.

Unlikely as it would have seemed only a few days ago, Tennake had become fond of Sarah, appreciative of her company and her lessons about the herbs of the wilderness.

Strange how God sets a path, Tennake thought as she stroked Sarah's damp forehead. *She, the daughter of Dominie Barent Nagel, was to go through the gates of eternity with Sarah wearing a magical pouch about her neck.*

She found herself wondering if Jacob had made his way to the town safely whilst he pursued the fish for them. Did he come upon Mr. Herrman's other Negro; the one Will called the dark giant? She could not remember if the slave was clearing wood at her brother-in-law's house or if he had gone to the town with Jacob. She whispered a short prayer to the Almighty for them both.

Everyone gasped and unconsciously nudged closer together as a thunder of gunshots erupted in the distance. Tears came into her eyes as she thought of her husband, and her absent brother-in-law who had not cared to breakfast with them earlier, saying that he would go directly to the Fort at first light for any news to be had of Resolved. Now, sensing that this was God's chosen time for her and her charges to die, she must accept that she would never see Resolved or his brother alive again.

Silently she began to pray that the Almighty Lord would make her courageous and that their deaths would be swift. She thought of her unborn child and her heart ached.

If only she could see Resolved's strong face just one more time, her death would not be so difficult to endure. If she knew that her man had been spared his life because of his absence from her now, then this would be a blessing in the midst of such treachery.

Would not the Lord grant her a small gift then? Would the knowledge that Resolved was alive be enough to soften her sorrow?

She looked at the children, and then at Sarah who was nearly in an absent trance. Finally, her eyes rested upon the small, pure face of little Aeltie. She touched the softness of the little girl's arm while pulling the child closer to herself. "Hold on to me, little one," she soothed.

Aeltie began to fall asleep with her thumb in her mouth. "Jesus will send his angels to guard us," Tennake whispered.

Sarah closed her eyes, her lashes seeking refuge against the well bordering the exquisite arch of her face; but peace suddenly evaporated amid a frightful turmoil of furniture being tossed about below.

Within seconds came the dreaded sound of footsteps ascending the stairs. Momentarily, five feathered and painted Indians stood before them, as demons would, their black eyes fixed with a purposeful violence.

Aeltie awakened crying, and as Tennake drew the child closer, she heard the alarming toll of the bell of St. Nicholas in the distance.

One of the wild men reached for Aeltie, attempting to pull the child from Tennake's arms; but she held firmly crying out to God, but whispering, "I beg of you, send Michael leading Thy angels that they take charge of these little ones. Another assailant came from behind, roughly taking her long braided golden hair into his hands, and while he raised his axe to strike the murderous blow, Tennake offered her soul up to God, knowing that within moments she would be in another world, a part of everlasting light.

She saw the arm rise to smite her, but before the blow could be struck, the course of her life changed. Her assailant's arm was held in midair as a third Indian interrupted his companion, screaming an urgent command that seemed to demand the would-be murderer withdraw his weapon.

The Indian halted immediately, though angry to be robbed of his conquest. He thrust his axe violently into the large trunk near Rebecca and her brother. Terrified, the children clung to one another as the Indian produced a sharp blade, which he waved ominously.

Aeltie fell to the floor as Tennake jumped forward, stepping between the glare of the blade and her children. This time the native did not hesitate. He seized her long braid and slashed it brutishly from her head, leaving her bare scalp exposed.

A scream erupted from Tennake's throat while the elder warrior shouted another angry command at those who had been rummaging through trunks that contained fabric purchased at the Kermis Fair. The three withdrew with Tennake's cloth and her red wool winter cloak draped over their greased shoulders. The others stood in front of Tennake appearing quite calm, speaking to one another in their native tongue.

Her sight blurred for a moment. She felt dazed and could feel the cool air at the back of her head, although she felt no pain.

Oh, sweet God, she thought. *They discuss taking us captive, perhaps to torture us all slowly before we are to be granted death.*

Her courage began to slip away. She had not been afraid when she had prepared herself for her own death or a swift death for Sarah and the children. But she could not bear to see them tortured to death before her eyes. She had heard all the terrible stories of such crimes here in the Americas; women violated, and then made to work as slaves. The savages often took hostages for ransom, but God only knew how they would be treated.

A new wave of terror swept over her as she wondered if they would cut her child from her belly and then roast the babe on their fires. She had heard that this, too, had been the fate of a colonial woman years ago as retribution for the skinning of a young Indian girl alive by one of Director Keift's soldiers.

Her mind whirled. She had overheard her husband talking to his brother regarding the Indian woman that had been killed months ago in the peach field. Perhaps she and her family along with poor Sarah were to be slain to make up for the unspeakable offense of these white men.

"Lord, Jesus, remember Thy faithful servants" she called out, *"have pity!"* She repeated the words over and over, strongly and with great determination.

She reached down for the Bible and held it tightly to her breast as she shouted again,

"Almighty Lord, protect us!"

The two Indians looked at Tennake with alarming concern.

"Pity Us! Lord, Lord!" She could hear nothing now but the sound of her own persistent voice as she prayed earnestly.

Suddenly, an urgent summons was called out in a native voice from an authority on the street below them. As quickly as they had come, the Indians were gone. Before the last departed, he triumphantly waved her long yellow braid in the air for her to see his coveted trophy.

Tennake was soaked with perspiration, but felt no blood at the back of her head. She weakly crawled to Rebecca and William. As they looked up into her eyes she put her finger to her lips. Although the house now seemed silent, all remained in the loft together without moving for many minutes.

Finally, Tennake dared to make her way down the stairs. She proceeded slowly, not knowing what horror waited below. As she rounded the stairs to the room, she could hear shouts in the distance. Then gun shots from the direction of the Fort. But all was quiet in front of Augustine Herrman's house upon the Broadway.

She looked at Augustine's fine upholstered chairs, which were slashed apart, the fabric hanging loosely to the floor near shattered Delft dishes. The front door had been ripped off its hinges and was nowhere to be seen. Augustine's precious books were thrown about the room, the pages of open volumes rustling ominously in the air.

She walked toward the overturned table. The tapestry rug that had covered the table was gone. *Obviously, another trophy to be displayed tonight around the heathen fires,* she thought.

As she approached more closely, her hand rose to her mouth. Once again her stomach turned over. There, face down alongside the broken furniture, lay the bloody body of Augustine's dark giant of a man, his skull crushed, a large section of his powerful back carved away.

She felt her knees shake so violently that she feared she would fall into his bloody pool. She reached for the one standing chair to brace herself. *Poor Samuel,* she thought. *God bless him; may his angels carry him home.* He must have run to the house when the attack came, and his last thought was to save his master's guests.

She had to look away. The sight of his butchered body had begun to make her sick once again. Suddenly, she heard the sound of footsteps running up the front stoop. Her heart pounded faster. She stood with her back against the hearth.

"Thanks be to God. You're alive!" Joseph cried as he stepped though the doorway and over the debris.

Tennake stared as though seeing a ghost. "I thought the wild men had killed you."

"Where are the children, woman?" Joseph asked softly.

Tennake continued to stare.

"Tennake, where be Will, Rebecca and Aeltie?" Joseph asked more sternly.

Tennake looked toward the ceiling beams.

"The children have all been spared and are in the loft with Sarah. It must have been the hand of Michael that held back the axe. He protected us all, but not poor Samuel." Her voice trailed off. In a stupor, she bent down to pick up some pieces of broken pottery.

Upon hearing his uncle's voice, William started down the stairs. "Go back to the loft, Will. I will tell you when it is safe to come down," Joseph called.

Joseph did not wish William to see the mutilated body of the Negro. He anxiously searched the disrupted room for something with which to cover the man.

Tennake began to gather the scattered books. "The savages were about to murder us all, the axe was raised, yet instead they did us no hurt."

"Are you in pain? I see no blood," Joseph said while gently examining the baldness of her scalp.

"No, I have no pain," Tennake replied.

He took the books from her shaking hands and led her to a stool at the opposite end of the room away from the body of Samuel. "Sit here. Rest yourself, whilst I tend the children."

After seating her, he ran upstairs where he found Sarah cradling Aeltie. He tried to receive the child when she reached out to him, but the servant's grasp was fierce.

It was only after Will went to Sarah with his own boyish soothing words that she willingly released his youngest sister to him.

Joseph took Sarah's hand and led her down the stairs. She sobbed loudly as she looked upon Samuel's pitiful body. With tearful, questioning eyes Sarah looked up at him.

"Master, where is Jacob? Where is Jacob? Oh, Lord Jesus, is he gone from us forever like Samuel?" Sarah began to cry hysterically and could not be comforted though Joseph had pulled her to his chest, wrapping his arms firmly about her. After a moment he held her at arms length, "Listen to what I tell you Sarah, you will be calm. 'Tis a good sign I have not come across his body. Many have made their way into the Fort for safety. Jacob may well be among the living."

Tennake raised herself slowly from the stool and went to Sarah, embracing her. "Keep your faith," she whispered trying to smile.

Joseph could not bear Sarah's sobbing. What a foolish man he had been to take this venture into this brutish New World so lightly! Whatever he thought this wondrous adventure would be, he never dared to dream of the murderous sight he was witnessing.

Of what use is a learned man such as himself in the midst of such calamity? He still had possession of Resolved's pistol, though he was sure this would mean little if the Indians decided to drive them all from these lands. The only true defensive strength this family had lay dead near the hearth of his master's house.

Who am I for these women and children to place their faith in? If Samuel could not defend himself against his attackers, then surely I, too, am lost, Joseph thought.

His self-disgust for having failed to protect his brother's family crowded out every other thought from his mind. Perhaps if he had been in the house with Resolved's pistol when big Samuel had come to them; but he was not, a good servant's blood had been spilled. Looking around the disarray of the room he struggled to make sense of some plan, something that he could do to help them all to survive this terrible time.

He had been to the Fort to obtain any official information that he could from Captain Berger, one of the few soldiers that had been left behind. He was halfway back to Augustine's home when the attack had begun, forcing him to seek protection in the tobacco warehouse as the streets became overrun with the wild men from the neighboring woods. He had been struck with a fearful horror when he saw the great number of their attackers.

What he could not understand was why every inhabitant of New Amsterdam was not already dead. He had seen hundreds of savages everywhere, but, remarkably, he saw few dead settlers. The wild men could have killed us all, he reasoned, because there are too few of us to offer any effective opposition to such a strong campaign.

As if Sarah were reading Joseph's mind, she jumped up from her stool and ran to close the shutters over the windows.

"You are right, Sarah, we require more protection. Come, the both of you, help me to move this Kas in front of the opening."

The three pushed the Kas securely against the gap where the front door had once been.

"Does your master have any other firearms within the house?" Joseph asked.

"He keeps a pistol in his writing desk," Sarah replied as she ran to the bedchamber.

Within a moment, she handed Joseph the pistol, powder, and ball pouch.

"I know how to fire the pistol. The master showed me a long time ago," Sarah said proudly.

"Good, then you shall keep this one." He handed the pistol back to Sarah and looked around the room. "We have secured the house as best we can. We must await the return of the enemy."

"Do you think the savages will return?" Tennake asked softly, looking to her brother-in-law for his counsel.

The words were hardly out of her mouth when they heard the toll bell ring out urgently from St. Nicholas.

"We must go to the Fort, Master," Sarah said excitedly to Joseph. "The bell calls to us. It is the command that the way is clear."

As she urged departure, voices could be heard from the front of the house.

"Keep still, woman," Joseph ordered.

Ignoring his directive, she whispered, "They not be the wild men. They be white men from the way I hear the talk," Sarah peered through a crack. What she saw astonished her. "It is Izaac Abrahamsen, the Jew tailor."

"Ah yes, I recognize him," Joseph whispered back. "He was one of the men at City Hall the other morning. He and about twenty other Jews were protesting to Director Stuyvesant, angry at having been refused the right to enter the Citizen's Militia. But their arguments held no water with Stuyvesant or any of the other good Christian townspeople. I felt the same. It is seemingly unholy for Christian and Jew to fight in a battle together."

"Why does he come to us now?" Tennake asked.

"I do not know. There's another along with him. A young man. His son methinks."

All the while, Izaac Abrahamsen was shouting wildly. It was understood that his intent was urgent.

"I have a mind to think him speaking Portuguese," Joseph mused.

"Look, Abrahamsen beckons me to come out of the house."

"The Jew is injured," Sarah muttered with quiet concern. "See the blood on his arm."

"Then, if the man be hurt, in all good faith we must help him, be he Jew or not!" Tennake said boldly.

The boy, about fifteen or sixteen, ran up the stairs behind his father, a pistol in his hand. Speaking hysterically in Portuguese while he waved his gun toward the direction of the Fort, he urged Joseph to come out.

"How would he come by a pistol?" Joseph exclaimed.

"We must tend to him, Joseph," Tennake repeated. Having heard the concern in Joseph's voice, Abrahamsen barked a sharp order to his son, who threw down the weapon.

"We must tend to the injured man, Joseph," Tennake urged.

"I would think that Augustine would not have it so, nor would your husband, woman," Joseph whispered.

Sarah whispered, "The boy means only to plead for his father, Mistress."

"Joseph, please," Tennake's heart was in her eyes.

"Well, though it may bring us harm to have them among us, we cannot leave a wounded man on our host's front stoop, to die before our eyes. Come, we will move the Kas out of the way," Joseph sighed wearily.

The three shoved the Kas aside. "Come in and be quick," Joseph ordered as they entered the house, Tennake grimaced when she saw the arm of the injured Jew as he passed her.

Without a word Sarah quickly detached the sleeve from her dress and began to tend to Mr. Abrahamsen's wound as best she could.

"Methinks that he will keep the limb," Sarah pronounced after a few minutes of binding the arm.

Mr. Abrahamsen was still frantically attempting to urge departure. But Joseph did not feel that it was wise to leave the protection of the strong brick walls of Augustine's house with the women and children in tow. After some time had passed, he convinced the Jews to remain with them. He had begun to feel fortunate having them beside him. And they did provide two more pistols. He was grateful for whatever help the Lord would send, though he wondered at the bravery of these Jews who had come to offer their aid at great personal risk. What an odd assembly they were, Christian, Negro, and Jew armed together against the wild men.

What would become of their souls if the enemy would come again tonight and kill them all? Would Christ be merciful and reward this boy and his father for their kindness though they had never been baptized into the true faith?

He looked over at the boy who had fallen fast asleep with his pistol in his lap. The young man's father looked back into Joseph's eyes, but did not speak. *It is a pity,* Joseph thought.

Night covered the town as the hours dragged by in the cold dark of the house. At first light of dawn, Joseph thought that it was safe to remove the corpse of the unfortunate Negro that lay beside them. The women wrapped his body in the white linen tablecloth that had survived its place in the Kas.

Samuel had been a big man, well over two hundred pounds, and nearly five foot ten inches tall. It took all the strength that Joseph and young Abrahamsen could manage to move his body to the back of the house where Augustine usually housed his horse and wagon.

Cows, chickens, and pigs mingled in noisy confusion on Broadway. Fires smoldered everywhere, though mercifully there had been no fires set in Augustine's lean-to, or any part of the house.

Their sad task accomplished, they were turning away from Samuel's corpse when Joseph heard the distressed voice of Dominie Drisius calling to him.

"Joseph, how fares all at Augustine Herrman's house?"

"Our women and children are all unharmed, except for my sister-in-law, the wife of Resolved Waldron, who has lost much of her hair to a heathen's blade. Praise God, she does keep her scalp and her life. We lost Augustine's big Negro. He doth lay here," Joseph called back to the Dominie.

The Dominie crossed the road toward Samuel's body.

"Have you seen Augustine's houseman, Jacob?" Joseph asked.

"Yes, he follows directly," the Dominie replied. "Thank God that you have been spared, Joseph."

Joseph looked back toward the house. "Two Jews, young Abrahamsen and his wounded father, came bravely to the house to escort the women to the Fort, but I convinced them to remain with us."

The Dominie made no reply as he observed Sarah sweeping up the fine white household sand mixed with Samuel's blood.

More and more of the townspeople were venturing out onto the streets. Gerrit Hendrickson appeared with two of his Negroes saying he had lost only one of his slaves during the attack and he had shot the devil Indian that killed him.

When Tennake heard Gerrit's voice she bolted past Sarah down the front stoop steps of the house to him. "Mr. Hendrickson, is your wife safe? How fares Ann?"

Hendrickson scowled. "Ann has come to no bodily harm, though she doth lay silent on our bed without moving, her eyes open and wild as a savage."

While Tennake tried to comprehend what her neighbor told her, she reached to the back of her head, recalling the treachery that had befallen her. Tears welled up in her blue eyes.

The Dominie put his arm around her. "Thank God for your life, child. Your hair will grow back before the babe within your womb celebrates his first year."

Tennake nodded. That her life and the lives of her family had been spared had truly been a miracle.

"You must all come to the Fort at once. We have managed to get a messenger out by boat to Director Stuyvesant imploring him to return in all haste. I trust that he will have received our dispatch before this day ends, but for now we must go to the protection of St. Nicholas church."

Dominie Drisius could be heard by the crowd that had begun to gather. Tennake looked earnestly into the minister's face. "First, I must go to Ann Hendrickson. Hopefully, another woman's coaxing is all that is needed to bring her around."

Joseph's body straightened with alarm. "Nay, sister-in-law. You will go now to the Fort with the Dominie and your children and the servants," he commanded sharply.

"I will do as I think right, Joseph."

Joseph grabbed her by the arm. "Tennake be not the stubborn one. Mistress Ann is not your kin; the woman is not your responsibility!"

"I must do this, Joseph. You go with the children and Sarah and see them safely housed. I promise if she does not respond to me, I will not linger but come myself."

Joseph shook his head. He knew it was useless to argue further and waste precious time. "You have become a sword in my side, Tennake, yet I cannot force you to do my bidding."

Tennake smiled for the first time since before the attack had begun. She turned to the Dominie.

"Dominie Drisius, whatever may befall me during this terrible time, I beg you to recount to my husband that I take full responsibility for my own actions."

The Dominie took a deep breath. "I will do as you bid."

Colonists had begun to stream into New Amsterdam from the outlying boweries and patroonships begging water as they came through the wall for protection. Most of the weary survivors were old men, women, and children who had escaped into the woods after their homes had been attacked. Through the thick of the forest and under cover of night, they had frantically stumbled toward the safety of the Fort in New Amsterdam.

Dominie Drisius spoke to a man by the name of William Aldricks. He and his family were exhausted having traveled all night, thankful that the moon had been full, giving them enough light to make their way. Stopping by the well, Sarah had given the children water to drink while Aldricks hurriedly told his story.

"Yesterday afternoon, near to 3 o'clock, the savages caught us off our guard whilst I, and my elder son and twelve-year-old nephew thatched the roof of our barn. My son and nephew were brutally murdered, the barn burned to the ground; but somehow I escaped and ran toward the house to my wife and younger children.

"During the commotion, I saw my family running toward the back woods and quickly followed. I had to leave the bodies of my son and nephew where they had fallen."

He wept as he spoke of it, knowing the hopelessness of his situation. Aldricks could not understand this attack upon them. His family had treated the Indians well and had known many of them for years.

"Consider," he lamented, "we had nothing to do with the killing of the Indian woman in the peach field of New Amsterdam's orchard. Nay, we thought the Indians our friends.

'Many times they slept in our house at the foot of our beds. Why would they come at us in this way when they knew that we were innocent of any share in the wrongs that their people sought to avenge?"

The man's wife stood next to him, sobbing her agreement.

"We treated all the wild people with charity and there was no reason for this bloodthirsty attack!"

The Dominie listened with quiet sympathy. Her shaking voice cut like a sharp knife as she vowed an oath to her husband. "I would leave this country and curse this place behind me. I would sail upon the next available ship to Holland if only we had the fare. I will never take my children back to our bowerie. Never! I will beg in the streets of New Amsterdam for their food first!"

"We must go back, Bess. When our militia returns and all have been calmed we must return and give our boys a Christian burial," Aldricks said quietly.

"Nay, I will not," his wife insisted between sobs.

The Dominie patted the woman's arm. The family walked beside the minister toward the Fort.

Joseph joined Will, Rebecca, Aeltie and Sarah, and after they were safely within the walls of St. Nicholas, he returned to Gerrit's along with Jacob, who had miraculously survived.

While en route, the two had passed the jailhouse where they found the instigator of all their troubles, Van Dyck, the one who had slaughtered the Indian girl months before as she ate a peach from his orchard.

He lay dead on the floor of Schaefbanck's jail, an arrow through his heart. Both of his hands had been cut off.

Jacob looked over Van Dyck's mutilated body and said, "Master Joseph, God willing, those savages have what they came for. Now they leave us be."

"Yes, it does seem that we are rid of our bad apple, but the cost was most high."

"Look to me like the prisoner was in want of a guard," Jacob said. Joseph nodded.

"Our town's jailer fights the Swedes with Stuyvesant. He should have taken his blade to this one's throat before he left; or, better still, tied Van Dyck to a staunch tree outside of the walls of New Amsterdam and let the wild men do as they would with him. We could have been saved much destruction."

"Martha, Dominie's eldest daughter, says she saw the Indians come to us," Jacob added. "The wild men came up behind her father's house through the orchard by the water. Mistress Martha says she see more than sixty dugouts and five hundred wild men come in those heathen vessels.

"Then old Ann Bloom, she be the Negro on the Van Willer bowerie just outside the wall of the city, stopped me alongside the road and she say more than a thousand came through the wall near her from the wild lands."

"God protect us," Joseph breathed.

As they left the jailhouse and proceeded toward the Fort, the pair encountered Tennake and the wagon that held the traumatized Ann Hendrickson.

Soon the church was filled with terrified souls huddling together fearing the immediacy of another attack.

Joseph, however, prayed that the Indians were done with their killings here. The savages had taken many captives whom they would trade for a handsome profit. He desperately tried to block from his mind dismal scenes of torture, which might be inflicted upon the poor victims before any attempt at rescue could be made.

That night the colonists gathered in clusters and listened in horror as the wild men could be heard rejoicing in a song of victory. Rescinding their curse that Peter Stuyvesant should rot in hell, prayers were offered up to God for the salvation of all and the swift return of the militia from Casimir.

SEVEN

Resolved stared at the shoreline in confusion. Could this be Beaverwyck, the robust settlement that had shipped a staggering wealth of over six thousand beaver skins to Europe in the year 1654? Where were the great mansions of these merchants, the prosperous families belonging to the Calvinist congregation which supported the noble venture of transporting a pulpit that they had risked their lives to bring them?

As if he could read his friends mind, Augustine said, "Yes, this is the place."

The villages of Beaverwyck and Fort Orange lay beside one another along the high banks of the wide restless North River. Resolved had half expected a golden doorway opening to a flowering mecca for trade where the roads would be paved with Holland's finest yellow brick. Instead, as their sloop approached Beaverwyck's shoreline, he saw a pitiful village of no more than forty houses whose roofs were thatched with straw, the frames crudely constructed of wood obviously taken from the vast surrounding forest of tall pines. There was not the smallest stockade guarding the settlement, yet more savages awaited them than he wished to see during a lifetime. However, Resolved was grateful for the Mohawk attachment that the good Dominie had arranged for them. Their voyage up the river, upon which the Englishman, Hendrick Hudson, first sailed his little Dutch ship, "Half-Moon" nearly forty years before, had been uneventful.

Resolved's eyes rested upon Elizabeth Beekman who stood tall and graceful, a brave figure beside her brother, and then back to the line of pathetic dwellings along the river bank. He wondered what Tennake would think of this primitive hodgepodge in the wilderness.

"'Tis a merry greeting, thanks be to God," Augustine said.

Resolved nodded his agreement, momentarily speechless. The enthusiastic, joyous welcome of the natives astonished him and before the crewmen had lowered anchor, nearly one hundred Mohawk Indians were paddling toward them through the cold, September morning waters.

Within the hour passengers, led by clergy, had climbed down the side ladder of their vessel into waiting canoes for transportation to the shore.

As Resolved disembarked, he recognized—amid the beached charred remains of a Dutch vessel—a face from his past life in Brazil. A young soldier stood quietly among the frenzy of wild men who now surrounded the minister. "Arnet VandenBergh, can this be you?" Resolved asked cautiously.

"Waldron?" the young man dressed in formal blue and orange uniform answered, uncertainly.

"'Tis you, to be sure," Resolved laughed running toward the Corporal.

"This is indeed a pleasant surprise for my eyes to feast upon. How do you come to be in this miserable hole?" VandenBergh asked as the two embraced.

"Oh, the luck of the draw," Resolved replied.

The Corporal made a sour face. "My lot was not so well cast. Nowaday I am left behind to guard the pigs and the cows, while my comrades are off to fight the Swedes."

"Take heart, I, too, was left out of the merriment."

"'Tis their loss," VandenBergh said, his frown disappearing.

"How long have you been at this post?" Resolved asked.

"Six months," VandenBergh replied.

Resolved nodded. "I have just arrived in New Amsterdam with my family. Barely did we set our feet upon dry land when I was assigned the duty of overseeing the transporting of a fine pulpit for your church."

VandenBergh began to laugh heartily. "And I am to see to its proper installation, a tedious duty I had thought—until now. There is no glory in guarding this deserted Fort or wet-nursing the pride of our beloved minister. But although I had longed to fight the Swedes with Stuyvesant, I shall now have the company of my old rascal friend, Waldron; and I see that the sun begins to brighten."

"It is good to see you, Arnet," Resolved replied warmly.

"How is your good wife?" VandenBergh asked.

Resolved looked away. "My Rebecca died shortly after we returned to Fatherland, God rest her soul."

"My condolences I give to you. I recall her to be a goodly woman"

"Yes," Resolved responded quietly.

"Whom do your children stay with in New Amsterdam?"

"Ah, well, God was good and gave me another wife who is in New Amsterdam with my children. She soon will give me another child."

VandenBergh pushed his long blonde hair behind his ears. "I am sorry to hear the news of your first wife, but praise God for his generosity in finding you a second good woman." He slapped Resolved's arm.

"I am fortunate," Resolved replied gently.

"I, too, have hopes of finding a good woman, but the good ones are few up here in this wilderness. How long will you stay in Beaverwyck?"

"Not for long as I wish to return to my wife and children in all haste. The wild men from the south are on the war path and like your village, New Amsterdam is a lonely chicken plucked of every feather."

"New Amsterdam is a strong fortification," VandenBergh declared.

Resolved shrugged. "What of those burned vessels?" he asked pointing toward the debris along the shore.

"I do not see heathen mischief there," the Corporal replied.

"Nay? Not the mischief of the savages?"

"Nay, the local wild men are friendly. The Munsee Indians brew up violence in the south, but these fires could be the foulness of one Dutch farmer and his three brothers who live across the river in Rensselearwyck village. Though there is no proof."

"Why do you think thus?" Resolved asked.

"'Tis in my mind," VandenBergh said, pointing to his head, whereupon, Resolved noticed a large bruise to the right side of the Corporal's temple.

"Many times we have troubles with those people living yonder under the protection of the Rensselearwyck patroon and their patroonship courts. Tenants, employees and officials of Rensselearwyck are not bound under the jurisdiction of the Dutch West India Company courts. They must answer to Director Stuyvesant on your island of Manhattan," he said.

"What foolishness! How can this be?" Resolved asked.

VandenBergh shrugged. "I'm told that it is the way of it since the beginning back in 1652, when Stuyvesant first came to establish this village right here upon the patroon's lands. Methinks that the patroon did not take kindly to this infringement of authority and insisted upon keeping his own court. The patroon and our Director knocked heads from the start.

"So now our little village of Beaverwyck has its own court and is responsible for Fort Orange as well as other areas. I tell you this is not a favored assignment here. As you can imagine, it is difficult for a soldier to live under two roofs. These no-good fellows come across the river to make mischief and then run home to the patroonship, whilst I stand helpless with my thumb up my nose!"

Resolved scratched his head. "Your village is far from what I expected."

A far cry from what many expected. It is a strange bed in other ways, too. You will care little for the other Dominie that is with us. It will not take you long to see that Dominie Schaets constantly puts his nose where it does not belong. He continues to interfere with civil matters on a regular basis siding with one authority, or the other, as may please him for that day.

"I hate the thought of him standing behind that new pulpit and so will many others. Last year, before I came over, some of the people of Beaverwyck tried to have him removed, but we are still stuck with him!" VandenBergh lamented.

"Bad business," Resolved muttered as he looked through the crowd and saw Augustine approaching them.

"Ah, Augustine, I wondered if you had drowned between the sloop and the canoe or if one of these friendly savages had knocked you on the head. Corporal VandenBergh, this is my good friend, Augustine Herrman, who persuaded me to come over from the Fatherland."

"Good to meet you," Augustine said heartily.

"I am honored, Sir," the Corporal replied bowing slightly. "Of course, Mr. Herrman, you will both take lodging at the Fort barracks will you not?"

"We would be very grateful, for apparently the good Dominie has been carried away by his beloved natives; so we entrust our keeping to you," Augustine replied.

"Pray then, do follow me," the Corporal invited.

"All duty cannot be dull and lifeless in this northern port," Resolved commented. "Come; tell us of what enlivens you of late, Arnet? Do you have any sport save putting your finger in your nose?"

Augustine pressed for an answer.

"Yes, what sport is there to be found that will keep us amused? Your old friend here was recently sworn in as Assistant Sheriff of our fair town and he has much excitement awaiting his return, especially controlling our pig settlers."

"What is your problem with the pig settlers?" Arnet questioned.

"Yes, the pigs are a problem to be sure," Resolved answered, trying to remain sober.

"We have plenty of amusement, too," VandenBergh interjected. "Just last night, I was forced to arrest fifteen year old Dirk Groesbeck who attempted to break down the door of the Widow Wendel after all others had long since retired to their beds."

"Fifteen and not marched off to fight the Swedes?" Augustine mused.

"He and a few others were left to hold the Fort, should they be needed. The Lord Almighty protect us all if it comes to that."

"Small help will the boy be to you locked in irons," Resolved reminded him.

"The lad got into some of his uncle's brew. The uncle had left with the others, leaving young Dirk to his own devices in the small hut that they share together at the edge of the village. Young Groesbeck's father passed into the hands of the Almighty some months ago, and since the boy had no other relatives, save one uncle, the duty of providing Dirk shelter fell to his father's brother.

"The uncle, Joannes Groesbeck, is a brutish man, drunken most of the time, and on those occasions beats his nephew mercilessly. These beatings, mind you, are unjustified," the Corporal lamented.

"This bad treatment of poor orphans should be stopped," Augustine interjected.

Resolved nodded his agreement.

"Could not the boy be apprenticed out to a local tradesman thereby plucking him away from his cruel uncle?" Augustine asked anxiously.

"Once again I am forced to put me finger up me nose," Corporal VandenBergh replied in exasperation. "Having come from Holland three years prior, Dirk's poor father had been a signed tenant farmer at Rensselearwyck. I am told that Peter Groesbeck was a good man, whilst we well know that many good men fall and the worthless live a long life."

"My brother will be looking for an apprentice," Resolved suggested as the three continued toward the Fort.

"The lad might well be a pot full of troubles," the Corporal replied thoughtfully.

"What did you arrest the youth for?"

"Lust," the Corporal replied seriously.

"Lust?" Resolved queried, bursting into laughter.

"Methinks that the criminal sounds to be in good health, Resolved," Augustine said smiling.

"I do not jest," VandenBergh said pointedly.

"I can see that you do not," Augustine replied soberly.

"Though warned repeatedly, the youth forces himself upon the timid Susanna Wendel whenever the opportunity does arise," VandenBergh continued.

"A wild boar is he?" Augustine asked.

"If you were desirous to take him to New Amsterdam you would have to hog tie him and then drag him forcibly from our village. What a bother to you he would be!"

"Pray tell us, Arnet. What did he do to this young blushing Mistress?" Resolved asked.

The Corporal's face remained serious. "Last night, Dirk was determined to profess his love, giving not a thought, or course, to her mother and the other children in the house. Not that I cast a blame upon him for his feelings of affection toward Susanna Wendel, for every eligible man in Beaverwyck wishes to wed her."

Augustine turned toward Resolved and winked as the Corporal continued. "The fool used a great log which he had found in the nearby brush to push in the door of her house, making enough commotion to wake ghosts of heathen Mohawk ancestors as they sleep in their bark longhouses across the river."

"No doubt his desire overcame him," Augustine murmured.

"I was armed to do battle," said VandenBergh, his tone displaying vexation. "Whilst on Rattle Watch, I had my sword, musket and rattle, which when used is enough to wake our dead as well as the ancestors of the wild men."

Resolved laughed knowingly as the Corporal continued his story. "But alas, I alone could not get hold of young Groesbeck who is twice my size. Dirk kept up his mischief and I shook my rattle briskly, though I knew not who would respond to my summons. Soon, the prattling rattle and the abominable noise of this culprit awakened an angry Widow Wendel, who thrust open her door and stepped forth with broom in hand.

"She, too, was most anxious to do battle and began beating the drunken Dirk most resolutely. Unfortunately, I, too, was in the line of her fire, and she caught me sharply with a determined blow thus producing this sore bump you see."

Both Resolved and Augustine examined the Corporal's swollen brow.

"Now came forth all of her sister housewives armed with spoons, sticks and axe, some taking great pleasure in beating the boy whilst others stood about in a fit of laughter. Well, the 'reinforcements' and I contained this criminal and carted him off to the barracks. Methinks Dirk will think more properly of his beloved come the morrow," he concluded.

Augustine and Resolved could not control their laughter. "Methinks that Dirk Groesbeck will not be so quick to break down a maiden's door in the future," Augustine pronounced.

Resolved looked at VandenBergh who was beginning to smile. "You must learn to laugh more often, Arnet, and laugh hardest at yourself or believe me you will grow old before your time."

Corporal VandenBergh laughed in spite of himself. "Resolved, you are still a stalwart old bear and I am happy that your heart is as light as it was in Brazil."

"Methinks it best to be merry," Resolved told him. "Laughter is strong armor. But take heart my friend, for I too will soon be on night duty with rattle in hand in New Amsterdam."

The three then retired to the protection of Fort Orange. The next few days, after enlisting the services of the patroon's slaves, they worked undisturbed while setting the pulpit, installing the weather vane on the peak of the blockhouse church, and loading lumber for the return trip to Manhattan Island.

Thankfully the Mohawk, unlike the more southern tribes, loved the Dutch. It was enough to fight the Swedes and the Munsee tribes without having to fight the tribes of the Iroquois. Resolved saw why the Van Rensselear patroon had trouble enticing colonist families to work his lands. Who would want to grovel in the dirt when the beaver money flowed like water? Trading for furs with the Mohawk allowed white men to earn a good living without the hard work involved in wilderness trapping.

The one striking similarity between the settlements of Beaverwyck and New Amsterdam was the abundance of brew houses.

It was at the Widow Lansing's Tavern that Resolved and Augustine met one of the most charismatic, coarse old traders that ever nested in those northern woods. VandenBergh's guests were happy for the suggestion that they sup at the tavern on the eve of their departure.

The door to the Widow's small log and sod structure had been thrown open. Whilst they dipped their bread into the communal bowl of chicken broth in the center of the table, a wild looking white man with a long dark curly beard and a long scar down the right side of his face appeared in front of them.

"Are you Corporal VandenBergh?" the unseemly intruder asked in poor Dutch with a strong French accent.

"I am," VandenBergh replied looking up briefly from his crust of bread.

"I am Jacques La Croix, from New France. I now make my home to the north in the land of the Cayuga who are the younger brothers of the Mohawk on the North River."

The Corporal looked up into the weathered scarred face of the Frenchman. "Yes, I've heard of you, La Croix. Were you not captured by our loving brothers, the Mohawk, some years ago? You survived their beatings and were adopted into their tribe. Are you this La Croix?"

"I am the one," La Croix replied.

VandenBergh wiped his mouth with his sleeve and stood up from the table. "I am honored to meet you, La Croix," he said.

La Croix bowed awkwardly.

"Would you sit with us?" VandenBergh asked. "This is Resolved Waldron and Augustine Herrman who have come from New Amsterdam."

La Croix nodded at the two strangers beside the soldier. "I am thirsty and would take some of your good Dutch beer," he said pulling a stool to the table.

VandenBergh looked toward his companions. "La Croix is an honored brother to every Mohawk within our colony and beyond, a position of respect that he earned from the wild men many years ago. He was captured during an Indian raid upon his father and mother's small trading post in the north, near Montreal.

"His mother and father were killed whilst he and his brother were taken captive and then forced to run through two parallel rows of Indian women and children in the Mohawk village. The tribal peoples were armed with clubs and sticks; and he was beaten severely.

"Others, who had been taken captive by the wild men during different assaults, had fallen to the ground exhausted after their ordeal and those poor souls were led away into the woods where they were tortured to death. Two of them were roasted alive. But La Croix and his brother, having survived the gauntlet, were spared. This man is known to the Mohawk by his Indian name, Onoda."

"All that you say is true," said La Croix quietly. "My name, Onoda, means "great hemlock." He accepted a large wooden tankard of beer from a serving maid.

VandenBergh nodded and went on.

"La Croix was fortunate to have been adopted as a son into the tribe by one of the powerful families, thus replacing him for a son they had lost in battle. Although I never met you, La Croix, I know you well, as you are considered one of the greatest tribal negotiators within New Netherlands."

"I have been a son to my Indian father since I was twelve years old," La Croix said smiling.

"We are honored to meet such a great man," Augustine said.

"Truly," Resolved added.

"I assume you seek me out with good reason. Do you have news from beyond our settlement?" VandenBergh asked.

Resolved felt his chest tighten. "You have news of New Amsterdam?" he asked.

"Yes," La Croix answered, "I fear I have unhappy news to report to you. This morning I learned from my Iroquois brothers that the South River Indians have attacked your Fort at New Amsterdam. Many have been killed. Many are taken captive. I have come to offer my services."

Augustine was stunned. "New Amsterdam? Impossible!" he shouted.

"I cannot believe this," VandenBergh murmured.

"When did they attack?" Augustine asked.

"Two days ago," La Croix replied.

Resolved exploded. He jumped up from the table, overthrowing his stool. Dazed, he staggered for the door, muttering that he must leave and return at once.

The short, but powerful La Croix, placed both of his hands tightly upon Resolved's broad shoulders and then spoke with compassion.

"Perhaps your family is still safe. In any case, you cannot help them by leaving in unplanned haste. My Mohawk brothers and I will go with you to New Amsterdam and we will help your people."

"Calm yourself, Resolved. This man is right. If there be hope, you will find it with him," VandenBergh said.

Resolved trembled. "God protect my family!" he cried out.

"Listen to me, old friend," VandenBergh pleaded. "Have faith in La Croix. This Frenchman has brought many whites out of captivity."

Resolved tried to think clearly, yet he could only see Tenny's long golden hair lying bountifully against her pure white breast, and he groaned at the thought of his unborn child sleeping within her tiny frame. One by one, he saw the glowing innocent faces of his children and his brother.

Has he come here out of a false pride and not a true duty at all? If his family is dead, how will he ever be able to forgive himself?

Augustine, VandenBergh, and La Croix immediately returned with great urgency to the barracks where news of hostile Indian attacks had preceded them. Though the trouble was far to the south, the people of the village knew that Fort Orange was as defenseless as New Amsterdam. Many argued that the Munsee Indians would never dare to come so far north within the strongly guarded realm of the Mohawk. Still, who would have thought the savages would go against the city of New Amsterdam?

Doors and shutters slammed shut. Like their counterparts in New Amsterdam, the women who were operating their husband's business quickly abandoned their posts and scurried to the protection of the Fort.

Later, as if he were an angel with a divine message, a lone soldier arrived unharmed at Fort Orange from Fort Christina. He brought news that New Sweden had been defeated without a single shot. The fine advantageous port and fertile valley with over four hundred Swedish colonists were once again under Dutch control.

The next morning Corporal VandenBergh, Resolved, Augustine, and La Croix, along with ten Mohawk braves, boarded the sloop for a solemn return to New Amsterdam.

EIGHT

Two days had passed since the attack upon the city of New Amsterdam. The sanctuary of St. Nicholas with its bright lemon-yellow brick had become a bleak tomb, binding together over four hundred terrified colonists and slaves.

Tennake shuddered as she looked at the desperate group covering every inch of the church's cold brick floor. She wondered if the pursuit of any land was worth the price of so many innocent lives.

Sarah gently took the hand of her mistress into her own.

"I heard Mr. Aldricks' wife say that the heathen have burned the settlement at Kent Island."

"Are you sure that Mistress Aldricks said Kent Island, Sarah?" Tennake asked anxiously.

"Yes," Sarah replied, adding quickly, "though it is believed that some may have escaped."

"Let us pray that Resolved's kin survives," Tennake sighed as she repositioned the sleeping Aeltie in her arms.

Sarah's face tightened. "I will pray for all who are in misery, Mistress, but methinks that our tears will fill many barrels before this terrible time comes to rest."

The women watched as weary survivors from attacks outside the city continued to enter the church. Everyone spoke of the fires that burned all over the New Netherlands. With each accounting, Tennake's heart turned over with renewed fear for the fate of her husband. If her anguish became a truth, how in the Lord's sweet name would she ever be able to carry out her noble promise to care for these children by herself?

She knew that Joseph would stand by her, but he would be able to do little if forced to support both his brothers' widows and the combined orphaned children. She feared that under such terrible circumstances she could not stay in the colony. Yet she could not go home either, since the winter would soon be upon them.

There would be only one answer, which was; of course, she would be forced to remarry immediately. This was a harrowing thought that left her sick at her stomach. To be sure, if her husband did not return, there would be several immediate proposals of marriage as she was still a young woman, pleasant to look upon, and had proven her fertility with a babe growing within her womb. A good healthy wife in the colony was said to be worth a maid's weight in gold.

Was it only a week ago that Augustine had laughed, warning Resolved to take care not to insult his wife or leave her alone too long, for there were plenty to replace him beside such a fair creature? She had blushed when he continued, saying that there were twenty men to every one woman in the colony, and even the poorest of the indentured girls could better themselves in marriage. Tennake closed her eyes and prayed again for Resolved's safe return.

The attack upon New Amsterdam had been a severe, unexpected shock to everyone. The savages were more enterprising and perceptively cunning than any of the colonial leaders would have thought, for they successfully struck at the heart of the Dutch colonial empire. Surely, the great Peter Stuyvesant did not think the wild men capable of such action, or he would not have left his city so vulnerable.

Tennake looked over the remaining food that she had hastily gathered within her apron as she passed Augustine's home on her way to the church. She had left the side of Ann's wagon for a moment to fetch a few apples, a small loaf of bread and a bit of cheese that had miraculously survived within the built-in cupboard on the side of Augustine's hearth.

Now, little food remained, though she had watched the portions prudently, dividing them equally among the children and Sarah. Wearily, she now began to break the remaining crust into small equal pieces.

She was so tired, although sleep had been impossible for her. Her eyes wanted to close, but she could not permit herself the luxury of blocking out her terror, for it was her responsibility to keep the vigil.

Ann lay motionless upon a black wool robe, her terrorized blood-red eyes staring blankly at the large oak timbers supporting their holy refuge. She barely moved as Tennake's eyes discretely followed her empty gaze toward the beams.

She wondered if her new friend was not silently witnessing the Demon of Vengeance, the serpent who performed a wicked dance that slowly drained the life of his helpless victim below.

With every breath Ann expelled the black vapors of death, her shallow breathing the only sign of life that came from her still body. She was a pitiful sight, her red hair wetly matted against the thin delicate blue white skin of her heart-shaped face, and ice-cold hands that both Tennake and Sarah hopelessly tried to warm with their own.

During the first night, Isaac de Forest's wife stood over Ann Hendrickson shouting accusations of possession; but it was Mistress de Forest, herself, who Tennake thought looked as if she had lost her mind. Unfortunately, everyone listened to Marie de Forest because Isaac was one of the wealthiest men in the colony. As the wife of a prominent citizen, Marie would be supported by the others, be she reasonable or not.

Sarah had protectively wrapped her arms about the comatose woman so as to shield her from the poisonous vile that sprang continuously from the lips of Marie de Forest.

"Put Mistress Hendrickson into the street," the prominent townswoman had screamed." Give this brew master's wife to the savages whom she loves so well. Everyone here can see that she has been cursed by them."

Marie's daughter had pulled her away, but not before the crazed woman spat upon Ann's smooth glazed face, which despite all the insults remained unchanged.

"Mistress de Forest is not alone in her thoughts, Mistress," Sarah said as Tennake wiped Ann's face clean with her torn sleeve.

"Why do you speak thus?" Tennake asked.

"I hear the other women whispering together. Many of them have lost their wits and I fear that they would do harm to this poor woman. They say the devil has made a home in Mistress Ann's breast. Methinks that this could be true, for the devil is strong among us and he can put himself into a body if he has a mind," Sarah said assertively.

"You must collect your wits, girl. Have faith in the Lord God and know that there is no demon within Mistress Hendrickson. You must believe me and not be fearful of her."

"I will try, Mistress," Sarah replied softly.

Tennake knew many believed that the Devil could plant a terrible sickness within one's soul that would also spread to those who were within reach of the victim. It was believed that the only way to cleanse the stricken free of this evil was to burn that foulness out with the fire of purification.

Tennake sighed and watched as Sarah cradled Ann.

"Methinks that spells and witchcraft are the work of Satan and I'll not have any part of the talk of frightened foolish women. Has not the Lord Almighty cared for us thus far? Lift up your heart to him now, Sarah, and remember that prayer to Christ brings forth only goodness," Tennake whispered.

"Me speak what I hear, that is all," Sarah said quietly.

"Do not listen to them." Tennake handed the dark girl a piece of apple. "It is unholy to think that because Ann's hired man killed a savage during the attack, a curse has come upon Ann from the victim's brother. Do not believe in the heathen power of a vengeful wild man."

"You have been in the colony but a few days, Mistress. According to Mistress de Forest, the Indian that spoke the curse is the 'Keeper of the Faith' and is very powerful in his tribe. It is said that he placed his curse upon the hired man, Mr. Jensen, and Mistress Ann."

Tennake rubbed her burning eyes. She did not believe that any savage, though he spoke a thousand oaths of revenge, could lord his heathen power over anyone who was as fine a Christian as Ann. *These women have given in to their fears,* she thought angrily.

"This woman is blessed and not cursed," Tennake said looking down into Ann's face.

"I am afraid, Mistress," Sarah murmured.

"Do not fear, Sarah. Our Director and the militia should return to the city before the night falls."

"Me hope to God it is so."

"What is Mistress de Forest's grievance against Ann? Why did she say that Ann should be placed outside the wall with the savages that she loves so well? I do not understand," Tennake asked.

Sarah looked anxiously about the church and seeing that everyone was occupied with his or her own trepidation, she began to recall what she had witnessed over the last years.

"Methinks that Mistress de Forest holds hatred in her breast for Mistress Hendrickson."

"Yes, but for what reason? What terrible plague has turned her heart into stone?"

Sarah twisted the sweet bag about her neck. "Mistress Ann is a kind woman who loves all children as if they be born from her own body. She cares not if they be white, African or Indian," she said softly.

"Why would anyone hold a hatred toward a woman who loves children?"

Sarah shrugged.

"Methinks because of the wild children. The Esopus savages killed Mistress de Forest's sister and her husband five years ago when they were working their fields down near the Walkill Creek; and now she would have vengeance against any savage."

"I would not want to imagine such a death for any of my own good sisters," Tennake said thoughtfully.

"Many have died here, Mistress, but not everyone holds hatred in their hearts like that woman."

"Five years is a long time to be bitter," Tennake reflected.

"Mistress de Forest's husband holds a grievance toward Mr. Hendrickson, who like his wife, also treats the wild men fairly in all the trade. Me cannot understand why the savages came into Mr. Hendrickson's house to make a fight. Master Hendrickson and my master are good men!"

Tennake touched Sarah's arm indicating caution. "There are many good people."

Sarah shook her head. "More that are bad, Mistress, and many are not good as you think. They beat their slaves and servants for no just cause. Soldiers kill the wild men and throw Indian babes into the river to drown. The white soldiers stand on the river's bank laughing while the Indian women try to save their little ones.

"These same white men sit behind Director Stuyvesant at service in this church and say to all that they fear God Almighty. They think themselves innocent of crimes, but methinks they be murderers, cruel men who should have the sword taken to them."

"Hush Sarah, your words sound as mad as Mistress de Forest," Tennake admonished.

"Not so long ago," Sarah continued, "Director Keift's soldiers tied an Indian boy, who was no more than twelve years old, to a post in the center of the Green where they skinned him alive. The colonists cheered. Mistress de Forest yelled louder than all the others Jacob told me.

"My people talk of this time of darkness to this day, and although it is said that some whites hold a shame within their hearts, many do not consider the death of a Negro slave any more than a butchered hog."

Tennake had tears in her eyes. "The horror is too much for my ears."

Sarah persisted. "The old Negro says to the fresh slave off the ship, 'You watch that you do not anger your master or else your head will be atop the master's mantle as an ornament for his good family to look upon.'"

"I cannot believe all this, Sarah. In truth, you must want to frighten me for your amusement." Tennake spoke briskly.

"You must learn how things be here, Mistress. White people do not trust other white people who stroke their servants or their slaves with kindness. They say, 'give a cookie to a heathen child and watch him bite off your finger.'"

"This cannot be the way of it."

"I speak the truth, Mistress."

"Mistress Ann was here during those black times that you speak of, was she not?" Tennake asked.

"Yes, Mistress Ann has been in New Amsterdam many years," Sarah replied. "She and her husband came over during the time of blood when Director Keift was here. Methinks that she has always been very brave, for she went against the Director by protecting an Indian man and his woman, and she would have given her life for them. That is why me cannot understand why the savages come at them this way."

Tennake sat closer to Sarah. "Tell me the story, Sarah, though I will judge if this be mischief you speak."

"This be no mischief, Mistress," Sarah said defensively.

"Those wild men were peoples of the Lenape tribe who Master Hendrickson traded with. The wild men had slept by their bed and shared their oysters with them. It was Weequehla, who showed Mistress Ann many good ways with the herbs of the forest. She showed her how to make a fine sweet bag to hang about her neck, which pleased Mistress Ann's husband greatly. Weequehla showed the Mistress how to brew a fine lemon balm tea for drink, the same that I gave to you when you first did taste my cookies."

Sarah paused with her story while she finished her piece of apple.

"Once when Master Hendrickson was near to death with a fever, old Weequehla brought him back to life again with her powerful secret waters," Sarah said.

Tennake smiled. "Secret waters?" she asked dubiously.

William pulled himself closer, taking an interest in the story.

"Tell us what became of Weequehla. What were these secret waters that you speak of, Sarah?" he asked.

"When Sarah a child," she answered, "the Indians lived close to the river, not far from this settlement. Weequehla's drink was secret."

"From whom did Mistress Ann protect these Indians?" Tennake asked.

"It was the Mohawk wild men from the North Country, who were seeking vengeance for the death of another Mohawk brother. They came to kill Weequehla and her son who were innocent of any such crime. But, because they belonged to the same tribe and to the same family as the savage who had done the killing, it is Indian custom that they must be accountable."

"One savage must make amends for his brother?" Tennake asked.

"Yes, Mistress, this is the way of it. Our Dutch leaders have long ago made brothers of the Mohawk and will stand by them in their deeds. But, Mistress Ann did hide Weequehla and her boy within her barn for over two weeks until it was safe for them to travel forth.

"It was good that they escaped because the next year the rest of their tribe became sick with a pox and most of them died. They, too, would have died, either by the hands of the Mohawk or from the pox; but now I have hope that they live someplace beyond the forest."

"You did not see Weequehla or her son again?" Will asked.

"No."

"Does Mistress de Forest know of the deed?" Tennake questioned.

"Only my master and his uncle knew of the Indians hidden in Master Hendrickson's barn," Sarah said. "I belonged to my master's uncle back in those times and lived at his great house which was just beyond where the wall of planks stands now. I was only as big as young William, but I can remember my master telling his uncle that he knew the wild people were hidden in the brew master's barn."

Tennake looked at Will, "You must swear that you will never repeat Sarah's tale," she instructed.

"I swear," Will replied enthusiastically.

Sarah paused for a moment to look at Will before she went on. "My master's uncle would have raised Cain, Mistress, he being so angry that his nephew stood by Master Hendrickson; but he did not disclose the whereabouts of the hidden wild people to the authorities."

Aeltie crawled into her older brother's lap.

"Methinks they must be dead because no one could survive the wild forest," Will said, handing his slice of apple to the three-year-old.

Sarah's lips curved into a slight smile. "Many live in the forest, Will," she said.

"Where would they have gone to live safely?" Tennake asked.

"Some go past the land of the Erie people, but others go far to the south, to the Carolina lands."

"I have never heard of such places."

"It be far away, Mistress."

Sarah looked into Tennake's eyes. "Mistress Ann taught me and the orphaned children our Bible. Many of the Dutch do not like to hear another white speak for the Indians and they do not teach servants the Word of the Almighty Lord."

Tennake patted Sarah's hand. "I am glad of heart that Mistress Ann has given you the lessons Sarah, for you have been a great comfort to me over the last days."

The two women looked into the dull, expressionless face, laying in Sarah's lap. Sarah's eyes were moist as she put a wet rag to Ann's dry mouth.

"Mistress Ann must live. It is because of her that I learned to speak proper Dutch, how to cipher, and properly tend to market. There is not a merchant in all New Netherlands who will cheat me," she said proudly.

Tennake's eyes sought out Rebecca who was playing in a far corner with two other young girls. Near to her stepdaughter, she noticed a cluster of women whispering together, occasionally looking over in her direction.

She was at her wit's end. She did not know if the knot in her belly was hunger or God's warning to her that these mothers, daughters and sisters who had banded together meant to give up Ann to the wild men beyond the wall.

Once again she turned her thoughts to prayer and thanked God for the good news that Stuyvesant had defeated the Swedes. He had received his colonists' cry for help, whereupon he had immediately initiated his return to New Amsterdam.

Later, the Dominie gathered them in a prayer of thanks. The jubilation that followed was as bright as the sun's rays filtering through the windows of the church. Several women encircled Ann Hendrickson, asking the Lord to cast out the evil that filled the woman; however, despite an hour of such devotions, Ann's condition remained mostly unchanged. Yet, Tennake thought that a stream of light was illuminating Ann's face, and a warm encouraging glow of hope washed over her.

Tennake could see that many of the women had departed from Mistress de Forest, apparently ashamed of their previous conduct toward the stricken woman. She heard some begging the Lord Almighty's forgiveness for having cursed her and being too quick to point a finger. Now a fire of guilt, a painful retribution of its own kind, burned within their spirits.

Suddenly Sarah jumped. "Mistress has moved!"

Tennake looked down into the blank staring eyes of her neighbor. "I will not believe a demon has entered your spirit. You must come back to us, Ann. Please, I pray you. Come awake," Tennake whispered.

As the sun faded into the darkness and then reappeared again the next morning, none of the men had as yet returned to save them. Despair began to return.

Tennake overheard two of the old men talking. The number of captives was great, whilst any thought of a rescue could not be considered until the return of their leader and their men.

Sarah, who had left Tennake's side for a moment, brought back word that Joseph, along with four Jewish men, had risked their lives at dawn by leaving the Fort in search of food. They had been somewhat successful and left what fruit and vegetables they had gathered for the Dominie to distribute.

Sarah, as well as several other servant women, braved the walls of their church to draw water from the city's common well.

At ten o'clock that morning, Ann Hendrickson opened her eyes and murmured Sarah's name.

A peace that comes only after total exhaustion settled into Tennake's weary limbs. She was limp and could no longer deny the needed sleep her own body and the child within demanded. She gathered Will, Rebecca, and Aeltie closely to her side and allowed herself to drift away to a joyful place of safety where the tall grasses swayed in a refreshing breeze, and the playful teasing laughter of her sisters caressed her lovingly.

Although hours had passed, it seemed to her that she had barely closed her eyes when she was awakened by the touch of a gentle hand upon her cheek. The rough large frame of her husband knelt in front of her.

An unbidden tear escaped from her eyes while she thought of her mother's words, *"Your faith in God will sustain you."*

NINE

The sweet, delicious aroma of freshly baked Oliebollen fruit-filled doughnuts permeated the warmth of the Waldron house on Broadway. Tennake gazed with satisfaction upon the Lenape woven reed basket stacked high with the pastries.

A sense of harmony surrounded her as she watched her infant sleeping peacefully in his cradle next to the hearth. She placed the last cake to cool. All was quiet but for the steady vibration of Resolved's snoring through the drawn bed curtain. Sarah had taken the elder children to visit Martha, Peter Stoutenburgh's Negro cook on Whitehall Street, who promised to give each of them a sugar cake. For the moment, Tennake's world was a serene nest of tranquility.

She wiped her hands clean of the pastry's syrupy stickiness. She had only one more letter to write, and although she had saved it for last, she considered it to be the most important. Exhausted, she pulled up her stool beside the smooth oak surface of her beautiful new table and began to write:

19 December, 1656
Dearest Cornelia,

I know not how to begin except to give to you the most joyous of news, which is that a son has been born to me whom we have called Barent, of course, to honor my own dear father. Recall you that it was my intent to do so, and my good husband heartily agreed, be the babe a boy.

Born after the midnight hour, the first day of December, the child was small at first, methinks that he came into this world before his appointed time, but I am happy to say that he grows and is robust. Out neighbor's Negro girl, Sarah, acted as midwife, and together we brought him forth, shedding tears of joy as we listened to his first cry.

My husband was attending to his duty as Assistant Sheriff in the town the night Barent was born, though Sarah awoke young Will and bade him fetch his uncle that he may relieve Resolved from his post.

Upon receiving the news, Resolved came in all haste, making a great amount of clamor in his entrance. He was most pleased that this one be another boy—for what good are girls he teased—though I take notice that he spoils them both to no good.

I am sorry that I have not written to you until now, but you may have heard of our Indian troubles and I prefer to send news of joy and not sorrow for my first correspondence. At some later day, I may write to you of that terrible time, but for now it is better to tell you that we are all safe and all is now quiet with the savages.

I have so much to tell you, Cornelia, yet I have little time. You will laugh when you hear that I have made the Oliebollen this year. Yes, it is two weeks before the New Year celebration, yet I have broken with traditions of the homeland to make them now. I can see you scolding me, but it is only right that we celebrate in this household!

Sorrowful news that I will share is that Resolved has been unable to locate his brother's family at Kent Island. The Indians attacked that place and within the whole of the Island only two children, those belonging to English settlers, have been found; and they now, being orphans, were put to live at the Orphan house on Williams Street here in New Amsterdam until a good family may be found to take them in. But, we cannot seem to find a word to be spoken by anyone with regard to my husband's family, and since no bodies have been found, we regret that they may be captives of the savages.

With this in mind, you might think me wrong to prepare a feast now; but still, I baked the Oliebollen because I do not wish to keep a sad house that will burden my husband further; and I thank God for sparing our own lives.

Tennake shuddered as she thought of Resolved's five nieces and nephews who had vanished along with their mother and her new husband. She had heard many stories of the gruesome fate that awaited those taken captive by the Indians; and although Mr. La Croix had reassured them, she did not believe they would ever be found.

She continued writing Cornelia's letter:

Methinks that even your free generous spirit would raise an eyebrow if you would be here come Sunday. On that day we will all enjoy a great feast in this house and share our blessings with new friends, among who is Mr. Abrahamsen, a Jew widower, one of the many Jewish colonists who were expelled from the Dutch colony in Brazil and then forced upon our good Director, Peter Stuyvesant. I know that you will not understand how different things are here, nor will you sit still when I say to you that I will have Mr. Abrahamsen and his son to sit at my table despite the cold tolerance of my husband. But again, this is another story to be told another day.

Dearest, how I wish that I would be back in Fatherland to share a sugar cake with you. What wonderful blessed work of Christ it would be that you would be able to hold my child and to be godmother as we so often spoke while we were girls. Knowing that this is impossible, I have asked a good neighbor woman by the name of Ann Hendrickson to stand for my child at his Baptism. She is a kind person who you would find pleasant and we have found comfort in each other's company, though there is no other woman on earth that will ever take your place, my dear friend.

I must now give you my love and ask you to thank your mother for the lace that she sent over to me. I will write again in the spring.

As Tennake folded the parchment, tears filled her eyes, and she wondered if she would ever see Cornelia again. However, she did know that if good fortune smiled upon them at some distant point in time and they should meet, their friendship would never be quite the same because more than mere miles separated them now. The girl who had departed Holland only a few months before had vanished. The ecstasy of her bridal garment had faded to distant memory.

She would never be able to explain the change that had come over her to her girlhood friend, for who among them fully understood the grace of God that Tennake knew came to her aid so many times since she had arrived in New Netherlands. Though she still delighted in the mysterious enchantment of the sweet air as she had innocently done the first day she arrived, she no longer feared that which she could not see beyond the trees, or the unknown sounds clamoring yonder.

She slept peaceably, believing that the Lord had spared her for greater tasks and looked forward to the newness of her surroundings, feeling at all times the strength of the angel Michael's shield.

Her new duties as a colonial wife provided a very different life than that over which her dear mother had raised her to preside. But she was grateful for Sarah and believed that the girl was more content at her house than at her own.

Sarah confessed that the sounds of young children were especially welcome to her. She resented old Jacob ordering her around and caring not for talk other than to bicker. He spent most of his time polishing the master's furniture that he had made.

Sarah was lonesome during her master's absences, further confiding that she believed Mr. Herrman had taken a fancy to a comely Yaocomaco woman in St. Mary's City. Sarah boldly said she believed his most recently completed portrait, which he proudly hung in his bedchamber, was a likeness of the woman, painted while he enjoyed the company of his English friends.

Not all of Sarah's time was spent tending to children, for Joseph had taken an interest in her. He took pleasure teaching her to wield her pen, writing her name expertly on a parchment. Having done this, he then took letters from his printer's chest and formed her name, pressing the wooden pieces into a sheet of parchment that he hung to dry on the crossbeam in his shop.

Later, Joseph presented her with what had been done as a gift. Although Resolved sternly warned Tennake not to be about stealing Augustine's Negro, Tennake sensed that he was pleased that Sarah wished to spend time in their budding household. Nonetheless, she paused uncomfortably when Joseph would not allow the girl to call him Master or Mister, but instructed Sarah to call him by his Christian name.

As she laid down her completed letter, Tennake glanced again at her newborn son. Satisfied that he was content, her eyes drifted toward the hand-painted tiles depicting Biblical scenes that surrounded her hearth, another generous gift from Augustine Herrman.

She especially loved the tile that brought to mind the story of Ruth, an account of unselfish love that had been close to her heart since she was a maiden. She now felt as though she shared a personal kinship with Ruth and often retold the events of this goodly woman's life to Resolved's children.

On such occasions, when she would recite, Tennake would hold Aeltie close and whisper to her, "In the Bible, Ruth said, 'Thy people shall be my people.' Now Aeltie, you and your brother and sister must know that this is how it is with all of us, for we, too, are now united families."

Sarah, also, loved to hear Tennake tell stories of their faith and it gave her satisfaction to be able to continue the training that Ann had begun.

Tennake poured herself a hot bowl of sage tea and remembered how all had settled down following the attack upon New Amsterdam.

In fact, her husband's heart had not skipped a single beat before putting his nose to the grindstone.

Will and Rebecca were enrolled in school where they would attend classes all year long except for holidays and weekends, a wonderful benefit of living in the colonial city. They still did not have a permanent schoolmaster despite the New Amsterdam council's repeated requests to the Company in the Fatherland to obtain one. But the Dominie gave proper instruction, and Resolved was glad to pay the instruction fee. If necessary, such educational costs would have been paid by the Dutch West India Company for young Will at least, but Resolved was determined that none of his children would ever be a burden to the church or the government.

Although there were some who would argue that money spent on a daughter's learning was a waste, Resolved disagreed. His girls would be suitable for the best of young men in New Amsterdam come their marrying time. He would see to it that they would be responsible women, well skilled and able to run their husband's business if need come, just as so many good widows now did in their city.

Why, if his girls had no education they would be as lost lambs in the wilderness and never be able to rise above their lot in life by marrying up. He wanted them to learn their prayers, the Commandments, and all else that the boys did learn. Tennake asked Resolved if he planned to apprentice any of his female children the same way as he did the boys; whereupon, her husband had become angry and for the first time in their marriage, he shouted at her.

Resolved's position as Night Sheriff required a great adjustment for Tennake and the children, although it was her husband who had bent the most to accommodate, both as new commander as well as the father of his family. Some colonists, still recalling her Resolved's English half, complained that he was not worthy of his appointment; but he was determined to prove them wrong, and by not letting the slightest offense go without a fine, many had come to call him hard-hearted.

Thankfully, few called him English any longer, for Peter Stuyvesant ordered the citizens concerned with Resolved's position to recognize his authority; and they had done so.

Tennake had learned much about her new homeland within the last months. She knew that when Peter Stuyvesant took over the colony in 1647, he announced to all the people that he would be as a father to his children. Clearly, Stuyvesant had seen fit to make Resolved Waldron one of his favorite sons, and her husband no longer laughed when his wife spoke of the grace that the angel Michael spread over them all.

Tennake sighed as she bent over little Barent to secure his blanket once again. She hoped that the troubles with John Bowne would rest as the babe now did.

In the beginning of the month Resolved received orders from Stuyvesant by way of Sheriff Tonneman to arrest the Englishman Mr. Bowne whose crime was allowing his wife, Hannah Feke, a Quaker, to hold religious meetings in their home with five other Quakers, a practice strictly forbidden.

Ann Hendrickson once told Tennake that if Director Stuyvesant had his way of it, there would be none other than Calvinists admitted to their fair wilderness city. Their Director endured the Quakers and the Jews, but had far less patience with them than he did his Negro slaves. However, he tolerated his pain and insisted that those of all faiths pay their tax to his office for the benefit of St. Nicholas church. Stuyvesant felt that he was fair in his treatment of those not of the true faith, because although he was firm that they financially support his church, he did not force them to attend its services. The Director would now use his current favorite Sheriff to do his dirty business.

It was unfortunate that Mr. Bowne could not return his converted wife to the true faith, but Tennake had heard that the woman said she would remain a Quaker whilst she drew breath;

and further, that she would use her home to hold her meetings if she was pleased to do so. Tennake had never seen the strangeness of such a wife toward her husband, but apparently the woman's husband was willing to die rather than leave her side or renounce the abomination of Quakerism. When the Quakers were discovered and reported to the authorities, Peter Stuyvesant's gentle tolerance toward Hannah Feke, and her followers, came to an end; and in an effort to teach Mr. Bowne to keep his wife in proper step, the Director had fined him steeply. Nothing could be worse for a man than to pay for his wife's misconduct with coins that were hidden away in the husband's private chest. However, Bowne shocked the whole of their community, and would not pay stating that he would hold to promised rights and the agreement for religious freedom previously signed.

With no remedy in sight, Resolved as an officer of Stuyvesant's justice, was sent to collect the fine with orders that if the fine was not paid immediately, Bowne was to be arrested. Tennake believed that it had been this trouble with Bowne, on top of the Indian attacks, which had brought forth the early birth of her infant.

Privately, her husband felt that the Director acted unreasonably; and for Resolved's own part he hated to go against Mr. Bowne, who had risked his life after the Indian attacks to join him and La Croix in their hunt for survivors at Kent Island. Bowne had also been one of the volunteers involved in the rescue of captives taken from New Amsterdam. He had begun to see that Mr. Bowne, though English, was a man of staunch convictions.

Several government administrators urged that Mr. Bowne be given more time to pay and repent, seeing that this harsh treatment of the Quakers was bound to anger their superiors in Holland. Such stringent actions were in direct conflict with the home office. They argued that Hannah Feke was not preaching openly in the streets but stayed behind closed doors in the privacy of her own home. They pointed out to Stuyvesant that John Bowne did pay his church tax and continued to worship at St. Nicholas. But the Director felt he had been patient enough in the matter.

Tennake's heart still ached when she recalled how Resolved and two soldiers went to persuade him to pay the fine and have done with it all; but Bowne refused, as Resolved knew he would.

John Bowne had answered the knock at his door with his newborn babe in his arms. As the arrest process began, Hannah, dragging herself from her sick bed took a firm hold of her husband's arm, wailing loudly that Resolved Waldron was a hard man. Her nephew, a boy of five, vigorously kicked Resolved and held on to his uncle's leg. One of the soldiers pried his small hands free, whereupon the little boy bit him severely, prompting the soldier to strike the child.

Until he saw blood spring forth from the wound upon the child's forehead, Mr. Bowne had been calm, but now he fought against Resolved's restraints like a wild savage. Amid abusive calls from the crowd that gathered by their front door, it took all of her husband's and his assistant's strength to drag him from his family.

Tennake heard Resolved stir as Sarah returned with the children. She quickly ran to the door, bidding them play for a short time in the snow that had begun to fall.

Sarah removed her cape at the doorway and shook off the snowflakes. "You have the look of one that is far from house," she whispered to Tennake.

"I was thinking of John Bowne and his wife," she replied thoughtfully.

"It is good that he has been sent back to Holland," Sarah commented; "and you should not worry so. Have you completed your correspondence, Mistress?"

"Yes, and I thank ye for taking the children. Did they receive their sugar cakes?"

"Every belly is full of two."

"When next you see her, thank cook for me," Tennake whispered.

Sarah smiled. "I be going now, Mistress, for you know that Jacob is miserable to live by, should I not return soon."

As Sarah departed, Tennake's thoughts drifted back to John Bowne's arrest.

She remembered her husband recounting John Bowne's words while he hung in irons for days in Peter Schaefbanck's jail, screaming that he would die before paying his unjust fine. Resolved had returned to the jail every day, imploring him to give up his useless and foolish fight, and pay the fine.

Her husband felt so strongly about the matter that he had contributed secretly to a collection that his brother Joseph had organized in Bowne's behalf; but the prisoner refused to accept their money.

It was apparent to many that Mr. Stuyvesant had met one as stubborn as himself, but the Director hoped he was not as clever.

On the fifth day of his imprisonment he told the jailer to leave the door to Bowne's cell open hoping that he would escape and give good reason to have done with him once and for all.

Tennake smiled to herself as she recalled the end result of Stuyvesant's plan. Mr. Bowne took the opportunity of an unlocked cell and during the day went home to see his wife and child but returned to his cell faithfully at night and closed his cell door.

This situation had become the joke of the town, but the laughing had stopped in Tennake's household as Stuyvesant summoned her husband once again and scolded him, saying that he had searched for a man that would not weaken in duty. He did not want to be disappointed in the trust that he had placed in him.

Her smile faded as she remembered her husband's bitterness upon his return from the interview with his superior. She recalled Resolved's words confessing that he was beginning to agree with his commander and wish that he had never laid eyes upon John Bowne.

She rocked Barent's cradle with one foot and thought of the Jews whom Peter Stuyvesant unsuccessfully tried to send on to the

English Bay colony, and who were treated with more scorn than were the Quakers. Tennake had been grateful that he had relented under pressure from the Company and allowed the Jews to remain in New Netherlands, for many Dutch settlers might lay dead were it not for their bravery.

She thought this bitterness against both the Quakers and the Jews unfair. It did not seem right that John Bowne was sent away from his home, nor that the Jews were forced to live in miserable quarters apart from everyone else in the city. She imagined that Mr. Stuyvesant felt that by denying their petitions over and over, eventually he would starve them away; but he had been somewhat surprised, for many colonists whose hearts had been softened toward the Jews in their settlement did trade with them.

Tennake was startled as she heard her husband's voice.

"To what far place have you flown?" Resolved asked as he threw aside the curtain to their small bedchamber built in the wall.

"I was thinking of John Bowne," she said. "Is there any word of him?"

"What word could there be, as he is still at sea on the Lysbet; and fortunate the man is to be there," Resolved grumbled. In a more jesting tone he asked, "Have you sent the children to the savages?"

"Nay, we be none so fortunate," Tennake teased. "They be by the side of the house and I was about to call them in but I thought that I would give ye a few more minutes of peaceful rest."

"You be peaceful yourself?" Resolved queried.

"Yes," Tennake replied.

"Tenny, concern yourself no longer for the good of John Bowne," Resolved said softly. "I am glad that he is on the ship, for now I may sleep nights."

"Mr. Bowne is one of our own faith, husband; or have you forgotten?"

"Who can forget in a house that chooses to remember Calvinists, Quakers, Jews, and Negroes—even stray pigs? I fear I will now be forced to put on armor for I arrested three more Quakers last night. They have now boldly taken to preaching in the streets." Resolved's voice had risen.

"I will pray for them," Tennake sighed.

"Do pray, woman, for there is no end to the grief that a Quaker can cause and methinks that I can tolerate the Jews better these days. I tell you that I cannot understand the reasoning of a man to take a Quaker to wife when he is a devout Calvinist. Bowne is fortunate that he has returned to Fatherland." Resolved looked at his wife in exasperation.

"How can you speak so crudely? I pity him and his wife. She is alone in this wilderness with her infant. Her sister is her only family here and she is a widow."

"You, too, are against me, wife? Recall you that Peter Tonneman advised Bowne at the bitter end that he could still pay his fine and all the charges would be dropped? But stubborn is the Quaker's husband, and it is he who has left his good wife in such a miserable position."

"Husband, I am not against you, for well you know of my respect for you—and my love," Her words were measured and patient.

"Then if this be so, do not concern yourself further for Hannah Feke or her husband," Resolved said sternly.

Tennake looked away.

"We will not see the Quaker starve. Ann Hendrickson, Marie Nagel and I will send food every week to her and the child. Or will you forbid me to do so?"

"Do as you wish," Resolved sighed.

"We will also pray for our Director," Tennake said quietly.

"I will speak no more of it," Resolved announced as he nestled back into his barrel chair. Aeltie had entered the house, and after removing her gray cape she climbed up into her father's lap.

Resolved reached for an Oliebollen and licked his lips as the fruit inside squeezed out when he bit into it. He handed another doughnut to Aeltie, who smiled contentedly, leaning back against her father's chest.

"Save some for the meal tonight," Tennake admonished.

"Methinks that I should have my fill before they all go out the door to Mistress Feke and the rest of the town," Resolved said reaching for another.

"I have made enough for everyone," Tennake whispered defensively.

"A man should have the right to do as he pleases in his own house."

"And so he should; so should every man or woman," Tennake replied.

Resolved turned around in his seat. He looked curiously at his wife and then he began to laugh. He knew that he could not champion the games of domestication with Tennake.

"Do not worry my songbird. John Bowne will come back for his wife and child in all glory, for our Directors across the waters frown upon bad treatment of those who risk all to settle themselves here."

Resolved licked the precious sugar from his fingers. "God help us, but we need the Quakers as well as the Jews here. John Bowne will be back, and his wife and child will be as fat as butter when they greet him at the wharf, thanks to you and your women."

Silently, Tennake vowed that they surely would be.

TEN

A powdery fresh snow continued to fall as Joseph discreetly watched Sarah through the frosted glass panes of the rear window of his tiny one room print shop. As she bent down, the hood of her bright green winter cape fell to her back, and once again he found himself curiously observing how the girl's long soft black curls suitably framed her angular light brown face, a wondrous mane that seemed to refuse all endeavor of capture.

Joseph smiled. Sarah often endured admonishment from his sister-in-law for leaving her cap behind while she collected firewood or frolicked in the garden, uncivilized behavior that seemed to cause Tennake considerable aggravation.

He wondered who this enticing temptress had sprung from, for to be sure, Sarah had come of mixed blood. At first he had believed that Jacob was Sarah's father, though he did not know when he first had conceived of this idea as no one spoke thus of Augustine's loyal old servant. Upon mentioning this thought in passing one evening to his brother, Resolved offered his own version of Sarah's lineage, saying he thought that she was a child of Dorothy Angolas' sister who died of smallpox when Sarah was little more than an infant.

Augustine had told Resolved that Dorothy and her sister arrived from the African Slave Coast on a Dutch ship when the two were young girls. Originally, Dorothy had been sold to a wealthy merchant who was a high-ranking official of the Company, while her sister was purchased by Augustine's uncle. They had been told that Sarah's father was a Company Negro who met a violent death while working one afternoon in the Company's mill. Sarah's Aunt Dorothy, freed from slavery for having saved her master's ailing wife from what all the physicians considered certain death, had cared for her sister's infant until the child was old enough to work in the household of Augustine's uncle. Years later, after his uncle died, Sarah became the property of Augustine along with everything else in that fine house.

Joseph had never believed the tale because any man with an eye would know that the girl came from a mixed seed bag; but better to keep this thought silent as no good would come of dispute over such a matter.

There was much rabbiting about the colonies, and whether the girl was sired by a white was of no importance since white men often begot children with slave women, although no respectable Dutchman would ever admit it.

As Joseph approached the side of the window, he watched Sarah pile into her slender arms the split wood from the stack that he and Resolved had cut. He admired her strength for a woman so slight of figure, as he also respected her knowledge of native herbal remedies. Was it not Sarah, who two years ago pulled the arrow from his shoulder, dressing the wound twice daily with that magical mixture of mud and herbs? He had healed completely in a few short weeks.

Sarah had taught him much in return for the small kindness he had shown her. She spoke the local tribal tongue and had shared that talent with his brother and himself, teachings that had proven worthy on many occasions since they had arrived.

Joseph wondered if having the tongue of an Indian, Sarah did not also inherit the blood of one. The Lenape people intermarried with Dutch, French and Swede, whilst the offspring of these marriages often married with other Indians or freed Negroes, begetting a strange breed.

The palms of his own ink-blackened hands began to sweat as he pressed closer to the window taking in the fullness of Sarah's breast. Now nearly twenty years old, the young Negro men had often admired her as she passed; yet proud Sarah never looked back at any of them. Joseph laughed to himself when he thought of how distressed Tennake had been when he called Sarah the "Dark Mistress of the Island of Manhattan".

He recalled hearing Sarah say to his sister-in-law that African field Negroes working in the master's orchards were no better than the dirty wild beasts that roamed the streets. But Tennake's reply was always swift as she admonished Sarah sternly to cast out the pride within herself. Augustine's Jacob was always quick to agree with the mistress of his neighbor's house, but Sarah cared little for the opinions of the haughty senior houseman.

Dear God, that girl shows a powerful burning within herself, Joseph thought as he dragged himself from the window. However, the truth was that Sarah did not burn alone.

Once, months ago, after she had brought him a basket of hot food from Tennake's fire, he had looked up from his press to find her standing idly in front of him. His apprentice had gone on an errand to City Hall, so for the moment he worked alone. Shyly she had come forward, took his hand, placing into it a sweet bag, a small pouch containing lemon balm, mint, and dried petals of lavender to be hung about his neck.

He had tried to refuse her gift, but Sarah had pressed her finger against his lips as she hung the bag about his neck and gazed deeply into his eyes.

At first he responded without thinking and roughly pulled her to himself so that he could feel the closeness of her against him, but had quickly released her seeing that she was frightened by his return of affection. Then as quickly as she had come to him, she had hastily turned and made her way promptly back to the house, leaving him bewildered.

He thanked the Almighty that there had been no more incidents. It was a brief intrusion, no harm had been done; but now once again she was filling his thoughts. Her face, even from a distance, warmed him.

I must be losing my mind, he thought sharply. As a Christian, he knew that any connection with a Negro slave woman was improper, foolish and even dangerous. A Christian who commits fornication with a Negro is shunned by his Church and officially fined so heavily that he would be fortunate to have anything left at all with which to support himself.

Yet, what harm was there in watching the girl from a distance and enjoying her attractiveness? As usual, this morning when she brought him and his young apprentice, George Wallace, hot corn cakes and a quart of rum to keep away the cold chill, he found himself wanting to touch the smoothness of her face.

Unable to stay away from his window, he returned to silently watch her as she walked upon the icy white of winter's frozen ground. She stopped to gather a few apples that lay in the snow at the base of the tree and then carefully followed her own tracks in the snow to the edge of the forest behind the Waldron dwelling.

Joseph discovered the purpose of the withered fruit as she stopped to call out to a doe and her young who hungrily approached her, unafraid, and ate lovingly from her palms. It was a peaceful scene that blended together under the cold gray winter sky. *A piece of time that should be painted so that those back in Fatherland could see the untouched loveliness of this land so far away from the soil of our birth,* Joseph thought.

How long would he fight with himself over his feelings for Sarah? *Must I obey the laws that were made for men who live in a civilized world, but do not make sense in this world?* He wondered. What was there about this Negro girl that drew him so? If Sarah were a proper Dutch woman possessing skin the color of freshly made cream, would she still stir his blood? If she were one of the fine widows who had been presented to him by well meaning friends over the last years, he would probably not have had a rat's hair of desire for them. And now that Resolved owned Sarah, the bargain with Augustine having been struck some time before, he could not get away from the girl long enough to think clearly.

Tennake openly voiced her disgust for slave holding, but having become fond of Sarah's company as well as her extra pair of able hands, she pleaded with Resolved to purchase her for their household. Although Augustine was reluctant to let Sarah go, he had agreed to the sale with the stipulation that Sarah would continue to cook his meals as well as those of the Waldrons.

So it came to pass that the path between the back of the Waldron and Herrman's houses became known to all as, "Sarah's Lane".

"First Skating Day must be very near," he heard George say as he looked toward him. The ice on the back creek was frozen solid and soon they would observe the Old Dutch holiday, which had been celebrated by many past generations. It was one of the few days all year that work and school were forgotten and everyone played on the ice.

Joseph remembered the first skating day that they had observed in America. Tennake had just given birth to her son and was unable to skate, but she had wanted Sarah to skate with the family so she strapped her own wooden base upon the bottom of Sarah's boot securing it firmly with the low spikes into the sole.

How they had laughed as they watched the children holding up the wobbling black slave girl while they pushed her forward on the ice. Rebecca had become angry that they laughed. She took Sarah's hands and gently pulled her forward.

They all watched in amazement as Sarah sailed alone against the crisp winter air. But not everyone skating on the frozen creek that day was pleased to see her skating with her master's children. The icy stares of some of their neighbors rivaled the coldness of the day; and Joseph recalled how some of them had left the ice in disgust.

Tennake seemed oblivious to the sentiments of her neighbors, or so she did pretend, Joseph thought. In the same way, she ignored the whispers against her for her kindness to the Jews and continued to pity them despite the possibility of a stiff fine for such a kindness.

When scorned, Tennake told her sour neighbors that a happy heart and a pious soul were the ingredients of a successful household. Joseph believed that she had come a long way from her father's house, much further than the distance of only one ocean.

Joseph went to his table and poured himself a tankard of hot rum. He should find a woman, a good staunch Dutch woman from an upstanding family, he thought. He had been in the colony long enough to do so.

"God love and protect the colony," he toasted, as he swallowed the rum, George joining him with a drink as well as a toast: "God keep your brother's children, be they alive."

Joseph's thoughts of Sarah faded as he painfully remembered those terrible early days that followed the Indian attack upon New Amsterdam. He recalled the crowd's angry rage, which had inspired Director Stuyvesant's first order commanding every Indian village within one hundred miles of the colonial city to be burned to the ground; but thank God some citizens kept their heads, imploring the wisdom of mercy that would lead to peaceful negotiations. After all, it was the freedom of their captive loved ones that would be lost in foolish retaliation.

Finally, La Croix offered his leadership, organizing several citizens and handpicked soldiers into small diplomatic groups who would be sent to the tribal councils with offers of goods for ransom.

When La Croix had arrived in New Amsterdam with Resolved, he learned through investigation that many of the local Indians who had been in favor of attacking New Amsterdam were willing to assault the settlers only until they found Van Dyck and slew him. This white man's death would be satisfaction for the killing of their young woman in the peach field. The Indians insisted that they meant only to frighten their white neighbors; but unfortunately, the attack had gotten out of hand.

Peter Stuyvesant would listen to no heathen excuses for the shambles that he had found in his town upon returning from his trouble with John Rising. For over seven years he had worked to build New Amsterdam into an independent Christian city of excellent promise; and within a few hours his colonial children's blood had been spilled, dozens were taken captive and his own barn was burned. He had no patience for savage lies, and he intended to send a very clear message to the offenders.

Jacques La Croix risked beheading as he argued with the Dutch administrator for leniency for the Indians living in the immediate vicinity of the Island of Manhattan. La Croix reasoned that the tribes had become accustomed to white rum, the axe, and European guns; and it was the Esopus from the far Western lands who did the worst of the treacherous deed. So why punish all the tribes, especially since many more colonists would have been killed had it not been for the intervention of local tribal people.

"Help me to save your captive people," La Croix had pleaded. "If you burn all the villages and hunt down every Indian within one hundred miles, then with whom will your merchants trade?"

Most of the people of New Amsterdam had been spared, though none knew whether it was because of intervention of local tribes or the news along the trail of Stuyvesant's imminent return that softened the Indian's attacks. Some hostages had been returned, yet even though Joseph and Resolved never gave up hope, none of the Waldron kin were found.

Persistent warfare with the Indians was expensive for the struggling colonists, and they had worry enough over encroaching English that constantly pushed at their Dutch borders. They needed no further aggravation. Since King Charles was reinstated, Englishmen were flooding the New World, all trying, Joseph supposed, to escape their own turmoil. There were ten Englishmen to every Dutchman in America, a perilous situation for the sons of Holland.

Still, everyone agreed that it was good that Stuyvesant worked steadfastly toward a resolution to the problem of the wild men before being overrun with the English; but his resolution might well prove to be a very undesirable pudding.

George had been drinking his midday rum by the window. "A soldier approaches the shop," he said.

Joseph opened his door to a young messenger from the office of the Director General. He handed him a parchment and quickly took his leave.

Joseph received weekly requests from the Company office at the City Hall, orders that paid him handsomely for the service of his trade. He had been so busy that he considered hiring another indenture to assist him, and if all went according to his plan, he would require the youth's service for several years. It would provide a wonderful opportunity for himself as well as the boy. The Company would pay the ship's passage, and food was plentiful in New Amsterdam.

George had only two more years to serve him and had already spoken to Joseph of his desire to seek work in his trade in Boston town. With this thought in mind, he planned to write to Tennake's brother in Holland so that her nephew could take advantage of his offer.

He brought the dispatch closer to the light of the window so that he could read the instructions for the printing of one hundred new regulatory forms. They would be used by every Captain of all the slave ships passing through the port of New Amsterdam.

Feisty Pete was unable to keep a proper accounting of the numerous ships that passed under his nose and he wanted a form that would register the ship's name, her captain's name, port of origination and all other information regarding the cargo she carried. Stuyvesant needed accounting since most slaves did not remain in New Netherlands, but were exported to the Virginia colony. A Dutch colonial tax of ten percent per head of the slave's value was imposed.

Joseph had begun to wonder lately whether or not George had the right idea in leaving New Amsterdam. He hated the corruption that Peter Stuyvesant forced with his foolish rules and burdensome taxes that benefited no citizen but himself. Although this order for forms would bring a goodly amount to be put to his cause, he was beginning to think that he would rather take his chances with the Catholics or the savages that remained within the borders of the Dutch colony.

"Stuyvesant demands one hundred forms to be completed in all haste," he called over to George who had returned to sorting out the wooden type.

"In all haste it shall be," George replied.

Joseph sighed. It would be years before he would have enough money to make another life away from New Amsterdam. He would invest some of his profits in another lot at New Haarlem, a village three hours walking distance from town where a garrison had been placed with hopes of protecting that end of New Amsterdam from hostile Indians. His friend, Dan Tourner, had already purchased four lots there, and had turned a good profit on two of them, which he sold last spring.

Joseph glanced out upon the vacant depressions in the snow where only minutes before Sarah had been feeding the little doe. He wondered if his own life reflected the same shallow emptiness as the footprints.

He recalled the words of his friend, Jacob Steendam, who was the first poet to live among them in New Amsterdam:

"'Twixt failure and success the points so fine,
Men sometimes know not when they touch the line."

Joseph repeated the lines to himself, and then whispered, *"And where do I next step?"*

He nailed the recent order to the overhead beam and returned to work.

ELEVEN

Resolved sometimes felt that his good wife more resembled the fierce black bird of prey than the sweet songbird who, five years prior, had accompanied him to New Amsterdam.

But he also was a changed man. Perhaps her critical sharp tongue had some merit, though by God, he needed not to hear her complaints so often. She frequently despaired that his children did not know their father's face when assignments took him away from home for months. He had argued that a wise woman would be glad of her husband's trusted position and thank the Almighty that he was valued so highly by his superiors. Tennake should have no complaints, but would do better to count her blessings.

Resolved paused and lit his pipe. When he was troubled, he often left his noisy household and walked alone beside the river's edge, although he imagined that his wife thought him passing his time at Pieterson's Tavern. Twenty years ago this would have been true.

He looked up into the pale dusty blue of the afternoon midsummer sky. She had agreed to their marriage knowing that her husband-to-be was not a minister of God who would be at their table every eve as her own father had been; nor had she been so innocent as to not know what her future wifely duties were to be. Did he not keep the promises he had made to her when they were wed?

Through his dedication to colonial duty he had secured them a respected position in New Amsterdam, a snug home, and fine furnishings. Not once had any of them gone hungry, and he felt that she should be glad he was willing to stretch out his arm and pluck the ripest apples from the trees. He understood the pain of persistence and he had assumed that Tenny would also.

Although Tennake complained, she had proven to be a staunch helmsman who dealt bravely with his restless burning for uncharted lands. She tended his children lovingly with a heart full and pure; but still he would rather not hear her complain.

His chest tightened as he thought of the Indian troubles and the constant English border disputes that had kept him away from his family and New Amsterdam so often. How would he retain all he had acquired in this land of opportunity if peace was not forthcoming? Protection for the struggling outlying farms that lay great distances apart from one another was impossible to manage without the Company soldiers. At Herrman's Kill, more than sixteen persons had been killed and five children taken captive by a murdering band of Tappans. Resolved groaned. Though no one wanted a repeat of the Peach wars of five years ago, he secretly thought that the Director General had gone too far in his treatment of the savages; and his resemblance to his madman predecessor, Keift, was frightening.

Resolved knew that both the Directors in Holland and Director Stuyvesant were growing weary of the constant assaults and did not want thousands of Indians swarming over their city in the New World again. He could understand a staunch stand, but Stuyvesant was enraged by the attack at Herrman's Kill and had lost his ability for calm decision-making.

The complaints of his colonists, who feared that the savages were becoming more aggressive, had lit a fire in old Peg Leg's heart that burned out of control. Action had to be taken or there would not be a man willing to take his family beyond city limits to the boweries, nor would those farms produce enough to feed a single family. Peter Stuyvesant would take the only course he felt was left to him.

As Thomas Kalm's sloop sailed by, Tom waved and called out a greeting to him. Resolved recalled the last time he had seen him was during the spring at his son Johannes' funeral. Indian raids and sickness had dispirited many colonists over the last year, but Tom was a tough man and he stayed. He, too, would not sell out. *Brave the storms,* Resolved thought; and he waved back.

Around the lands of Wiltwyck, which were approximately eighty to ninety English miles north of New Amsterdam, entire settlements had been destroyed, colonists had been burned alive or scalped and children taken captive, just as had his brother's. Dutch traders traveling in the north reported seeing two young girls in one of the Indian villages near Wiltwyck.

A Frenchman named La Barge had been on a hunting expedition and later insisted that he had spoken with the children who gave their names as Deborah and Anna Waldron. Although six months had passed when this news of his nieces reached his ears, Resolved, Joseph and their neighbor, Benjamin Bullivant, immediately pursued the lead with renewed hope. A month later they returned home thoroughly disillusioned. It was as if his brother's family had been absorbed into the untamed earth along with the spring rains. Still, Resolved had sworn never to give up his quest, and this hope of their discovery had made him eager to join Stuyvesant's campaign into troubled Esopus land.

He and Augustine along with the La Croix brothers were to meet with the Esopus chiefs at their village that lay beside the riverbank two miles south of the Dutch village of Wiltwyck. Their party would travel by foot and canoe to the Indian village where they were to deliver an invitation from the Director to partake in peace talks. They would be followed by a sloop carrying a garrison of forty of Stuyvesant's best soldiers.

When he told Tennake of his assignment to bring news of a planned peace talk between the Esopus natives and the Dutch, she wept, saying, "I do not look forward to being a widow in this wilderness."

He had tried to cheer her. "Do not arrange the celebration of the merry widow or accept any proposals of marriage, for I promise that I will be home to table while the little ones still wet their pallets."

Tennake managed a small smile. Seeing this opening in her sentiment he declared, "Wife, we must have peace with these savages, for if all continues upon this same course, Pete Stuyvesant will have no further use for a Night Sheriff, as our streets will be barren! Be hopeful, for can there be a better man for this duty than Frederick or Jacques La Croix?"

She had smiled bravely as he knew she would and whispered, "I am always hopeful."

Tennake respected the La Croix brothers and had fed them at her table many times in their early years. Because they had lived as Indians, she trusted their experience with the natives. Jacques La Croix and Resolved had become good friends since their first meeting in Beaverwyck.

Frederick had once been married to an Esopus woman who bore him three of his children long before he married tall Anna the Swede and fathered six more. It had been Frederick who taught Will the language of the Mohawk. Tennake felt that there was no one more qualified to smooth the way to peace with the wild men.

Resolved pondered his boy's eagerness to join the campaign. He had discouraged him even though Will would make a fine companion during the journey, for his son had made friends among the Indian boys who had taught him the art of night fishing and catching a wild turkey, skills that would be helpful while in the wilderness. He could also speak both the Munsee and Iroquois language better than he or Joseph.

Yet, Resolved had felt better knowing that Will was at home watching over their family.

Resolved inhaled another smoke. He noticed the shimmering green flutter of a hummingbird as it invaded a nearby wild honeysuckle plant. He recalled young Rebecca's request that her older brother capture one of the West India Bees. She needed a bird very soon if it were to be pressed and dried so that her gift would be received by her uncle in Holland in time for Christmas.

His thoughts returned to the day of departure. Tennake prepared a pouch filled with fresh bread and dried fruit and chided that although he may die on the journey, it would not be of starvation. She had also prepared goods to be carried in one of her most precious baskets purchased at Kermis the first week she had been in New Netherlands.

Jacques thought that it would make a fine peaceful gesture if she sent along her best Mohawk basket; but it had been Tennake's idea to fill the basket with a brick of her cheese.

Resolved's heart ached as he thought of how wrong everything had gone with their mission. He painfully recalled that the whole of the Island of Manhattan was on the alert due to another uprising of the Wickquasseeks. Early on, Augustine decided they should rest the first afternoon and night in the village of New Haarlem. Jacques and Frederick had agreed and the four took their lodging with the Sheriff of the village, John Slot, who told them that yesterday two more farmers had been murdered by the savages at Van Keulen's Hook.

For miles around, the settlers had become afraid to go out to the fields to plant their crops since the beginning of April; and he had no idea how they or their live-stock were to survive the winter without food. If the Indians did not kill them, they would all starve if they stayed in New Haarlem, Slot said in disgust. Many of the farms were deserted and falling to ruin, their owners returning to the safety and comfort of their city properties in New Amsterdam, some retreating all the way back to Fatherland. Although Mr. Slot thought it might be too late for diplomacy, he was glad to hear of the good intentions because he felt that everyone had enough of the bloodshed. Even the Wickquasseeks, who had once been peaceful, were tired of war.

Resolved and his companions left New Haarlem at dawn and later arrived at Wiltwyck bone weary. They left their canoes at the shore and walked two miles to the Indian village where they entered the native settlement without hesitation.

Frederick made himself known immediately to the startled Esopus by inquiring in their tongue of the whereabouts of his dead wife's kin. While he engaged the natives in conversation, Resolved, Augustine, and Jacques followed with their hands outstretched, away from their weapons. Soon, Frederick was made cautiously welcome by his first wife's cousin and their party was invited to eat with them.

Frederick noticed that the Esopus looked weary and there were no strong young warriors to be seen in the village. Jacques commented that, most likely, they were absent, causing mischief somewhere else. The Indian village was filled with old men, women, and children with gaunt eyes and swollen bellies.

Resolved felt that Frederick held within his chest a silent sympathy for these people, for he could see the Frenchman's dismay as he looked upon the starving young. To be sure they were a pitiful sight.

Earlier in their journey he overheard Frederick speak of his desire to convince the Esopus to accept Stuyvesant's terms. His voice had trembled as he told Jacques that he came on this journey not out of love for the greedy Dutch, but to save what was left of his children's kin from the harshness of Dutch blades.

Resolved believed that if his dead wife's relatives did not lay down their weapons, they would be gone from the face of the earth. Everyone in the colony knew of Stuyvesant's institution of a bounty for Esopus scalps or heads. He had issued the same directive years before, for the scalps of Raritan Indians and now a Raritan scalp was scarce to be found.

Both Resolved and Jacques looked sharply not only for kin but for any white captives whatsoever. They found none. Still, if the two La Croix brothers could survive their boyhood with the savages, then it was possible that a Waldron child might be able to do the same. So they continued to look.

When Frederick had been recognized, some of the women began to make them welcome, leading the Dutchmen and the Frenchmen deeper into the village.

As they approached three elderly chiefs, Augustine pulled out rum and presented it to them. The gift was acknowledged and given to one of the women who disappeared with it into a roundhouse.

Resolved pulled from his backpack the woven Mohawk basket that his wife had sent which contained the cheese. He knew that clever Jacques had more than hospitality in mind when he suggested Tennake part with her basket, for it was immediately recognized by the Esopus chiefs as a sign of Dutch alliance with the Iroquois.

The northern Mohawk Indians had long been enemies of the Esopus South River people and had terrorized them whenever they could. The war-torn Esopus did not wish to ignite further warfare with the Dutch that would bring the wrath of the Iroquois federation.

The chiefs laid out mats upon the ground and the four strangers were invited to sit and make talk, while the rest of the tribe hovered about to watch the proceedings. Two young boys appeared with a fresh caught rabbit, which the Indians roasted over the open fire, politely sharing both the game and the cheese with their French and Dutch guests. The rum, Resolved noticed, had been put aside.

Upon conclusion of their meal, Augustine proceeded to deliver the message from Peter Stuyvesant exactly as he had been instructed. As he spoke he looked directly into the tired eyes of the enemy, waiting prudently after the conclusion of each sentence for Frederick to translate:

All attacks upon the whites and their farms and settlements must stop at once and all white captives, Dutch or English, must be returned without any exceptions; the Esopus were not to keep any "favorites". Even if an Esopus man had taken to wife a white woman, she must still be returned along with any children that were a result of that union. Also any captured white children that had been adopted into the tribe. Of course the Dutch would pay a handsome ransom to the Esopus for any white captives returned, but it must be understood that no white was to be prevented from being a part of the ransom settlement.

At this point the chiefs began to confer among themselves. Augustine held up his hand to signal his command for silence; and after a deep breath he began to speak again.

"On the other hand," he said, "the Director General of all the New Netherlands, His Honor, Peter Stuyvesant, urges all Esopus to come to the settlement of Wiltwyck in three days time for the negotiation of a peace between the Dutch and their people. If you do not come to Wiltwyck, I have been advised to tell you that every man, woman and child in this village will be destroyed."

Frederick completed the translation of the message staring angrily at Augustine. But Augustine persisted. "Tell them they should not allow false pride to cloud great wisdom. Tell them that as we sit to make this talk, a great ship has sailed northward from New Amsterdam and is by now moored at Wiltwyck. Many soldiers have been sent to do as I say, should they refuse to come," he said.

"Augustine, I would not insult these people further, for they have known of the reinforcements at Wiltwyck for two days now," Frederick stated.

Resolved recalled the outrage of the chiefs. They knew their people could not endure another attack by the Dutch or the Mohawk at this time. They did not trust the Dutch, but La Croix had fathered an Esopus and they trusted that he spoke the truth.

The chiefs having already received word that more soldiers were in Wiltwyck, knew the round little Dutchman did speak the truth.

After a brief discussion, they decided to go to Wiltwyck as the Dutch ordered, so their women and children would be spared. But they would not give their answer at the talks. When their warriors returned, they would consider what had taken place at the council.

Augustine insisted that all the people of the village must go to Wiltwyck with their chiefs. Finally, after many hours of discussion and Frederick's encouragement, the Esopus chiefs agreed that in three days time, they, along with their women and children, would go to Wiltwyck for the council.

The talks would be conducted by Captain Steenwyck representing the Dutch government. As a sign of good faith, Frederick La Croix would remain with the chiefs and would again act as interpreter at Wiltwyck.

As Resolved, Augustine and Jacques left Frederick, they embraced him, confident that a peace appeared to be a real possibility.

Augustine returned to New Amsterdam to make his report to Stuyvesant who awaited the results of their meeting. Resolved and Jacques continued northward to Fort Orange to complete their personal mission which had been delayed because Resolved's entire family had come down with the fevers. Augustine's household had suffered as well, and he still mourned the death of his beloved Jacob who had lingered for months. It seemed that not a house in all New Amsterdam had been spared a visit from the angel of death.

Resolved and Jacques had been anxious to survey a vast timber-filled acreage near the small village of Half-Moon, just northwest of Fort Orange. If all were agreeable, Resolved would purchase this land from the savages and establish a Mohawk trading post that Jacques would manage.

The lands surrounding Wiltwyck had to be made safe because the South River Indian Territory was the halfway point for all trade between Fort Orange and New Amsterdam.

Resolved and his brother already owned three lots near the post at New Haarlem, but he wanted a part of the rich northern soil as well.

His position as Assistant Sheriff provided a good salary, yet the path to wealth and power he envisioned for his sons was not through this minor political post. Five long hard years of bowing low to people who he did not prefer, was a drink that did not go down smoothly; but he had done what had to be done. He had hung his hat on the Director General's wall where now it was a familiar and welcome fixture.

Meeting Jacques in Beaverwyck years before had been a blessing. Resolved had always respected both brothers but he especially liked Jacques for he was a robust, amicable fellow with a quick wit and great enthusiasm.

Jacques came to New France in 1637, after spending most of his youth with Mohawk Indians. He had been lured, like so many, by the flirtatious smile of the little beaver, he told Tennake.

When he first came to the Americas, he lived in the great northern woods, a paradise stocked with beaver, wild cats, and the great bear. After becoming a young man he made his home with a Cree woman, who as a child had also been captured by the Mohawk. She gave him three sons and they lived happily for many years on lands that were twenty English miles north of the small village of Montreal.

He once boasted to everyone at Resolved's table that during those years he had trapped more beaver and fox than any other white man in that territory, claiming that he alone had supplied over 20,000 pelts for the Russian hat market. He enjoyed good hunting because he was brother to all Mohawk and Cree, as his brother Frederick had become brother to the Esopus of the South River valley.

As his Cree sons grew into boyhood, Jacques taught them to night fish and trap animals. But, in 1649, his wife and their sons perished from the smallpox, whereupon Jacques moved away from his land and the Mohawk to live alone in the land of the tall pines. Eventually, he came to live with the Cayuga Indians where the village was a short distance from the Half-Moon settlement.

Had it not been for the Voyager, as Jacques was known, nearly one hundred colonists would never have been recovered from captivity after the Peach war.

After leaving Frederick with the Esopus, Resolved and Jacques traveled north in their canoe. Before leaving, they had asked the local boat keeper, Martin DeHaan, to arrange for the safety of Frederick's canoe until he could return for it three days hence. DeHaan had agreed to do so.

They rowed steadily with the tide, eventually making camp along the bank of the river. There they made a fire and prepared to fish as Jacques had learned as a boy from his adopted Indian father, Peeka. Feeling more comfortable within friendlier Mohawk lands, they quietly waited for the fish to peek out from the glassy water's surface in search of the light of the torch that Resolved held high as he stood on the edge of the shore. It wasn't long before their inquisitive finny friends arrived and Jacques had skillfully reached into the cool water, securing the evening meal.

As they sat on the shore enjoying their catch, they observed the far off light of a passing sloop. The Frenchman called out his merry greeting and waved his fiery torch in the blackness, causing its light to dance far across the water. The vessel's captain signaled his reply. Resolved and Jacques stood beside one another and watched as the vessel dimmed and was finally swallowed by the night.

Before sunrise the two were again enthusiastically pushing northward. When the sun did come up, it was warm upon the skin of their arms as they rowed. They took this to be a good omen.

Near Fort Orange, the powerful North River became a liquid highway cluttered with every kind of floating craft. Rows of great Iroquois longboats were anchored upon the grassy slopes beside the shore; and in the distance they could see Indian women working the fields. Large flocks of wild turkey roamed the small hills beside the bank, while the honk of wild geese in the sky above, heralded their arrival.

As their canoe approached the wharf, Resolved noticed how much more of everything there was in Beaverwyck. Colorful sloops lined the shore and although the sun had begun to set, both white and black servants continued to load and unload their master's goods in compliance with sharp instructions barked by their overseers. Beaverwyck had grown since Resolved was there in 1657.

Upon arriving, Resolved paid the local boat keeper for safely mooring their canoe near the end of the wharf until their return. The following day they would make the last leg of their journey on foot in a direction of north by northwest; but for this night they had agreed to share a feather pallet with a clean Lindsey woolsey cloth at the Inn of John Paul Rapin.

After agreeing to meet at sunset at the Inn, he and Jacques separated. Resolved longed to visit the Dutch Calvinist church, while Jacques made arrangements with their Mohawk guides who were two of his adopted father's nephews.

Jacques was a Catholic. He boasted that he was indeed a devout Christian but he would not have his head covered by any church. Although Resolved thought there was some humor to this, he wished that he could persuade the Papist to see the light of the true faith, for God only knew what was to become of Jacques's soul upon his death.

Within the hour of arrival, Jacques was hurrying toward Rapin's Inn where the congeniality of a fellow Frenchman awaited him;

but it was not only the flamboyant conversation of old fur traders that beckoned.

The courting or attempt to court a woman was all so strange to him, and he found that he was a boy around Marie; for other than their French blood, and the fact that she was a widow and he a widower, they had little in common. He had never known a French woman or any other white woman intimately. There had been his Cree woman, whom he had not married, but to whom he was bound by tribal law. She had been a good woman but that was so different, a time that belonged to the young La Croix.

Now was a new time. His cabin near the great falls at the place which Algonquin people called, Cohoes, had been empty long enough and he would like to have a wife again. How he had longed for this widow with the face of the Virgin Mary and a body that stirred his blood so completely that he could not sleep at night. She was right for a man like him, for Marie was not a skinny girl but a fully blossomed woman.

The Inn was, as usual, an oasis to all French traders who did business; or, if they had no business they still looked for good cheer and well-cooked food. After spending the day in a town where even dogs barked in Dutch, and tired of hearing their brutish tongues, Rapin's was a welcome respite apart. Not that Rapin would hold anything against anyone who confessed to be Dutch, certainly he was happy to take their stivers for his rum.

He had tenderly fashioned a garden of flowers behind his Inn. Tables were placed conveniently beside shade trees that were most inviting to the parched weary traveler. In the warm season, the patrons sat late into the afternoon enjoying their drink in the freshness of the open breeze as they had done in their old countries. Two years before, Rapin took his sister in after her husband was killed. His brew house had more than doubled in customers.

Beaverwyck was growing and now hosted several brew houses, a baker's shop, a tailor, and over one hundred and fifty houses.

Beaverwyck, Fort Orange, and Rensselearwyck boasted of a total population of over one thousand settlers.

Captain Van Tricht had been killed in an Indian skirmish and Elizabeth Beekman had married a wealthy Dutchman named Van Bergen whose two brothers were killed by Indians. Jacques told Resolved that Mr. Van Bergen built a great manor house near Poeten's Kill for him and his bride. Elizabeth was well and would soon give birth to their first child.

Resolved knew that Jacques believed in their dream that a trading post for lumber from the thick forest, and not the pelt of the beaver, was the way of the future. The Europeans had been settled in this part of the country for over forty years and the Indians complained that the beaver had been hunted to near extinction in many areas. As the beaver became scarcer, fur trading declined because the Indian hunters, with whom the white men did business, were forced to widen their search. Although many reasoned that beaver would flourish for another thousand years, Resolved insisted that timber would be as valuable as gold to the powers in Europe.

Resolved tossed a stone out into the river and watched the rippling of the water as he had done as a youth. *Why dwell upon all of this?* He had allowed his grief and misfortune to make him a brooding, miserable man this past year, but no longer. He would make amends with his wife.

TWELVE

The big Dutchman and La Croix, his French collaborator, awoke before Henry, Will Waldron's prized fighting rooster, crowed, and long before the morning's sunrise secured the promise of a warm and misting dawn. The anxious pair rose quietly and gathered the provisions needed to travel deeply into the thickness of the wild.

Departing Rapin's Inn and the village of Beaverwyck, they embarked upon their journey northward toward French lands, tired, but full of optimism. The evening before, Rapin's tavern had been a gay whirl of song and frivolity as some thirty brash male voices sang and toasted the little beaver well into the night.

"A bear growls in my head this morning," Jacques La Croix moaned.

Resolved grinned. "I was only too happy to retire early; though little sleep did I get with all the clamor. Those wild days of old are gone for me," he said as he navigated the rocky path toward the shore of the great North River where the two were scheduled to meet Jacques's nephews, Metacom and Tonkawa.

"Methinks that you should not have drunk so much, Jacques, for it would be a pity if that thirsty, growling bear confuses you so much that you forget your way."

Jacques laughed. "Fear not, for you will see the land of my Iroquois kinsmen. You will smell the tall pine." The Frenchman knew well the geography of the landscape underfoot. More than a few drinks of rum would be needed to render him incapable of leading this Dutch investor to the desired plot of land beyond the great waterfalls of the Cayuga tribal people. But, Jacques admitted to himself that he would be happy to see his Indian nephews, for they knew the paths around the Falls better than he. However, conveying such information to Resolved Waldron on this beautiful sunlit morning was not necessary.

Jacques winced as Resolved tripped over a large tree stump.

"It is clear, Dutchman, your youth is spent! While I am still in my prime."

La Croix stopped to lean against a tall gray oak. He spit into the thicket brush behind him and wiped beads of perspiration from his forehead with his sleeve.

Resolved turned to confront the scarred and weathered face. Jacques's warm, dark eyes awaited a reply, sparkling with familiar jesting challenge. Resolved loved this little bull's staunch spirit, but he also loved to provoke the French Voyager.

The duo was in a playful mood, since the events of the last few days had been encouraging. They surmised that Frederick La Croix would, by now, be sitting in tribal council, his steady, deep diplomatic voice proclaiming soothing promises to the savages. Both were confident that his sincere friendship with the natives was weaving a binding belt of peace that would last for generations.

Resolved took a deep breath of new spring air and decided that this morning it would amuse him to pull the little bull's tail while the Frenchman's older brother, Frederick, saved all that was good and glorious in the New Netherlands colony.

"I watched you, whilst you watched her last night," he slowly began while observing his target keenly for reaction.

Jacques looked up toward the budding leaves of the oak, ignoring the provocation.

Resolved continued with a smug grin. "I fear your wits have become dim with your foolishness, great Voyager."

Jacques cocked his head. "And what did you see last night through your wise old eyes that I did not?"

Resolved bellowed a haughty laugh. "You are wasting your time on that woman for she will never have you, Papist! Though, in truth I believe you are the poorest and most wicked Papist whom I have ever known. It would be better for your cause if you were suffering from the terrible fevers; perhaps then, when Marie saw you in the clasp of death, she might give you a smile or a word as she knelt to say a prayer of farewell."

Jacques La Croix stopped grinning. "My head hurts today, Resolved, and my tolerance is not great, so make your meaning plain."

As Resolved proceeded down the hill toward the river, the silent pleasure of catching the Frenchman by his horns warmed his belly.

"Do you know that she is a Huguenot, and her father and brother are in the colony to avoid the French courts for crimes against a Catholic nobleman? Her kin are of the real reformed of France. I have met Marie's father, who used his sword upon the Frenchmen. He lives in New Haarlem village where he is under our Dutch protection."

Jacques was unconvinced. "How can a Huguenot live under Dutch protection in that village?"

"Methinks the man has connections in high places," Resolved replied winking. "As you know, it is my duty as a sworn officer of the colony to have knowledge of such crimes so that I may protect our good people here.

"Although her father is peaceable now and offends no one in our country, others in his own Fatherland would this day see him dead. Forget this man's daughter in Beaverwyck and find yourself another, for Marie will only break your spirit Jacques."

Jacques snorted as bulls do when flustered. He resumed making his way down the path.

"We are far from Europe, Resolved. If you think that I fear any man, much less the virtue of this woman's Huguenot soul, you are mistaken!"

"If I were you, I should fear her brother as well." Resolved became serious. "He might eagerly take his knife to your throat while you sleep in one of the soft beds of his inn; although a paying guest is desirable, a Papist as suitor for the position of brother-in-law would be far from welcome.

"Take care that he does not notice how your eyes glaze over when his good sister enters the room. The Huguenot may wish to carve them out of your head and use them for seasoning in his soup."

La Croix was grinning again. "No," he said, "Huguenot woman or Papist woman, all women of the world, they are all the same for a good man. I will win her affections as well as her hand. The day shall come that Rapin calls me brother-in-law."

Resolved raised his eyebrow.

"I will wager you my beaver skin hat that you will never be invited into the beautiful Marie's bed."

"Ah, a Calvinist that wagers. A rare man, you are indeed, and one that will wager with a Papist such as my lowly, graceless self. I can see that ours will be a partnership that shall yield a great crop. I will accept your wager. If it is agreeable with you, I shall say that I wed her before the next summer."

"Agreed," Resolved called out.

At the North River's edge the travelers were joined by Jacques' nephews, who greeted them warmly. The four continued traveling several miles through the woods, yet near enough to the shore to view the activity of the traffic upon the river. The great waterway linked trade for all the settlements between New Amsterdam and Beaverwyck; but north of Fort Orange the river grew more turbulent, and the vessels traveling upon her were smaller and fewer.

After some time, they departed the riverside and followed a small, curvy path up and over a small hill to the right of their course. The trail widened into a large opening where they came upon the settlement of Barent Van Oblienis, Jacques' nearest neighbor. In the center of the clearing stood a large house and barn surrounded by a pen that contained some twenty or more hogs.

Jacques caught the stride of the big Dutchman. "Ah, we come to Barent's place," he said.

"Praise God," Resolved whispered.

Smiling, Jacques said, "You will find Van Oblienis' family pleasant. Each year another is born. There are now nine daughters, but only one son who was born last August. Van Oblienis was so overjoyed when blessed with the boy that he covered the entire door to his house with blue ribbon. It must have been stored in his trunk for many years. One must hang the white ribbon for the girls and blue for the boys. This is Dutch custom, is it not?" Jacques asked.

"Yes," Resolved replied. "This has been the custom for as long as I can remember."

Jacques nodded.

"Van Oblienis was so grateful to have a son that he gave a great feast that went on for over two weeks. I stayed with his family for three days during which time the child received the holy waters. Guests came to celebrate with them from as far away as Hoorn Hook. We had a grand time."

"There is nothing so pleasing to a man's soul as a son."

"You speak a truth."

"Of course, children keep a man young," Resolved boasted mirthfully.

"Oh, so I grow old, but you remain the cavalier of your youth!"

Resolved studied him. "My friend, it is impossible to grow old with a young wife who births a new babe in my house every year. I am like your neighbor here in the wilderness, although I have been fortunate: God has sent me an equal amount of both male and female children.

"Methinks nine daughters would be more than any man could tolerate. Take my advice and give up the useless pursuit of Marie. If you want to keep the fire in your blood, find yourself a young wife who will serve you well. You do not need the trouble that comes from a seasoned woman with a sharp tongue."

The day was growing to a close as their party approached the Van Oblienis homestead. Soon half a dozen lively girls surrounded them. The daughters, who ranged in age from two through fourteen, made no coy attempts to hide their delighted enthusiasm when they welcomed their visitors. And their mother was enthusiastically inviting everyone to come hither, the woman obviously happy for the prospect of news of the outside world that the visitors would bring with them.

It was apparent to Resolved that the children knew their native guides well, as the smallest one had thrown herself with childish vigor into the welcoming arms of the younger Mohawk. The two Indian brothers tossed the giggling little girl from one to the other while older sisters playfully grabbed the buckskin breeches of the Indian's legs, attempting to pull him over.

Jacques laughed and shook his head. "They are wild little cats, are they not!"

"Ah, if only they would stay this way, but all too soon they grow tall and sullen," Resolved answered thoughtfully.

Followed closely by his Negro, the master of the house approached them clapping his hands while he called out admonishments to his daughters to leave the poor young men alone.

"Do not concern yourself. Our braves can defend themselves well enough," Jacques called out.

"I fear my daughters behave worse than our cow when she is in the grip of her milking time. Greetings to you, Jacques. Welcome, and good it is to see you again," Van Oblienis said warmly.

"Your girls grow more beautiful each time I set my sight upon them," Jacques continued in a complimentary tone.

"Ah, you mean more bold and strong; and that they are. God help my newborn Michael John, and me, for I fear that he shall be my only support in this den of maidens. God protect him from his sisters."

Jacques slapped his back affectionately. "Take heart, neighbor. The tide has turned with the birth of your son and you are still a young, vigorous man. Surely God will send you more."

"No, Jacques, my wife says that she has done her duty and I dare not press the matter for fear that I would lose her. I cannot be without my good wife."

"You shall hope for good son-in-laws, then," Jacques said.

Van Oblienis turned toward Resolved. "I know you, Sir."

"From where? Do you recall?"

"We met once at the funeral of my cousin, John Dyckman in New Amsterdam some years ago. You do not remember me?" Van Oblienis asked.

"No, I am sorry," Resolved apologized. "Although well I remember your cousin, John. He played a grand game of nine pins."

"Yes," Van Oblienis recalled. "He played well before his sickness took hold of him."

"'Twas a pity."

"Well, friend, I will not turn you away because you remember me not. It is understandable, for there must have been more than one hundred guests invited to his funeral, and, of course, his widow and sixteen children."

Resolved nodded and added that he knew the widow has been fortunate to remarry quickly. He recalled that she and her new husband had moved themselves to New Haarlem along with ten of John Dyckman's children. "The good woman has produced two fine boys for her second husband."

Van Oblienis held his hand over his chest as he fell into a fit of coughing mixed with laughter. "Mary always was a fertile field. But then, come into my house, all of you. See why I cannot complain on that account myself. We have plenty of room for you all at the meal table. Just this morning my Negro man, Anthony, trapped six rabbits and we have plenty of turnips and fresh bread to share. Come, my wife will have both my ears if you do not share all your sights and news with her, for what woman does not long for news of civilization?"

"We thank you for your kind invitation," said Resolved.

"Before you thank me for my kindness, I would ask that you see how you endure the good intentions of our favors," Van Oblienis replied as his daughters crowded around them.

The girls immediately descended upon Jacques, all speaking at once to him while they pulled and pushed the bowlegged bearded man through the wildflowers as if he were their pet goat.

"I welcome the company of your family, Mr. Van Oblienis," interjected Resolved, "for they fill me with the familiarity of my own house where I have four children, a brother and his good tradesman.

"My wife Tennake, and our Negro girl, Sarah, set two tables for the supper hour for we are unable to be seated all at once. So please, make no apology for your healthy, noisy family. God bless you all."

"You have a Negro servant wench in the city? A house girl?" Van Oblienis queried.

"My friend is not high born, just high minded," Jacques called over.

"Nay, I am not, but I am glad to have Sarah and I can tell you that my wife would never let her go. Tennake urges me daily to find Sarah a husband, and then I am to build our Negro couple a cabin on the back of our lot so as to keep them fat and happy in our service." Resolved laughed.

Van Oblienis looked over his guest.

"Thank God for the Negro, eh Waldron? I have sleepless nights wondering what I shall do with all my lands when Anthony has his freed papers in five years time.

"I made the bargain that he would work with me on this place for ten years. He has already given me five, and all too soon I fear I must honor my oath if it kills me. He will get his pair of hogs and an axe. Though I doubt that he will go very far from here without Betty."

"Your man has a wife?" Resolved asked.

"Yes, last year I gave him my permission to marry. I bought her cheap through an Indian trade to work the tobacco crops, not for a house servant; but my wife got her hands on her and now she says that Betty is her Negro."

Resolved smiled. "Methinks I know that tune," he said.

The farmer nodded. "Two months ago Betty produced a daughter that they call Elizabeth, so the crop was fruitful you see. I will be keeping Betty, marriage or not, for I made no such bargain for her papers," Van Oblienis said with a stubborn tone to his voice.

"I know of only one other man who makes such terms with his Negro, but you need not have made any such arrangement at all," Resolved said. "Recently, Peter Stuyvesant announced that in the English Virginia colony it is law that a Negro is a servant for life by nature of the color of the skin."

Van Oblienis stopped walking and looked down at the ground thoughtfully. "I had not heard of this ruling before."

"Though you gave your honorable word as a Dutchman, I presume," Resolved mused.

"That I did," Van Oblienis replied.

"And so?"

"And so I will keep the bargain. What care we what the English say or do? Anthony has worked well for me and he is not a heathen, having received the holy waters many years ago. Still, I wonder what will be our fate.

"This farm sits on over one hundred acres of land owned by Van Rensselear, only seven of which are cleared. Five of those seven acres that now grow grain were cleared by my Negro man and my older brother now deceased, so I cannot in clear conscience go against my word. Though I must say, an honorable spirit seems to do little to help me sleep peaceably in my bed at night.

"Jacques speaks the truth when he hopes I may find good son-in-laws, for it will be my only hope for survival. My eldest daughter, Mary, is nearly fifteen years of age and has been asked for by the Lockerman's son. Although I mean to have him over here and not she over there. Well, God's will be done, right Waldron? I fear that I have burdened you with my troubles. Come meet my good wife!"

That night they enjoyed familiar Dutch company, feasting on mint tea with warm crullers and corn pudding, along with freshly caught roasted meats. They slept peacefully, both white man and Indian lying side by side on the soft quilts that had been spread out upon the freshly scrubbed plank floors. Van Oblienis and his family did not think that unkind savages would ever touch their lives. For nearly twenty years Van Oblienis had rented the farm from the noble Kiliaen Van Rensselear; and they had never been attacked by hostiles.

In the morning, Resolved, Jacques, and their guides Metacom and Tonkawa departed the house much refreshed. They proceeded northward in silence, each of them vocally exhausted from all the conversation of the night before.

Living in the wilderness country, deprived of neighbors for miles, had rewards; but a life as such had disadvantages also, Resolved thought. Things that a man living in the city of New Amsterdam took for granted, such as news from outside the colony and the opportunity of education for his children. These were impossible for homesteading outlanders, as was protection from the savages by the garrison.

In spite of their kinship to Jacques, Resolved still considered Metacom and Tonkawa heathen. Watching them at all times, whilst keeping a hand free to draw one's sword was wise, he thought.

Resolved's mind returned to the conversation he and Van Oblienis shared the previous evening, and though Resolved had been a public servant all of his life, he saw something of himself in the farmer.

Van Oblienis came to America as an indentured servant at the tender age of twelve, along with his older brother, Jeremiah. It was a trip made possible by the Van Rensselear patroonship. For a few years, they worked in Van Rensselear's mill at De Laetsburg, a small fort located on the shoreline of the North River near Fort Orange, which provided grain for the garrison.

Eventually, they became tenant farmers on their own land in the patroonship. They cut timber from their two acres, hauled the lumber by ox cart to the river where Kiliaen Van Rensselear provided his sloop for the transportation of cargo to New Amsterdam.

They paid handsomely for the boat and had to pay a portion of their profits from the sale of the lumber, but since half of the proceeds belonged to them, they were satisfied. They made enough to purchase a Negro field hand from an Indian slave trader in Beaverwyck and still had coins to hide in the floorboards of their new two-room cabin.

Considering they had come from Holland as orphans, the brothers felt they had achieved much. Anthony was the best investment they made, Barent Van Oblienis boasted, for as he and his brother planted and harvested their cleared land, Anthony cleared two additional acres of land the first year he was with them.

Soon, Barent married Mary, a childless blue-eyed English widow, two years older than himself who bore him a house full of daughters; and now, finally, one son.

The first year of their marriage was marred by tragedy when Jeremiah drowned while racing his sled against his brother and his sister-in-law who was with child. With Jeremiah gone and everything left to his brother who was then barely eighteen years old, Barent forged a kinship with his Negro; and now he felt obliged to keep his oath, even though it was made before his brother's death. The man worked hard and had suffered much. Silently, Resolved wished Van Oblienis well.

As Resolved and his party came within earshot of the great Cayuga Falls, a magnificent water power that burst forth where the North River joined hands with the Mohawk's waterway, Metacom tapped Jacques on the shoulder. He pointed to the distant side of the river below, where a brown mother bear played with her cubs in a pool of clear water.

Looking at Resolved, Jacques smiled, and over the deafening roar of the cascade shouted, "My nephews are happy. They say to tell you that our expedition has been blessed."

"Why do they say this?" Resolved shouted back.

"The Mohawk people believe that the great bear is the spirit of a powerful brave, and to meet him along one's journey is most fortunate."

Resolved smiled and waved at the two braves next to Jacques, nodding his pleasure. They continued around the falls, proceeding west by north west for approximately three miles. There they came upon a spot that Resolved thought would be well suited to build a cabin.

Although Jacques would be there to support the venture, Resolved would send his eldest son, William, who was old enough to start out on his own and was an excellent hunter with a natural love for the waterways. By managing his father's portion, he, too, would soon have gold coins to hide in the floorboards.

Resolved imagined his logs floating over the falls to the river below and then onward to market. This land that was abundantly covered with pine, hemlock and oak, was everything and more than Jacques had told him it would be. As soon as arrangements could be made with the local tribe, he would purchase two hundred acres with good strung wampum that would more than satisfy the savages.

It would be done!

THIRTEEN

Once again the clouds of death and despair pressed down upon the Dutch New Netherlands; and as another December made it's wintry entrance, a lingering bitterness filled the hearts of the colonists. The highest born merchant as well as the lowest servant was weary of the tyrannical leader, who with his hard-handed tactics had begun to represent an unjust master with rod in hand. No benevolent loving father, Peter Stuyvesant was digging his colonial children into early graves; even his staunchest supporters had begun to worry for the longevity of their colony. In the seclusion of their homes they prayed for a merciful change, but publicly kept a still tongue, for to protest Stuyvesant's justice was worth their lives.

Months earlier, Resolved had returned home to New Amsterdam in high spirits after purchasing land in the north, where he had left Jacques in charge of the building of their small trading post. However, his festive mood was short lived when he learned that while he and Jacques had enjoyed the hospitality of Van Oblienis, a force of two hundred Dutch soldiers and hired Mohawk braves led by Captain Steenwyck had murdered every Esopus while they slept in their village near Wiltwyck.

The peace talks had never taken place and Frederick La Croix had been killed during the bloody skirmish. The death of the

Frenchman was blamed upon the savages. However, one soldier who had drunk too much of Pieterson's brew one night, wept as he confessed seeing Frederick die by the hand of a white man while trying to protect an Indian woman and her child.

The massacre had lasted only twenty minutes and afterwards Steenwyck's men burned everything, the sickly sweet smell of burning human flesh floated through the warm spring air that night, an odor that the young soldier would not soon forget.

A few women had escaped the flames and ran into the forest, but were soon rounded up by soldiers who dragged them back to New Amsterdam. Three weeks later they were placed aboard a Dutch slaver bound for the plantations on the Caribbean Islands.

"Justice," Resolved said to himself disgustedly the morning after he again questioned the soldier at the Fort, who, in the presence of Captain Steenwyck, said he could remember nothing of his foolish words spoken the night before.

Although there had been an official Company inquiry, no one would admit to any inappropriate action; and so, after a short deliberation by Peter Stuyvesant and his nine city officials, they agreed that La Croix's death had indeed been the doing of the savages.

During the remainder of the spring and through the summer months, reprisals from Esopus warriors who had been absent from their village during that murderous time, continued.

Eight more Dutch soldiers were captured while on patrol in the wilderness lands and burned alive. While these troubled times continued, any thought for a new business venture in the rich North Country was foolhardy, for venturing more than a mile outside of the safety of New Amsterdam's walls would bring a good chance of death.

Resolved sat with his Dutch Bible open in his lap and tried in vain to find a reason for the terrible events of late. Surely there was a more diplomatic path that could have been taken, for when Augustine, Jacques, and he had left the Indian village; the heathen were ready to talk. He did not understand the need for such a slaughter and he cursed Peter Stuyvesant.

Resolved thought of Jacques, who now swore never to return to New Amsterdam while Stuyvesant drew breath, saying if he came to Manhattan Island, it would be to see that the Director swiftly left the earth.

Perhaps the heretic thought of being blessed by the great bear had doomed he and Jacques, or perhaps it was as his brother, Joseph had said, "They were all prisoners of a political whim; sorry victims of a man gone mad with power."

He looked at Joseph who sat across from him rereading the letter from Tennake's brother, which conveyed news of his intention to come over. Obviously, his wife's kin, who were seeking a position for their second eldest son, had not received his letter warning them of the danger of embarking upon such a journey at this time.

"You know, Joseph," Resolved said abruptly, "The prophet Isaiah says that if we call upon the Lord he will answer, but I have called repeatedly and still I find no peace."

Joseph looked up and nodded.

"There is not a man among us that will have peace here. I cannot understand why we are being ignored by the colony's shareholders back home. Although they may care not what becomes of us, they should be attentive to their dwindling profits. Their neglect makes me as sick at heart as does Pete Stuyvesant's incompetent rule. He would do well to recall Keift's fate and treat the wild men accordingly, for I think that of late we are more the savage beasts than God-fearing Christians.

"What good can be said of men who, after offering opportunity of peaceful negotiations, disregard their invitation and murder the enemy in their sleep?"

The elder brother paced the room.

"Joseph, I have no answer for these atrocities; and I, too, believe that Stuyvesant has lost his wits. However, we have planted ourselves in the soil of this country and although this ship begins to sink, I will bale out the water with my bare hands if necessary before I will go back to Holland."

From the corner of the room where she had been tending to her sewing, Tennake looked at the two men. Although she spoke not a word, her annoyance was obvious.

"My apology to you, Resolved," Joseph said softly. "We should not press upon this matter any further as it only leaves us in bad temperament."

Tennake raised her eyebrows knowingly, but forced a smile in her husband's direction. He softened his voice. "Joseph, forgive my anger. It is only that my heart aches so! I have guided my life in an orderly manner and obey the order of the law, but God help me, Peter Stuyvesant is the administrator of a law of which I am ashamed. Of late I am pressed to feel an allegiance to the man; but his has become a hard leadership to follow. Anger soars within me; yet, I recall how Peter's word was my armor against sharp tongues which opposed my appointment."

"I remember," Joseph admitted.

"We know that harder times are coming for us," Resolved continued, "and it is best that we remain united in the face of such troubles.

"Apart from allegiances, my blood boils at the senseless death of poor La Croix, whose brother now carries such pain within himself that he swears never to step foot into New Amsterdam again."

"We have lost the aid of two good men," Joseph reflected. He poured himself a soothing cup of hot apple cider, and as he leaned over the table to reach for a slice of Tennake's fresh pumpkin bread, the drink spilled over his chin disappearing into the curls of his thick dark brown beard.

"I will leave you, brother," he said, smiling, "to ponder your own thoughts; and will go argue the value of the heathen soul with Isaac Abrahamsen."

"Take him a cake from me," Tennake requested.

"Not only will the bread give him pleasure, but your kind thought as well," Joseph replied.

"My brother, Joseph, the grand philosopher," Resolved sighed dryly after his brother had left the house, cake in hand.

"He loves everyone," Tennake said sheepishly.

"What do you mean to say, wife?"

Tennake put down her needlework. "I say nothing, but that you should go softly with him."

Resolved took the tobacco jar down from the shelf and began to fill his long stem pipe, whose enjoyment he had learned from his Indian neighbors, growers of the tobacco plant since ancient times.

He sat back in his favorite chair and drew in the smoke, enjoying the tranquility of an exceptionally quiet house, for his children were at afternoon Bible study. Sarah, too, was absent having gone to the slave quarters in the town center where she nursed sick Negroes, or so his wife had told him.

Tennake sat quietly working by the window, attempting to catch the dwindling light.

As he smoked and thought about the peaceful land among the tall pines of the Cayuga people's country, Resolved recalled how he had returned to Fort Orange after the paper was signed, feeling as grand as if he were riding upon a fine horse. The Cayuga Indians were eager to do business, and after a few days of bargaining he had purchased a beautiful piece of property located near the Half-Moon settlement. The cost had only been a few tools, glass beads and two quarts of rum.

He had remained with Jacques for three more days, and with logs cut from hemlock and pine, they began to build their small cabin upon the highest point of grassy knoll. Jacques' Indian nephews proved that, if encouraged, they could work as hard as any Dutchman.

A young native named Croton, from the nearby village of the
Cayuga tribe, assisted them. Immediately upon entering their camp
the boy told everyone that his father had been a Dutchman.

Croton's skin was as fair as any of Resolved's children, his hair
black, and his eyes seemed darker still. Resolved had seen the
mixing of the flesh many times among the French and the savages
in New Netherlands; and he knew that in Brazil the Portuguese
men preferred women of dark color, but never before had he seen a
half Dutch Indian. Croton was the only one of mixed color in his
tribe as his mother had long since remarried within her own kind
and bore several more children, all full-blooded Cayuga. Perhaps
Croton had come to their camp out of curiosity because of his
white kinship.

Resolved had looked upon this boy with revulsion, knowing
that one of his own kind made a union that could only be likened
to a pox. Making a "half-breed" was a great sin upon a Dutchman's
soul, but Resolved decided that judging was also a sin. Resolved
Waldron, too, had many sins of his own that needed accounting.

Croton proved to be an asset to their camp, in addition to his
native tongue he also spoke Dutch and French and worked faster
than anyone else and never complained. Despite Resolved's initial
revulsion, he found himself liking the young man, as did Jacques.
Metacom seemed jealous of the attention Croton received and
quickly pointed out that the Cayuga's were of a lesser tribe than
the great Mohawk, a complaint largely ignored by the Voyager.

After learning of Frederick's death, Jacques's usually happy
heart had become somber and little could be done to comfort him.
Resolved had begun to believe that the French widow with the face
of an angel in Beaverwyck might not be such a terrible match for
his old friend after all. Hers was a face, he reasoned, that could
bring a man back from the dead.

Resolved looked at his wife, who was once again round with
child.

"What is it?" Tennake asked softly.

"I was thinking that in all these years you have never once asked to go home to Fatherland," he replied.

Tenny looked down at her needle that she had begun to thread next to the light of the candle.

"I do not ask because I am home, husband. It would please me greatly to visit again someday, but my home is in New Amsterdam. Now that my father has gone to the Almighty, were my mother in better health, I would have her come over for a year's time, but I fear that the long voyage would be too burdensome for a woman of her age.

"Had Father not been so ill, he would have come the year after we did. But it was not God's will and I never had the heart to go back to Holland alone without my family. Someday we will all go."

Resolved took his pipe from his mouth and stared into the glow of burning tobacco.

"Someday," he mused. He thought this was the wistful desire of a patient woman, but he wondered if they ever again would see the shores of Holland. Although it would be good to see his birth land again, he could not afford to pay the passage for all of them over and back; nay, not even for one of them.

He thought bitterly of the heads of the Esopus, which had adorned the walls of the fort until a few days ago, trophies brought home by Stuyvesant's great conquering soldiers. He and several other town citizens complained to their Director that these gruesome prizes were terrifying their young children, and finally they had been removed.

"I wonder to what home I have brought you," Resolved said gently.

Tennake looked at him tenderly.

"God has protected this family through terrible times before, and he shall do so now," she replied assertively, folding her cloth.

Resolved smiled. Whenever his heart grew black and withdrew to the deepest loneliest part of his breast it took but few loving words from this good woman to renew his spirit. She humbled him with her faith, which was as big as the sky. He had come to count upon her comfort as one of the blessings in his life that he could not do without.

"I will never believe that Stuyvesant gave orders to murder the Esopus," he said suddenly. "Steenwyck must have drunk too much that night. Captain Steenwyck was stuck with love for the daughter of a farmer who lived south of New Amsterdam. His fierce passion would surely have ended in holy matrimony; but the girl was killed by the Esopus in a raid upon her father's farm last year. Young Steenwyck had sworn vengeance. Many who attended the Holt christening heard him speak a sacred oath against the wild men. Do you recall?"

"Yes, I do," Tennake replied softly.

"Pete Stuyvesant knew this man's heart and should never have put him in charge of this command," Resolved declared.

"I doubt that the Captain's temperament escaped Peter Stuyvesant," Tennake observed. "Nor do I believe that he intended to sit meekly within death's palm and speak words of peace with the Indians. He had set his mind to cleanse us of this hellish plague by way of a murderous lesson."

"You may be right, and although a lesson was needed, I would have taught it differently. I have no love for the wild savages that continue to attack our boweries and kill our settlers, but I would not have the blood of sleeping women and children upon my hands."

Resolved put another log into the fire.

Tennake sighed. "I, too, pity their poor souls, although what is done cannot now be changed. You must resign yourself to calmness or lose your wits as has our Director."

"How can I be calm?" Resolved asked in exasperation. "We cannot endure more warfare with the savages for we do not have the soldiers to fight both the Indians and the English. Our Director knows this situation well, and could have spared us the retribution of the wild men if he would have waited until the Company sent more soldiers."

"Husband, the words you speak are those of a reasonable man, but it matters not since the vile deed was done. Of course, as a woman, I understand little of such matters, but it is unimportant whether a crazed young man or the leader upon whom we depend is responsible. We must all live with the consequences and pray God's forgiveness for wrongs committed."

Tennake came to her husband and kissed him lightly upon his forehead. "You are a good tender wife," Resolved said.

"You are not Director in this colony, Resolved, and therefore you cannot take his burden upon yourself. Although you have taken no pleasure in this matter, you followed Peter Stuyvesant's orders and departed to Wiltwyck. Had you known of this terrible injustice, you still would have followed the same course and obeyed your commander.

"Thankfully, you did not know of his plan, for then you would have become a part of this murderous act and your heart would have been heavy for the rest of your life."

Resolved smiled wearily. "By God, I am thankful that you are mere woman," he said.

"Have done with it then and return your heart to me and the children," Tennake coaxed.

"You are my life, Tennake." He kissed her strongly on her lips.

"Your ardor compliments me, husband," Tennake said gently pulling Resolved's long red beard.

Resolved ran his hand affectionately across his wife's belly. "You have done much that is worthy of praise," he said.

"Our children need us both, husband, and though I am happy to keep him home, our eldest is not happy about a delay in his quest for the wild North Country."

Resolved uttered a small groan.

"Will must learn patience. In this time of turmoil, safe passage to Mohawk country would be impossible."

"When did his father wait patiently for safe passage?" she asked.

"Would you have me send him out then?"

"Nay, nay, only that you must speak to Will about this and not leave him in silence."

"Keep your heart, woman. I shall speak to him and I shall try to remember the impatience of my own youth."

"He is your son, Resolved. One you could never deny, and that be a truth. Though I did not know that impatience belonged only to those without beards or budding breasts," she said, smiling.

"Wife, as you know, patience is not my strongest virtue," Resolved replied.

Still with a smile upon her lips, Tennake added, "You have other virtues that are much to my liking and we shall not speak of those that are not."

Resolved laughed robustly. "Nay, remember this to be Sunday and only a few hours ago we both took part in the Lord's Supper."

Tennake's face began to redden. "I meant no vulgarity," she said. *If these thoughts be sinful, would her husband also be held accountable for ravishing his wife on the night of the Sabbath?*

"What think you about this?" Tennake asked raising one eyebrow.

Resolved tried to sober himself. "Methinks with your superior wit I will lose this match," he replied.

"I must be allowed a few victories," she concluded.

"You may have all the victories that you wish," he said softly. She seated herself on a stool next to his chair and as she looked up into her husband's eyes he squeezed her shoulder affectionately.

He ran his finger tenderly along the softness of her cheek and realized that he had finally found the peace he had searched for in the verses of the Holy Book. He had asked God's help and received his comfort as was promised in Scripture.

"Why did you say, earlier today, that more bad times shall come? What were you thinking?" Tennake whispered.

"I wonder what direction our English friends will take now that Charles II is restored to his father's throne.

"Augustine tells me he hears from St. Mary's City that the new King of England has many relatives and friends who would like to fill their pockets, and our Colony could well be the purse that the King has in mind to plunder.

"If the English make their move against us, we cannot withstand their attack for they are many and we are the few here in the New World. Our sleeping enemy knows that our forces are weak from these Indian uprisings."

Tennake patted her husband's hand.

"Again you concern yourself with that over which you have no control. Would you take the burden of the English government upon your soul along with the responsibility of our Director General in New Netherlands?

"We have survived warfare with the savages, Resolved, and we shall survive the English should they come with their guns against us."

Resolved nodded soberly, although he knew that the day would come when their English neighbors would sail into New Amsterdam's harbor and shout their demands for Dutch land. He knew as well, that the time was nearing when he would be forced to call Charles II, the King in New Netherlands.

FOURTEEN

As Tennake passed her thirtieth birthday, it seemed that the sun rose and set more quickly than she remembered from her girlhood days in Holland. Each new day was a repetition of the one before, the monotony of household chores broken only by Sunday church services, a wedding feast, a funeral gathering, or a christening celebration.

Poking at a simmering log, she looked over at nine-month-old Cornelia, her plump infant thumb tucked securely in her mouth as she slept peacefully in her woven basket by the hearth. While her household slept, she leaned over to pull the bright red and blue Indian blanket more securely about the babe.

It was late October, and outside her snug house on the Broadway the leaves of the tall trees glistened brilliant colors of yarrow yellow, burnt red and golden peach and while they were beautiful to look upon, the chill of a foreboding winter filled the New Amsterdam air. She ached as she looked at her little daughter. Nearly two years ago she had lost Adam, her second-born son, to the cold of the winter winds. As he died in her arms while she rocked him, she understood the pain that tore out the hearts of so many of the women in the colony. She did not think that she or her husband could survive that kind of hurt again.

Resolved, who in the past had been her strong rock, had been lost in his grief, and had left her that spring for two months while he went to St. Mary's City with Wynant Van Zandt. Although he claimed that his absence was unavoidable, she suspected that he had asked Peter Stuyvesant for the duty.

For a long time she had believed that Adam's death was her doing. It was God's punishment for her prideful recounting of the many attributes of her small son, Barent, to any neighbor who came to her door. She loved Barent more than she could ever have imagined possible, and although she loved Will, Rebecca and Aeltie, she could not help but love Barent more because he was the child of her body.

When Adam was born, the anguished midwife told her that her infant would not live to see his first birth date, but she would not believe her though even she could see that the child was weak. Her tiny boy had survived ten days. Surely she had done something to incur the wrath of God.

She saw the same pinched look in the midwife's face when she handed the swaddled blonde Cornelia to her. But sweet Cornelia fooled the midwife and had proven herself to be a staunch Dutch girl. This afternoon Tennake renewed a silent pledge that she would not allow another of her children to slip away. It was a promise that would be difficult to keep for only the strongest of the babes would survive the harsh New Netherlands winter to delight in the tiny incessant fluttering of the little jade hummingbirds come the following summer.

She recalled how she had loved the winter with its sparkling glow of frozen water droplets that clung to the branches of the trees. As a girl in Holland, she had yearned for First Skating Day and the gaiety of the sleigh races, which embraced the joyous spirit of the weeklong New Year celebration.

Now, the season of colonial winter proved to be an unbearable hardship which took the sparkle from the droplets and brought instead isolation from the comfort of friends and neighbors who lived just beyond the wall. The ice that clung to the branches of the trees also clung to the chests of the old and the tiny babes, foreshadowing the fevers of death, which to her seemed to follow the fall of snow. This was a truth to be written in her book of memories that she would pass onto her children so that they would know how things were during these times.

She cut a slice of bread and poured a tankard of steaming hot apple cider. Standing near the window Tennake enjoyed the warmth of the cup, becoming lost in a silent moment of reflection Today she and Sarah planned to make apple butter, and Rebecca and Aeltie were scheduled to attend their lace-making lesson at Mistress Phillip's home.

As Tennake gazed out, she thought of peaceful walks through the tall grasses of Fatherland and of the excitement that she and Resolved had shared the day their vessel had first entered the waters surrounding this island. Vaguely she recalled as many details as she could of that first day, a lifetime apart from this moment.

Last week, Resolved had returned from Maryland country and immediately resumed night patrol duty in the city. This morning he would sleep soundly for another hour before rising, a small miracle considering the noise of children that would soon fill the house despite her admonishments.

She liked her husband's position as New Amsterdam's night officer, for his situation offered her an opportunity to have his daytime company to a small degree. Through his engaging tales of travel she was offered a pleasing escape from the binding walls of New Amsterdam, from which throughout all these years she had never ventured further than twelve miles.

Resolved, who had always been a flavorful storyteller, knew how to sweeten his tale. It was good to see him laugh robustly again at his own recount of travel; and she savored the intimacy in which her husband spoke to her in trusted confidence on many subjects. Resolved was an astute diplomat and nothing reached the ears of his neighbors that he did not want them to hear. This virtue of discretion had brought him high honor and great endearing value to Director Stuyvesant.

Tennake wrapped her hands around her still warm tankard as she thought about the story Resolved had recently told, one she had been unable to forget. Three weeks ago he had been a guest in the English south country at the great manor house of Mr. Philip Calvert at St. Mary's City. Since his return, he had amused her and Rebecca with tales of his visit with the most powerful family in all of Maryland.

All the same, she remembered how she had been against his going on this assignment. Resolved, still on the mend from a knife wound he had received while breaking up a fight between a Dutchman and a Swede, had departed upon this journey with a heavy heart. Tennake had wanted him to delay the rigorous venture into the wild southern countryside that lay between New Amsterdam and St. Mary's, until he was healed; but her stubborn husband would not hear of it. His obstinate nature, which in her youth she thought to be charming, had now become a curse. She often worried that Resolved was pushing himself into an early grave.

Before he departed from New Amsterdam, they had shared harsh words, which Tennake regretted as she had come to understand such discourse was a waste of God's good gift of breath. When she had asked Resolved if this journey could not be assigned to a younger diplomat, he had exploded louder than any of the cannons posted at the Fort.

"Do you not think me capable of doing a man's full day of work? By God, I am fifty years of age, but I can hold my own with any of the other young bucks!" he had shouted. Despite his wounds, Mr. Waldron would tend to his business.

Her husband's sore words wounded deeply. Sometimes she felt that the man she had wed in Holland was married more to the Company than he was to her.

Of course, her heart healed when he returned and confessed that he left upon that assignment with a heavy heart, partly because he sensed her lack of faith in his abilities, and partly because he suspected that Joseph was secretly meeting a Puritan girl. Tennake found this amusing, since she had introduced her brother-in-law to every suitable woman in New Amsterdam. However, her brother-in-law would have none of her or Resolved's recommendations, but would instead choose a girl that he could not bring to house. Although Resolved would suffer the Jew for the debt owed him, he would not have a Puritan as part of their fold.

"Better he should wed a Quaker, rather than a runaway Puritan from the deceased Cromwell's Commonwealth!" Resolved had bellowed. His fury caused Aeltie to weep and William to rush out of their house. Tennake hated words spoken in anger for it went against both their natures; and it was certainly rare for her husband to spew foul words in front of their children.

Happily, the distance placed between them had been a proper antidote, since other than the disruption of the initial day of homecoming, Resolved had returned to them refreshed in spirit, cheerfully describing every detail of St. Mary's City, making a colorful word painting that she could envision well.

Tennake sighed. Despite his lack of divine solutions to all their problems, their Moses was a most courageous man for whom she held a great tenderness within her breast. She smiled as she thought of Resolved's concern for his brother. As a man nearing forty, Joseph did not need a keeper, and even though Resolved, being the elder, took the responsibility of his brother's welfare with grave seriousness, it was time for her husband to allow him to make his own bed.

Her mood improved further as she thought of the beautiful blue fabric tablecloth embroidered with a flowered design of tiny golden stitches that he had brought her from the Mistress of the Manor at St. Mary's City.

"A gift from one queen to another," he proclaimed sheepishly as he handed it to her.

Her thoughts returned to his description of the Calvert's manor house. *How this wife would love to trade places with her husband and let him stay to home tending six children, Sarah and his brother. If the Almighty Lord God would see fit to send her to be waited upon and served as a Queen at the fine table of the wealthy powerful Calvert, she would be grateful for the rest of her life.* Foolish dreamer, she chided herself.

Judith Stuyvesant might be that fortunate, but Tennake Waldron would be blessed just to see the top of Anna Grossman's table on the other side of New Haarlem.

Still there was no harm in dreaming, for her dreams had given her a light heart and she was happy that she had married a man who traveled to distant parts and brought her wondrous stories which quenched her thirst for knowledge of the outside world.

Although there had been a time when she resented his long absences, she now felt far more blessed than most women. She could have married Peter Luyster and been the wife of a farmer who never left his acres and could tell only tales of hogs and corn. Yet, if she never heard of anything but hogs and corn, perhaps she would be as content as Mr. Luyster's wife seemed to be.

According to letters from her dear friend, Cornelia, her own garden in the colony seemed to be the sunniest part of the entire world. Both England and Holland had gone through many difficult days of late, and the years of turmoil under Oliver Cromwell had taken their toll upon England and everyone who would do business with her.

Tennake remembered how her father worried over their powerful neighboring country and Cromwell who he considered to be a vile oppressor, claiming to be for his English people, yet stealing every joy from their hearts. He prohibited bowling Greens, cockfighting, wagering, and eventually had closed the alehouses, ruling in behalf of the stern, grim-faced Puritan minority. Finally, in 1651, he had introduced the most hated of all measures, the Navigation Act.

Tennake had written to Cornelia that she wondered if Oliver Cromwell and their own Director General Stuyvesant were not distantly related, for he too had, on occasion, forbidden all of the same amusements. Her dear father would not have loved Peter Stuyvesant so well, had he known the man by person and not just by rumor of valor in battle. Now Cromwell was dead and his son, Richard, assumed the role of Lord Protector of all England.

Cornelia replied that the Commonwealth had crumbled and Charles II had been restored to the English throne, which was old news to Tennake thanks to Resolved's most recent journey to the home of the English Calverts.

At first, all of New Netherlands had hoped this would be a glad tiding, but the news of the new monarch had only proven more worrisome for the Fatherland and the colony. Arguments over the borderlines had increased and King Charles' enforcement of the Navigation Act cut deeply into the trade lines of good Dutchmen even further. Words of war were on the lips of every Dutch citizen, Cornelia wrote.

Minor disturbances sometimes arose between Dutch and English neighbors on Long Island, but nothing so serious as to bring either to their knees. In America, far removed from the old country, Tennake believed that Cornelia's distress seemed exaggerated.

"Let her come to New Netherlands and live among the wild men for a time. Our savages will instruct her in fear so that she will know what true terror might be!" she had remarked in a letter to her friend, Elizabeth, in Beaverwyck.

Resolved had often spoken of the English as the sleeping enemy, but Tennake had far too many enemies pursuing her family that were quite lively to worry over one that slept.

"When the enemy awakens, advise me, husband," she told Resolved. "Until that time, I'll keep my hand upon my little pistol that I keep under my skirt, and pray to God to give me heart, if need be, to use it."

In response to Cornelia's letter, Tennake had written her a sorrowful letter one afternoon after witnessing a wild crowd cheer as soldiers peeled the skin off the back of one of Stuyvesant's captive Indian youth. She had gone to the Green to fetch William so that he would not witness the violence, but instead she had found him behind the Baker's house vomiting from the sight of the atrocities.

Upon her return she began her letter to her dearest friend:

"You know well, Cornelia, we have made our nest here by fighting savages, sickness and death. Dutch or English, French or Swede, Spanish—or whether our religious belief is Christian or not—we tolerate one another well. Say nothing to me of war with the English, for what is this to me? I care not whether Charles II or King Turkey with full feathers rules England! Some of our settlers fear that with this restoration of the Monarch in England, New Netherlands will be forced to turn over their lands, boweries, mills, and businesses to England and have Charles II serve as our Lord Protector.

Dearest Cornelia, my husband has just returned from Maryland where he sat to sup with the great English Lord Calvert himself and was treated warmly. His wife, Ann Wolsey Calvert sent Judith Stuyvesant and me a fine tapestry for my table and I care less than the sweat on a horse's backside that she is a Catholic, for her kind gesture was wondrously appreciated. I was very taken that this great lady from such a prestigious family would think of me thus.

Believe me, the English colonist has as much grief to tend to during the course of a day as we, and although there be trouble makers born to all sides, the majority of all the people over here want only a peaceful living. Many are in this country to increase their wealth in a short period of time and then return to their Fatherland in all great glory, be that Fatherland Holland, France, England, or any country.

Before Resolved had been a guest at the grand Calvert Manor house, he was an honored guest along with Augustine Herrman at the house of Mr. Symon Overzee. Resolved told me that the gracious Mrs. Overzee stuffed them so full of her puddings and cakes that they could hardly move!

On the third night of their journey, they were invited to the home of Mr. Philip Calvert, Mr. Overzee's closest neighbor. While they were there, a Mr. Doughty, previously of the Manhattans, called upon their host unexpectedly. Although after some thought, Resolved did not think that the call was unexpected at all as I am sure you will also agree after I tell you the tale.

Mr. Doughty is the father-in-law of Hugh O'Neal; and his daughter, May was the widow of the esteemed, Adrian Vander Donck, until after her husband's death. She remarried and relocated in Maryland. Resolved had met Hugh O'Neal a few years ago while he and Jacques La Croix were tracking down some of our people who had been taken captive by the savages. Resolved said that O'Neal was very much a bold swagger of a man.

After dinner at the Calvert's was finished, Mr. Doughty laid upon the table his maps and charts of this country, taken, no doubt, from his deceased son-in-law. One of the maps was printed in Amsterdam of old by direction of Captain John Smith who discovered the Great Bay of the Chesapeake.

The second map was also printed at Amsterdam at the time of Lord Baltimore, but the men did not know by whom it was drawn. Both maps differed one from the other, and Mr. Doughty wished to prove that the Dutch are upon English lands. Of course, the Dutch know otherwise! The boundary disputes went on for some time, the English always insisting that they held this land from the days of old, ever since the year 1584, and the time of Sir Walter Raleigh.

Augustine and Resolved argued that the Dutch took their origin and right to the land from the King of Spain, since he was the Netherlands' King at the time of the discovery of America, nearly one hundred years before Sir Walter's time.

"You have both lost your wits!" Mr. Doughty shouted at them.

"*Recall history, Mr. Doughty,*" *Resolved briskly retorted.* "*Remember that in those times Spain was our Sovereign, placing the Dutch fairly within this land. We liberated ourselves from Spain and after our victory; Spain legally conveyed full title to all property in Europe and America to the Dutch!*

"*I entreat you, Mr. Doughty, to look upon your maps once again, this time opening your eyes wider!*"

Resolved was disgusted with this abrupt little man who seemed to be so full of the fighting spirit. Cornelia, I would have laughed when he called him the little red cock, but I dared not to do so for he was upset to know that this Mr. Doughty was once a citizen of our Dutch colony, and the father-in-law of one of the greatest Hollanders that hath every lived. And now that his daughter is married to O'Neal, I imagine it suits him to argue against those who had once been kindred. He must support his daughter's interests, which also suits him very well!

My husband may have English blood flowing through his ancestral veins, but no stauncher Hollander do I know. Resolved did apologize to his host, Mr. Philip Calvert, as did Mr. Doughty, for the impoliteness of their heated moment. Glad was I of this, Cornelia, since had he not apologized; I most assuredly would not have seen the tapestry!

Resolved came home to me full of admiration for the English Chancellor who by all accounting seems to be a generous and peaceable man. He invited Augustine and Resolved to look over his vast number of books, putting them at their disposal while they were there. Resolved thinks highly of a man of intellect although he feels that a keen eye should be kept upon the learned Englishman, for according to my husband one thing is most certain: when an Englishman speaks of boundary lines he means country.

He feels that England's Lord Baltimore would gladly have the whole country of New Netherlands, not just a few additional miles of this disputed land. But alas, Lord Baltimore is far across the ocean's waters and has little heart for the people living on his lands. All everyone in this land desires is a convenient trade arrangement between our two countries, so that we may all go about our business."

Tennake completed her letter with news of those who had attended infant Cornelia's christening and regretted that Cornelia herself could not have been there to stand up for her namesake.

Finally, Tennake expressed her secret concern for the attention that Joseph was showing Sarah, for she had seen the looks that were exchanged between the two, which had made her shiver. She was not worrying about Joseph's interests in a Puritan, although she omitted this thought from her letter.

Tennake usually held her tongue regarding Sarah and Joseph because it was her duty to keep their home as peaceful and joyful as possible. Better to confide her fears of this unspeakable relationship to her old friend in Holland, although she knew that Cornelia would have no reasonable solution to the problem. She lived in another world that believed the keeping of slaves was unchristian.

Tennake had prayed daily about the matter of Sarah and Joseph. She had not confided her fears to her sisters because to do so would elicit taut, set faces with raised eyebrows, an unpleasant vision that sent pain to her temples. Cornelia was her only choice for unburdening her soul.

She could hear the children awakening above her head.

Another day had begun in the city of New Amsterdam, on the Island of Manhattan.

FIFTEEN

After Resolved returned from St. Mary's City, the boisterous debate of a probable English invasion of the New Netherlands never ceased between father, son, and brother in the Waldron house. The men folk's continuous cursing of the English Lords that suckled from their restored King, made Tennake and her daughters wince.

The colonists knew their troubles did not always find root with their colonial English neighbors, but some had begun to love them less. The English settlers in New Netherlands began to resent the high and mighty attitude of the Dutch. Although Resolved had come from English stock, he was thoroughly Dutch, and as the debates raged on at her table, Tennake pondered the history of her husband's family.

In 1587, Resolved's father came to Holland as one of Queen Elizabeth's six thousand English soldiers, and after marrying a Dutch woman had remained in the city of Amsterdam. Many of the English had stayed with the Dutch after their assignments ended because England suffered hard times during those years. The crops had not been good, and all of England whispered of what would become of their country when their aging Queen Bess died, since she was without an heir and had not named a successor to her throne.

When Tennake wished to torment Resolved, she would remind him that her family had been Dutch since the time of the Lord Christ himself. Still, the arguments persisted and oaths of English damnation grew more violent as Resolved claimed his right to the Fatherland as surely as any other man who walked the earth now or in glorious Fatherland at the time of Christ.

"And what if those English Lords crossed the ocean and came to our pretty little town here in the wilderness?" Tennake asked her husband.

She persisted sharply. "What if the English King himself came and relieved Director Stuyvesant of his duties and sent him back to Fatherland along with his Burgers and Dutch soldiers? Would the Waldrons then return to Holland, if, please the Lord God Almighty there would be Waldrons left alive to return?"

"They have not broken down our doors as yet," Resolved told her coldly, his jaw set.

Tennake thought that the English would come, and soon, and God only knew what would become of her family when they did. She had heard all the recent rumors that filled every tavern in their colony saying the English were now laying claim to all of New Netherlands. Would they be forced out of this colony as the Spanish had forced the Hollanders out of Brazil years ago?

Alas, if the English allowed her husband to retain his properties in the colony, how could a man who knew nothing but public service become a farmer or competent diamond merchant?

Resolved had not realized a profit from his earlier purchase of the northern lands because the warfare with the savages between New Amsterdam and Fort Orange had never been fully put to rest; and he dared not let William take the responsibility of a trading post in the midst of such disquiet.

Eight months before, when all was supposed to be quieting down with the Indians, John Montague's sister, Ruth, had been captured just outside Half-Moon village. She had been returned from captivity through the grace of God and the intervention of friendly Mohawk, but had not uttered a single word in all the months since her arrival back home.

So William had remained in New Amsterdam within a stone's throw of the Fort's soldiers, and Resolved's beautiful land of the abundant pines under the protection of Jacques La Croix had remained free of the lumberman's axe. The dream of future riches from her husband's northern lands might well remain a dream forever if the English took New Netherlands.

If the English removed her husband from his position, how would they feed this large family of six children, as well as Sarah? Tennake had spent many hours nervously pondering a course that might be taken.

One evening as he was enjoying his pipe, Resolved mentioned that Mr. Van Meteren sold off his house girl, Miriam, when his debts had become too great. Resolved's statement disturbed Tennake immensely because long ago in better times she had promised Sarah that she would keep her safe; but how would she be able to honor such a commitment should they lose everything?

Returning to the Fatherland was not a pleasant consideration either, because all they possessed was in this Dutch colony. Her mother had passed on to the glorious light of Christ last year, as had her eldest sister Rebecca when she attempted to bear her seventh child. Resolved had long ago bid farewell to any kin in the old country; so although she still had family there, her babes were here and she no longer had the desire to return.

The possibility of the English becoming their new Lords was a grim one that no person wished to face. She and Resolved had spoken of retreating to the country to take up residence on the lots that he had purchased in New Haarlem. The small village situated between the great forest and the city of New Amsterdam was thriving, thanks to Jan Van Bommel, a previous resident of New Amsterdam who now operated a successful sawmill there. Several Dutch families, as well as Van Bommel, had already departed to their investment properties rather than meekly return home should the English come.

Van Bommel wrote to Resolved, asking William to come to his mill to learn the trade while he waited for the situation with the wild men to improve in the North Country; but Will did not want to leave New Amsterdam.

Joseph, who had also invested money into a lot of land in New Haarlem, had once told her that the waters of the Hellgate were the sweetest of streams that ever gave charm to a landscape. Last spring, she had seen the place he had spoken of so affectionately, and agreed that the lush rolling lands of New Haarlem were as beautiful as any that she had ever seen put on canvas.

Since the neighboring savages, the Wickquasseeks, had signed a treaty with their Dutch neighbors vowing peaceful intentions, the gardens of the village women at New Haarlem flourished. Their produce had grown undisturbed.

Tennake had heard the story of Sauwenarack, the head chief for the Wickquasseeks, respectfully asking for permission from the Dutch to fish the waters of nearby New Haarlem. Unlike the northern wilderness lands, there seemed to be no threat from the wild people that bordered the village of New Haarlem.

A commons had been instituted to the west of the village where the cattle grazed peacefully under the care of an assigned herder, but most advantageous of all was the garrison of fifteen soldiers who were stationed there with the blessing of Peter Stuyvesant.

If the English invaded, however, Stuyvesant would be gone and so would Dutch protection for the little village that pushed at the doorway of the wild men. Still, since a peace had already been established with the Indians, New Haarlem seemed a much better prospect for the future.

Tennake did not want to move from her beautiful house in New Amsterdam where her babes had been born, but if she must, she would, because a blind man could see that all was not well here.

One evening, sleepless with worry over what would become of her family, she broached the subject of their future to her husband.

"Tenny, your worries speak poorly for your faith in a good staunch Dutch heart or the Dutch blade," he admonished. "Our High Mightiness in the Fatherland would see that no Englishman ever rules this colony," he assured her briskly.

"I have been thinking, husband,"

"God save us all from the thoughts of women. It is truly a dangerous sport," Resolved teased.

"I implore you, husband, allow me the right to a few words so I might explain my thoughts to you."

"I ask pardon. Please proceed."

Tennake folded her hands in her lap.

"How often have you complained to me when returning from your many journeys over the last years, of the terrible lack of any proper accommodations for the weary traveler? How often have you slept in a bed of leaves under a tree or nearly caught your death as you lay upon the damp ground in a spring rain?"

"Many times I have complained thus," Resolved chuckled. "The inns in this new country are few, and bright are the stars when a good hospitable neighbor invites us to spread our pallet upon his floor or offers a bit of fresh hay in his barn and the warmth of his beasts."

"Just so," Tennake mused.

Resolved wrinkled his brow. "What are you thinking?"

"If the English come and you lose your position, you will need to look in another direction," Tennake said tentatively.

"Good woman, perish such a thought at once!"

Tennake frowned. "Do not be annoyed with me, Resolved. You may not be a farmer, but you speak the English King's language and you could make use of this talent if bitter times do come to us."

Resolved burst into laughter. "Tenny, my sweet bird, New Haarlem may be beautiful to look upon, but be assured that life as a villager would not rest easily upon you."

Tennake pouted. "Did you think that I chose a simple undemanding life when I followed you over here? I would happily begin a new life there if the move would benefit our family.

"We could build a fine dwelling house of brick and also a bouwhuys under the same roof where our cattle would be housed, that travelers might find refuge from the weather. It would also be wise to build extra rooms that could be used as an inn for the more affluent travelers who would pass through the village."

Closing her eyes she continued on as if she were witnessing a beautiful vision. "Our guests that come from great distances will bring us abreast of news from those distant parts and when they depart shall tell others of our clean beds covered in fresh white linen where they rested undisturbed by fleas. I have been told that the best inns of England harbor more fleas than there are trees," Tennake began to laugh.

"No respectable flea would dare to enter the house of Tennake Waldron," Resolved mocked.

"Laugh if you must, husband, though I think you would not be finding the place so much the humorous as practical. We will have a coach drawn by four fine horses pulling up the guest to our front stoop. And you are the resplendent Inn Keeper, happy and prosperous, playing the part of the gracious host who engages his guest in good conversation so they would understand be they English or Dutch.

"When they return to their homes, they will speak well of us to their neighbors, especially after we offer them a goblet of our fine peach wine, freshly made from the fruit grown in our orchard."

"A peach orchard? I own but three small lots," Resolved interrupted.

Tennake continued as though she had not heard her husband speak. "I shall cook them as fine a meal as any that you have eaten at St. Mary's. Their mouths will water, as they taste my roasted rabbit smothered in parsnips and herbs, along with apple baked in sugar, sprinkled with lemon balm. And after one bite of Sarah's warm bread drenched in fresh melted butter, the men will hate to sit at their own wife's table.

Suddenly tears came to her eyes.

"I will tell you this husband, though this colony turn English and I am forced to leave this good house, I will always be Dutch. Potted tulips will always grace the window ledge of the house we sleep in, and I will speak Dutch in our house as will our children and grandchildren, or they will have no discourse with me."

Tennake smiled while wiping away her tears. "But of course, we would be as happy to take an English shilling as a silver Dutch daelder."

Resolved stared at his wife in silence. He had no idea she had such thoughts under her cap. He touched her cheek gently. "Your words move me; though me heart aches to think that you fear us to be so weak."

To himself he thought:

If only a Dutch defeat at the hands of the English would provide such a pretty little end for them; but he did not see the future as brightly as did his wife. He feared that the English crown would not leave any of them so much as a piece of cloth with which to cover themselves. He, as well as many other Dutchmen might be hanged, or at the very least, when the enemy took over their properties, they would become beggars in the streets. However, he would protect his sweet wife's dream.

"Tenny, your inn lifts my heart," he said brightly, "but we need not await the English to retire to the country. I think I would like to be the gracious Inn Keeper."

"You like my dream, then?"

"I do," Resolved replied. "You are a good woman, Tenny, though methinks that you should not worry. Are you not the God-fearing woman who has told us many times that Our Lord God will protect us? Did you not tell me from the first that we were a chosen family who would overcome all of the troubles put before us? Have faith now that we Dutch will stand tall against our enemies. Who is to know the future? Perhaps God wishes us to be diplomats in our old age—from our Inn at New Haarlem's village. What do you say of that?"

Tennake smiled. "I say this must be a truth."

"And I say that I should watch you very carefully wife," Resolved said emphatically, "lest you become another Margaret Brent."

"You mock me, now," Tennake protested. "I am no Margaret Brent, noble English Catholic lady; nor am I any man's mistress, but a proper wife to you I be, Mister Waldron, and a good mother to your children."

"I do not mock you, Tenny. Well you might be compared to all Mistress Brent's virtue."

"I wish I had the courage of Margaret Brent," Tennake said thoughtfully. "This woman who alone paid her passage over from England as well as passage for three others, and fought for her rights to her lands in Maryland, does stir my senses.

"Methinks she has been judged unfairly. Mistress Brent's relationship should be between the two accused, and God and I believe that she did her duty well in keeping the wishes of the Governor's will."

"Methinks the woman became as wild as the cats in the forest."

"You are too harsh, husband. Do you speak thus because a woman sold all of the properties without anyone's consent? Or because she stepped outside of the English laws? For my part, I believe that she wished only to do what was honorable and she lacked funds to pay the soldiers who had helped quell the rebellion in Maryland while her beloved Leonard still lived. She sold the land of Leonard's brother in order to raise the money to pay the debts promised to these soldiers."

"She should have sought proper advice," Resolved stated.

"Had she done so, Maryland may not have been established, and surely Cecil Calvert, Lord Proprietor and second Lord Baltimore living in London, would have been a happy man."

Resolved laughed. "Joseph thinks that the good Lord Baltimore owed Margaret Brent a great deal more than the few coins she took from his pile. He insists that this staunch lady paved the road for many of the 8,000 settlers that Maryland now has."

"Eight thousand English neighbors," Tennake replied.

"Yes, God spare us," Resolved sighed.

"Methinks that if we here in New Netherlands had Margaret Brent at the helm of our ship we would be far better off," Tennake said.

"Keep such thoughts to yourself," Resolved instructed.

"Who else hears me?" Tennake asked.

"Still, it was only right that she should be paid for her service to the Calverts, but asking to be admitted to the General Assembly, where no woman, not even the Virgin Mary herself was allowed, was very bold," Tennake giggled.

"More laughable than a Jewish King and a Catholic Queen disputing a partnership over a Protestant land."

Tennake did not think the comparison humorous. "Happy was every man in England when Mistress Margaret's petition was denied. She left St. Mary's to live in a new brick manor house that she built in the center of her vast tobacco fields in Virginia. She named her plantation, 'Peace' and I hope that she has found it," she said softly.

They heard the loud bang of the Dog's Head knocker against their front door.

Upon answering, Tennake bid Corporal Schuyler good day.

"Good day to you, Mistress," he greeted. "Is your husband in?" he asked, looking past her into the house.

"He is. I have tied my husband to his chair that he might remain to house for a time." Tennake smiled.

The messenger's face turned a subtle pink color.

"I am here, John," Resolved called. He arose and walked to the door.

"Pay no attention to my wife. A robust foul mood usually overcomes her each day at this time."

"I am here officially, Resolved," the Corporal announced with some hesitation. "His Honor, the right and prudent Peter Stuyvesant will hold audience with you at four o'clock today."

"Thank you, Corporal. I will be in attendance, you may report to His Honor."

Tennake closed the door behind the young soldier and watched him from the window. "What must people think of me," she said quietly. "My lips move, but sometimes my heart bids them be still."

"John holds you in high regard, wife. Did we not stand at the christening for his little Anna? I should think him bemused with your hearty spirit. I wonder more what old Almighty Pete has up his nose," Resolved pondered.

"In all likelihood, he wants every colonist above the age of five to take up arms against the English. In this manner we should defend ourselves, for we know that there are five or ten Englishmen to every good Dutchman. Methinks he would persuade you thus."

"I do not believe that the English council wishes to go to war," Resolved said, "nor will I have us move from our good house tomorrow morning to the village of New Haarlem as you would have us all do. If I can believe the word of Philip Calvert, and after all, he is the half-brother to Lord Baltimore, those Englishmen who lived this many years in America would see a peaceful settlement.

"At St. Mary's City, and again at Culvert's Rest Manor, and at Mulberry Grove, the same sentiment was expressed to us: that we men of the colonial land should find a way to resolve these border disputes. We must do a business of useful trade between the colonies.

"Remember, sweet wife, that Charles, who will be the third Lord Baltimore when his father, Cecil dies, is the first to live in the colony founded by his ancestors. He loves this land and would have peace. Thus, I have reported to our good Director Stuyvesant."

Tennake shook her head in disbelief. "One day you bitterly curse the English as sleeping enemies, and the next day they be an enemy that sleeps as angels in repose," Tennake whispered.

"But Tenny, haven't you taught me that men can be sinners one day, yet humble God-fearing men another?"

"Ah, I see. Well, on the morrow my words may be the kinder, but today I am feeling tired and wishing that we could be left alone and not concern ourselves with these English troublemakers.

"We were left alone many a time to fight the savages and wash the blood from our hands after we buried the victims of those wars. We were left alone to wipe the sweat from our brows after working from dawn till dusk six days a week. We were left alone to hear our belly growl when our ships filled with needed goods did not arrive. And now, our Fatherland chooses to leave us alone without a proper supply of soldiers to protect us from these English robbers."

Bitter tears squeezed out of Tennake's wide blue eyes, clouding her vision. "I know that you are more disgusted with the English than you will speak of," she said.

"Yes," Resolved replied, "many of them in and around our beloved New Amsterdam have become clever story tellers. Our own English settlers in New Netherlands are worse for the want of war than the English Catholics in Maryland, and the Dutch are being blamed by the English for all the Indian troubles which they have brought upon themselves.

"Only yesterday while in Pieterson's Tavern, I overheard a story being told by Captain Wikx, as it was told to him by Mr. Bateman, who in turn had heard it from Mr. Wright, the Indian Interpreter. It is claimed that the war raging between the English and the Indians of Delaware Bay, was caused by a Dutchman who incited the savages.

"He said that an Indian met a Dutchman in the Whorekill and told him that he intended to kill a Dutchman because his father had been slain by one. The Dutchman replied that the Indian's father had been killed by an Englishman and not by a Dutchman, and he should therefore seek his revenge on the English who had brought them evil.

"The Indian sought his revenge upon the English and they suspect that the Dutch furnished the gunpowder, ball, and guns. I asked Captain Wikx if anyone could testify to this matter but not a soul could."

Sadly, Tennake looked up into his face. "I grow so tired, Resolved. I am tired of the bad behavior of men be they English, Dutch, or Indian. Will this river filled with our children's blood never stop flowing?"

"No, no. Do not shed any more tears, sweet wife."

Hearing her mother's sobs, Cornelia began to cry, while six-year-old Barent, who had been playing a game on the floor using sheep anklebones, looked up at his mother with concern.

Resolved patted Tennake's shoulder and kissed her forehead. "Console yourself with the pleasant thought that I will be burdened with tasks every hour of the day. I fear that I will resemble a chicken that has lost its head."

Tennake tried to smile.

"Better still, think about the horse race soon to begin," Resolved continued. "The children have spoken of nothing else for the past many weeks. William will race, and Rebecca too, unless you tie the girl to the bedpost. Dry your tears, woman."

A little after three o'clock Resolved left her for his appointment with Director Stuyvesant. By the time Sarah returned from Ann Hendrickson's house with Aeltie and Rebecca, Tennake had composed herself.

Resolved was right. They would all go on somehow.

SIXTEEN

A diverse spectrum of color crowned the tall masts of vessel upon vessel sailing into the bustling harbor at New Amsterdam. These ships brought a continuous flow of new settlers from every corner of the earth, blending individual ideas and traditions, and creating a multinational town in the center of the wild men's ancient world unlike any other civilization to be found around the globe in the year 1663.

Local native Indians who roamed curiously through the streets of the city were but a small part of the colonists' daily concerns. The settlers traded freely with them, allowing the wild men to cheaply obtain the European goods to which they were quickly becoming accustomed. Every shop owner bid against his neighbor for the natives' catch of fish and wild game, while more than one Dutch iron pot fetched well-strung sewant or wampum beads from the coastal Indians. Some colonists would sell whatever they could to make a small profit in this cutthroat business environment.

Wampum was valued as highly by the Indians of New Netherlands as was gold to the Europeans, because in the northernmost part of the New Netherlands colony it was used regularly to pay for goods and services by both colonists and Indians.

Though against the law, and the cause of many conflicts, settlers would also sell their much sought after liquor to the wild men.

"One would be foolish not to accommodate the wild man's thirst," Jeremias Bout squealed the night he was arrested for his crime. Bout had sold liquor to five young braves on a Saturday, and at sunup the following day; the Swede Roelof Jansz's sloop was found burned in the harbor.

By nine o'clock Sunday night a neighbor had reported Bout's crime to the authorities and Resolved had put Bout in irons. Selling liquor to the savages was very profitable, while keeping the peace of New Amsterdam had become a relentless pursuit for those who were sworn to uphold the laws of the colony.

Although warfare had continued north of the city, the inhabitants of New Amsterdam lived harmoniously with their neighboring wild men, the Mohicans, the Manhattans, the Canarsees, and even some of the South River Indians who came to live outside of the wall of New Amsterdam so that they might be near the trade.

Most Lenape had been driven away from the outlying areas of New Amsterdam by the Mohawk, whose barbaric fighting services had been enlisted by Peter Stuyvesant in an effort to secure the colony.

Following his orders, the Dutch Company soldiers who sometimes joined forces with paid English soldiers, had burned Lenape villages. The few surviving clusters were destroyed by hired Mohawk who pushed undesirable natives further to the northwest lands beyond the Susquehanna River.

Although peace existed between the Europeans and the Indians, neither faction trusted the other. The Waldrons, as well as their white neighbors, carefully watched the "Praying Indians," as they were known, for although a wild man was baptized, everyone feared that the wildness never left his blood and the rite of holy waters could be forgotten before the sun rose on another day.

Tennake prayed for the wild people of New Netherlands every night, just as she prayed for herself and her family because she believed that salvation belonged to all. Yet despite her faith, she was ill at ease with her Indian neighbors' strange religious ceremonies, practiced even by those that had been baptized.

Summer nights, as she quietly called to God, she shuddered, covering her head with her quilted coverlet in a useless effort to silence their cryptic song during their "Feast of the Dead." Although Resolved lay motionless beside her, his breathing deep and rhythmic, she knew that he, too, heard the savage celebration that began at midnight with one of the leaders giving words of welcome to the ancestors of their dead. It frightened Tennake that the crazed pagans believed the living, as well as the spirits of their ancestral dead, did cohabit within their village, which was but a few hundred feet from her sleeping children.

Although she felt it sinful to allow her thoughts to dwell upon such an evil practice, fearfully she wondered if the wild people made a potion that truly brought back the dead. Their howling dance went on until dawn, keeping all of New Amsterdam awake—with the exception of her children who slept soundly.

Perhaps guardian angels closed the children's ears and they did not fear the ruckus of the savages, since they played games with them in the streets.

Both eight-year-old Barent and his younger sister, Cornelia, fished in the kills beside the native children. Their father cautioned his children to be on their guard at all times, but allowed them these friendships because he believed it was necessary for them to know their enemies should they once again turn against them. Tennake doubted that her little ones understood their father's true meaning, for how could they distrust the native children with whom they had played ever since the time they were old enough to walk. Despite her own misgivings and the confusion of the world outside, she was grateful that prayer, grace and salvation all abided within the secure walls of her home on the Broadway, as well as within the breasts of her husband and children.

Resolved had instructed her to beware of all of the wild men, even those who boasted to be Dutch allies. He had insisted that barbarous savages, especially those of the Iroquois Nation, could turn on them all within a moment's breath.

When Tennake protested his severity against the heathen, her husband warned her not to look for another of God's miracles to save her children, for although the savages enjoyed the Dutch goods, they were merely serpents in their Garden of Eden. She must take care where she and their children walked in the garden, and make use of the good sense with which the Lord God had blessed her when she received the holy waters.

Over the years Resolved had made an effort to learn about the natives' history, faith, and customs. He wanted to pass along this knowledge to William who would eventually move to his wilderness post in the North Country. Jacques still faithfully tended their land prospect near the great Cayuga Falls, without the comforts of a wife by his side.

The Iroquois, with whom the Dutch had signed a treaty in the year 1643, fought and overcame the native tribes in the northern country. The heathen wars had continued for over twenty years and had eliminated hundreds of Huron, Tobaccos, Neutrals, and Erie who had once lived in the western part of the colony.

Resolved and Jacques remained steadfast in their friendship during this time, even though Dutch allies of the Iroquois killed many Jesuits and French who were in their path. This was an uncomfortable situation for many settlers, for many Dutch grandmothers' cuddled half-Dutch, half-French grandchildren, as well as those who were half-Dutch and half-English.

The New Netherlands colonists were assured their safety from the Iroquois by their Dutch government, which had secured their friendship through staunch trade; but Resolved assured his wife that the friendly Iroquois, if provoked, would attack the Dutch in the same fashion as the South River Indians at the time of the Peach Wars.

During the years following the Indian attack upon New Amsterdam, the Director established many harsh methods of control to protect the settlement from further attack. His pleas to the Company in Holland for more soldiers to protect the colonists had gone unanswered, because after losing their colony in Brazil, the Dutch West India Company was nearly bankrupt and could offer little assistance.

Previously, Stuyvesant had used public monies raised through fines and taxes upon incoming cargo to pay English soldiers as well as Iroquois for their help. He felt, however, that the issue of possible attack had not been fully put to rest, and so with the help of two burgomasters he decreed that the town of New Amsterdam would hold captive within the Fort, Indian children seized from the South River region. At the first threat of hostile attacks, soldiers were instructed to slit the throats of every child.

Much to the annoyance of Resolved and other officials who followed the orders of their leader without question, Tennake and many other women protested this plan outside of St. Nicholas church one afternoon after the service. Resolved, who defended Director Stuyvesant's strategy, insisting that this was the best way to gain a peace from the wild men, gravely admonished the women to keep silent upon such matters which did not concern them.

However, Ann Hendrickson and Tennake regarded the use of small captive innocents as sacrificial pawns, very barbaric. Within the walls of their homes they gave their husbands no peace upon the matter.

"What manner of peace can be made under a bloody banner?" Tennake privately asked her husband.

Barbaric or not, Resolved's orders were firm and he cared not to hear of the women's tender feelings toward those at whose hands their own people had suffered over the years.

Tennake wanted to believe that some imaginative action would bring an end to the blood that poisoned the streams of New Netherland's outlands, but she had heard of the terrible fate of the wild men who had run from their burning villages. She knew that many had been massacred and she recalled the faces of those who were returned to New Amsterdam in shackles.

Many of the prisoners were children barely three years old, and Tennake had wept when she saw them dragged through the streets, their ropes so tightly bound around their tiny wrists that the twine was soaked red. She was not alone in her outrage, for many of the townspeople, both men and women, turned their heads away in disgust as Company soldiers, the Sheriff, and the Assistant Sheriff carried out their duty.

There were those, however, who jeered at the wild children and spit upon them as they passed. Many, who in the past had lost children of their own, knew of the wild men's love for their own children, and it was a valuable asset of which Director Stuyvesant would make use.

While it was generally agreed that the Indian was lazy and made a poorer worker than the Negro, they were forced to work in the Company's farm fields, warehouse and mills, while the owners of the breweries, specifically the burgomaster's brewery, received abundant free labor.

Joseph wrote a letter to Tennake's brother in the homeland stating that he believed that these Lenape captives, who stubbornly resisted the lash, would rather die than be lorded over.

Joseph also spoke against their enslavement, voicing his concerns to Resolved many times, but his brother argued that if he did not keep quiet; their whole family would be in a boiling kettle in the center of the Common.

Many of the Indians became ill very quickly and several died within the first few months of captivity. Now, some who had been in favor of holding the captives changed their minds, saying that their Negro slaves were a much stronger breed. But the debate continued and many other colonists insisted that these Indians provided cost-free labor with no financial risk, while Negroes were expensive to purchase.

Although many Christians did not agree with the reasoning of those who made use of the captive children, they all agreed that the children's imprisonment offered colonists an opportunity to save their little souls.

Within a few weeks Tennake and Ann Hendrickson gained an audience with Peter Stuyvesant's sister, a Godly pious woman, who at one time pleaded leniency to her brother, the Director General, on behalf of a Quaker prisoner; and therefore, Tennake believed she would be sympathetic to their concerns. She was known for her kindness, and Tennake and Ann begged her to intercede with the

Director, allowing them to hold a school on Sunday afternoons at the home of Mistress Ann who would instruct the captive children in the true faith of Christ.

Eight other Calvinist women who devoutly believed that God had spared Tennake during the attack upon their city—and later Ann Hendrickson, who surely had been brought back from the vapors of death for a purpose—accompanied them to the great house that afternoon.

Henry, Ann Hendrickson's driver, drove the two women to Peter Stuyvesant's manor house where upon arriving Ann was polite but insistent that the Indian children learn their Ten Commandments and be baptized as soon as possible. Before fifteen minutes had passed, the Director's wife, Judith Stuyvesant, who sat rigidly beside her widowed sister-in-law, had been moved to tears, promising that they would speak to Peter Stuyvesant that night.

The Director General agreed that there was a spiritual obligation to be shared by the members of their church toward his young prisoners; and being a pious man, he did not want to be noted to posterity as the one who kept Christianity from the savages.

However, it had taken three days of Dominie Drisius' preaching and Judith Stuyvesant's pleading before Peter Stuyvesant gave up his final objections. He argued that all good intentions and diligent work of the women might prove to be fruitless. His family argued that neglect would be more unpopular since, as his wife reminded him, it was the wish of his superiors in Holland that he show a policy of tolerance in all matters. Such a goodly gesture toward the savage children would most certainly impress the minds of those to whom he had sworn allegiance in Fatherland.

The following day, both Ann and Tennake received a dispatch from Judith Stuyvesant with instructions that the Indian children be schooled in the true faith; their lessons would be taught Sunday afternoons following the second service at St. Nicholas. The women would be allowed to use the religious books that were used to teach their own Dutch children.

Initially, Resolved had not been pleased with his wife's persistence, but upon seeing the personal interest that Peter Stuyvesant had taken in the matter, her husband had a sudden change of heart and was greatly flattered that the Director would call upon his wife to perform such a noble task.

Roughly escorted by Company soldiers, the children arrived together in one long line, with their wrists tied firmly so as to be certain that none ran away into the wilderness lands beyond the wall. At the conclusion of each lesson, they were returned to the barn housing the Company's tobacco and oxen.

When night fell on the Sabbath day, the captives slept on hay-strewn dirt floors beside the animals. After many weeks of lessons about Christ, a cold October wind began to blow through the cracks in the side of the plank walls of the barn. Some of the women took pity on the orphans and sent their old quilts to cover them in the damp of the night.

After a few weeks, Tennake and Ann began to notice festering sores and bruises upon the children's arms and legs, derived from what they believed to be cruel and unnecessary treatment of their students. Tennake was convinced that those responsible for the abuse would burn in hell; but the thought of their future demise did little to sooth the pain she felt in her bosom each time she looked at the sores upon the bodies of these frail children.

She complained bitterly to Resolved. After all, he was the Assistant Sheriff of the city, and could surely speak a word to the Director on their behalf.

"They are barely more than babes, Resolved, some our Cornelia's age. The Director's soldiers in whose charge these tender souls have been placed are unfit to care for hogs.

"I have been told that Captain Burmham served under Director Keift and makes no pretense about hating all Indians. He brags of playing games in the streets of New Amsterdam with the severed heads of his past conquests, and laughs when recalling the fate of a frantic Indian woman while she tried to save her drowning infant that had been tossed into the river for sport.

"I beg you to investigate these wolves who pretend to be lambs, for I know that even the most hardened heart of an honorable man would soften to see these children," Tennake pled tearfully.

Resolved held no remorse in keeping these children of the enemy as beneficial hostages, but Tennake continued to plead with him on the children's behalf. After he inspected the arms of two of the young girls, he softened and became silent in disgust. Afterward, he went to Nicasius de Sille, the chief Sheriff of New Amsterdam, bidding him inspect the condition of the children.

At first, the Sheriff was hesitant to interfere with the duty of the Company soldiers, but after one of the Indian girls was mysteriously found dead in back of Jon Hooten's barn, Stuyvesant himself called upon Captain Van Neer who was in charge of the captives to make an accounting. Director Stuyvesant ordered that the prisoners be treated fairly or he would have those responsible for the children's wounds, in chains. After that, the children were put under the direct care of the Dominie and housed at night at the quarters of the Company Negroes.

A year passed and the policy of holding Indian children was abandoned. However, few would have been returned to relatives. The people of their tribe had been dispersed and their villages no longer existed.

Tennake was horrified upon hearing a rumor passed along to her through Sarah by a Company slave. He said that soldiers had come to their quarters during the middle of the night and taken away three young Indian boys. Sarah believed they were taken to one of the ships in the harbor and shipped to distant lands where they were sold for plantation work.

Later, when questioned, the soldiers guarding the Negroes quarters said they knew nothing of any missing children and no accounting for the children was made.

In the twelfth month of their captivity, there remained but a handful of young natives who had learned the Dutch language and customs and were well versed in the Holy Bible. With their homelands dispersed, these children had no other recourse but to remain in the city to work as servants for Company officials or in the houses of affluent Europeans.

One orphan Indian child who had been left behind, was given the name of Ruth, by Tennake. She was a small, frightened, shadow of a girl when Sarah brought her to Tennake, and although she had known Mistress Waldron as teacher on Sundays, she remained withdrawn from her, fearfully wrapping her tiny arms about Sarah's dark legs. Though Sarah assured the child that all was well, for weeks Ruth would not leave the skirt of the slave.

Slowly Tennake won her trust and began to give her daily lessons in the faith alongside her own children; but Tennake had no easy task convincing her husband that the child should remain in their household. Although he had originally approved of the plan, he had witnessed the uselessness of it all and now had an uneasy feeling about housing his wife's protégé under their roof.

However, after much pleading, Resolved relented and Ruth was allowed to stay permanently within their household as a house servant, but under the constant care and instruction of Sarah who would have full responsibility for the child. Sarah told her master that she would make a fine cook out of Ruth someday, and would teach the child all the secrets of her herbal garden. Whereupon she immediately put her to task beside Cornelia, making the copper pots shine.

Tennake came to love little Ruth, who was no more of a hostage or prisoner in the Waldron house than were her own children. Though Resolved had staunchly told Sarah to keep the child close, within three weeks of her arrival she began to sleep upon the same pallet with Aeltie and Rebecca, wedged between the two—a protected little sister.

Ruth thrived upon roasted meats and cookies in her new home, becoming quite plump. Within a year she spoke Dutch fluently and knew her prayers.

The Indian child was baptized in the year 1664.

SEVENTEEN

A determined Joseph struggled against the slippery, narrow mud-soaked path that connected Augustine Herrman's fine yellow brick manor house with his and his brother's modest properties along the Broadway.

The thick black storm clouds that brought a nourishing downpour during the morning hours had disappeared by noon. Now, the musky smell of wet pine bark and the sweet fragrance of the June sassafras that straddled this woodsy trail, known commonly to neighboring families as "Sarah's Lane," pleasantly filled the air.

Joseph had been awake all night thoughtfully considering what he felt would be the most delicate conversation of his life. Joseph avoided the front entrance of the Herrman house, so as not to be intercepted by bothersome, unnecessary conversations that most assuredly would occur along the frequently traveled Broadway road. He yearned to put his awkward questions to Augustine Herrman as soon as possible, thereby putting an end to his constant painful anxiety.

Joseph Waldron, unlike many fellow Dutchmen residing in New Netherlands, had never longed to return to Fatherland. His work was regularly sought after by officials in the colony and though he was not a wealthy man, he was comfortable. He had found a new homeland.

Among his many friends, the one man he most admired was Augustine Herrman. After all these years in the city of New Amsterdam, Joseph had come to rely upon his friendship with the jovial successful surveyor. Their relationship blossomed into a strong bond of kinship as they discovered their mutual love of poetry and paintings while traveling to Maryland in 1660. Both delighted in the splendid colorful works of art, which illuminated the walls of wealthy Catholic noblemen.

Today, Joseph hoped that he would find the plump master of the Herrman house in an agreeable mood. He knew that Augustine took pleasure in confining himself to the perimeter of his home on Sunday afternoons. After Augustine had endured Minister Drisius' three-hour service at St. Nicholas and properly renewed his fragile soul, he could bask in the satisfaction that came from his profession of Calvinist theology.

With his soul shining as brilliantly as a newly baptized babe, this Hollander would be enjoying the true clarity of the bright daylight hours amid the companionship of his easel and canvas. Afternoons such as this, the wealthy owner of the tobacco warehouse could be heard joyously singing the psalms as he matched his uniquely mixed paints to brush and then to canvas, capturing the ongoing sequential scenes of life upon the Broadway in New Amsterdam.

Joseph anticipated that Mr. Herrman, who had also managed to remain a bachelor, would be passionately immersed in the ambiance of his own very intimate world. His illustrations were, as Mr. Herrman jested adamantly, "a most satisfying mistress who never gave him troubles."

"If only I could be as light of heart as he," Joseph sighed out loud, the bones of his shoulders sagging as another wave of souring guilt washed over his tall slender frame.

He could see the outline of his friend's house, and he paused to breathe deeply once again of the sassafras. He hated to be manipulative, for he found such behavior disreputable. The thought that he had stooped so low himself with one whom he considered his closest friend, grieved him deeply. It was important that he choose the most agreeable moment possible to approach the Dutchman.

Joseph needed answers to questions that left him sleepless for more months than he could recall. He wished to unburden his heavy heart that pounded during those frightening nights like a savage who maliciously beat a wrathful drum faster and faster until he could endure the terrifying sound in his head no longer.

Hating the blackness of the night and fearing the angel of death would come to his very bed to visit him, he took to lighting a candle and reading verse until the light of morn in hopes that the Lord Almighty would take pity on his wretched soul. But, alas, the Lord did not hear him and the shadows stayed by his side shouting, *Fornicator! Fornicator!*

Though the day was warm, a chill went through him, and as he sighed and ran his fingers through his long thinning brown hair, he began to walk slowly toward the house.

What had bound his affections so tightly to this forbidden fruit? For the first thirty-five years of his life he had walked a straight path. Where had the path separated? Surely, there be no hurt in his reading of poetry, or having the thoughtful concern of a master with student, nor an innocent discussion of herbal remedies with his brother's Negro servant woman.

When was the day that he had left that respected position of concerned master and entered the realm where he now stood, the primary character in the darkest of roles?

He thought of his lustful weakness in disgust. He had sinned, and though it did not have to be, should never have been, he had done this deed with Sarah most willingly at the time. He thought back over his sister-in-law Tennake's goodly ways and how she had tried to find him a proper match, but he would have none of her kindness. His eyes could see only Sarah.

Although men greatly outnumbered women in the colony of New Netherlands, he, who was fairly prosperous and in great demand by the maidens, was as yet unmarried. There had been many introductions to fine women in New Amsterdam, which would have allowed him to better his position, and any one of these would have been better for a man of his standing.

He had walked along the river with the lovely, gracious, Jane Holmes, widow of George Holmes who had been one of the earliest English settlers. Joseph knew that he should be flattered that such a creamy white dove would look his way, for he had never been one to hold any grievance against the English colonists of the town the way his brother had done in the past. There was not a man in the city that did not stop his work and cast his eye upon the young widow as she passed by.

But for all of her attributes, he could not muster up an interest in Jane Holmes, for when he had looked beyond her beauty and her properties, his eyes rested upon the smooth brown skin of his own brother's property. His forbidden uncontrollable desire for Sarah, a Negro wench, had placed him in this entangled web and was slowly driving him mad.

In recent months he had questioned all that he had previously thought to be solid and true. He no longer attended church services with his brother and family. Although to avoid any questioning of his faithless actions, it would have been easier for him to do so, but he could not abide the hypocrisy.

Resolved had prodded him to give reason for his sudden denial of the Lord Christ, because his turning away from all practice of their religion had left his family in a humiliating position in the community. Joseph would lay down his life for his older brother, but he could not give the reason.

Now that he had absented himself from Sunday services, he could not stand up and bear witness at the baptism of Van Curler's child, Ryckert, as he promised long before the child was born. His refusal to attend the rite of holy waters for the babe caused a sore rift between the child's father and himself, and had embarrassed his sister-in-law so grievously that she barely looked at him at mealtime.

Finally, Joseph gave up his usual seat at her table and dined alone in his shop or at the inn down the street.

How odd that with all her good intentions, Tennake had unknowingly further fanned the fires of hell for him. She sent her Negro servant woman to him with meals from her kitchen. Tears filled his eyes as he thought of Tennake's courage and constant goodness toward him. She had never failed to treat him with all the fairness and devotion of a sister, and he had repaid her kindness with betrayal.

Joseph's steps dragged as he recalled words of prayer, but they caught in his throat as he realized that prayer to the Lord meant to ask forgiveness for his sin of fornication.

He could not find regret within his heart for that which had been between Sarah and him. He sighed. He had become honest with himself in some small way for he understood that it was no longer lust alone that drove him, but the tender feelings that he possessed for Sarah. He dared not believe that he loved this woman and wished to keep her as his own. He knew only that he wanted to make a right of his wrongs and he sensed that his good friend Augustine, Sarah's prior owner, might be willing to help him.

Joseph stopped and leaned back against an ancient tall oak, his dark circled eyes following the one hundred-foot silver gray bark to the very top branches that seemed to touch the sky.

He recalled his terrible shame last spring when his young niece Rebecca had discovered her beloved Sarah lying on her pallet in a pool of blood, and the still tiny cold boy of her infant lying atop her breast. A terrified Rebecca had been unable to raise the limp unconscious woman, and immediately ran for her mother.

Joseph was certain that it was only through the grace of the Almighty Lord that Sarah had survived, though mercifully the issue of their sinful dalliance had not.

His chest tightened as he recalled how he had buried the babe in a grassy place deep in the woods some distance beyond the wall. No one in New Netherlands suspected that they were lovers. He had outwitted even the most tenacious Sheriff, his brother, and had found solace in the knowledge that Resolved would never have considered looking for a criminal within his own family.

Joseph banged his head hard against the bark of the tree trunk as he remembered Resolved's inquisition of the girl. Her master demanded with a fierce authority that she name the father of her dead child, but Sarah remained silently seated upon her stool before him.

His heart ached for his soft loyal Sarah as he watched his brother cruelly attempt to shake the truth from his slave. Joseph could bear the violence of his brother's wrath no longer, and although he had not admitted his part in the crime, he jumped forward to wipe away her tears with his sleeve and admonished Resolved for his hard-hearted manner.

Joseph knew as soon as the sharp words had left his lips that his indiscretion was a secret no longer, that suddenly all was clear to the investigative eye of the public officer.

Resolved was trembling with rage. His large muscular arms hung from his side, his hands opening and closing as if they were squeezing the breath from his brother's throat.

He put his face in front of Joseph. His words cut like a knife.

"Do you deny that this was of your doing?" he asked.

Joseph shook his head.

"The fault is mine," he said quietly.

Resolved slumped down into the barrel chair near the table. Sarah was sobbing and Joseph laid his hand gently upon her shoulder, an action that infuriated Resolved. He jumped to his feet. His face was bright red.

"Leave this house!" Resolved shouted.

He had banged his fist against the wall causing his wife's Dutch delftware to fall from the mantelpiece onto the floor and shatter into pieces.

Joseph did not speak with his brother for more than a month. During May, he had asked Resolved's forgiveness; but while the two tried to reconcile at Pieterson's Tavern he had further told his brother, after several glasses of beer, that Sarah should not be a part of his property, but a freed woman, whereunto he should have the right to take her as his good and proper wife.

Resolved had looked at him as if he had lost his wits. He retorted violently that perhaps Joseph should not be who he is either, that perhaps he should be the King of the whole colony. But they were all who they were. Once again they had parted in anger and had not spoken for the past seven weeks.

Joseph composed himself and briskly pushed away from the tall oak with a renewed burst of energy. The time had come to summon his courage and test his theory on Augustine.

As he approached the rear of the Herrman house, he saw old Daniel hunched over his budding plants in the garden. Augustine had purchased the Negro from Sam Dyckman after the latter's plantation in Brazil had failed. Joseph always suspected that his friend wanted to replace his fine carpenter who died more than a year ago. But, Daniel had not the gifted hands of Jacob, so Augustine had put the old man to the task of tending his large garden, while the slender fingers of "Dove" had taken over the duties of Jacob's magnificent clock.

Joseph believed that the aged Daniel and Gray Dove, an Esopus Indian woman, would be the only servants in attendance today. Yesterday, Sarah had told him that Augustine had lent out his slave, Moses, to Jeremias Van Rensselear, to assist the northern agent of the patroon in renovation work upon the manor house located in Rensselearwyck. Van Rensselear, who was short of workmen, was anxious to put his dwelling in order so that he could bring his soon-to-be Dutch bride over to suitable accommodations.

The thought of "Dove" warmed Joseph's weary heart. Augustine had named the woman Gray Dove, since he found her native name quite unsuitable to her peaceable, pleasing characteristics.

When Augustine had inquired how she had come to be known what she was called, she had replied in her native tongue that her father named her, "Place that Roars," because she had been born near a small fall of fresh water located on a branch of the great North River.

"Place that Roars," had spent three years in the service of the Director on his plantation near New Haarlem. She was a comely girl of sixteen or seventeen when she was acquired by her new master.

The young maiden, newly named "Gray Dove," was barely settled into the Herrman house when Augustine discarded the "Gray" part of her name declaring that there was little gray about his beautiful, spirited new acquisition who had proven to be a better cook than his former Negro, Sarah.

"Good afternoon to you, Sir," Daniel called out as he saw Joseph approaching. Joseph waved a greeting. He was sure that Daniel spoke to him in the Dutch tongue, but his speech was so brutalized with Portuguese and traces of his native African tongue that rarely could anyone understand him.

"Good afternoon to you, Dan," Joseph called back.

"Master Herrman?" Daniel asked anxiously as he struggled to his feet.

"No, no, I can find him. Stay to your duties," Joseph instructed.

Daniel bowed respectfully and slowly knelt down again into the dirt, happily resuming his work. At the same moment Dove appeared at the rear entrance waving Joseph forth. As Joseph passed her, Dove curtsied and pointed to Augustine who was engaged precisely as Joseph had expected.

Augustine looked up and smiled. "Have you come for a tank of Hendrickson's beer? Or perhaps some enlightened discourse that only two fortunate or unfortunate unmarried male souls may exchange on such a lovely peaceful day?"

Joseph folded his hands in front of him and walked toward the canvas. "I come for both, though today I will count us most fortunate of men, he responded examining Augustine's painting.

Augustine raised an eyebrow mischievously. "I shall agree with you," he said putting down his pallet and brush.

"Pray, go on with your work, Augustine."

"Nay, nay, Joseph, have no fear. The rains last night did little to cool the heat today, which hath come far too quickly since my colors seem to rebel against me this day. 'Tis best that I put this aside and refresh myself. Please come and be seated."

Joseph did as he was bid; sitting upon a stool by the magnificent wooden table that Jacob had made for Augustine so many years before. He recalled with both melancholy and joy the many times that he and Resolved's family had dined at this table during their early years in New Netherlands.

This afternoon the table was strewn with documents of official sorts, books, and many half completed sketches of Dove.

Within minutes Dove appeared with a pitcher of beer, then disappeared just as quickly—but not before Joseph noticed how lovely the girl looked in her gown of light blue silk.

Joseph had often admired the excellent portraits of this Indian maiden that lay propped up around the base of the floor. Augustine obviously took great pleasure in his subject and had painted her clad in various colored gowns, each canvas masterfully reflecting an accurate warm ambiance that Dove seemed to radiate whenever he had been in her company.

"I believe that you have come for more than the usual refreshment of body and soul today," Augustine said, rolling up two parchments that had been on the table, and stacking three books next to the documents. He then filled a goblet with beer for Joseph and one for himself.

Joseph smiled into his friend's eyes. "You are right. I seek your valued counsel," he replied.

"Your tone is more woeful than our good Dominie," Augustine observed. "Counsel, you say? Are you going to turn my beautiful afternoon into one of gloom and doom?" he winced.

"No gloom will shower upon you. I promise," Joseph replied. "However, I have problems to which I pray you will have solutions."

"Solutions? Heaven smile upon us. I confess, Joseph, your somber face has given me concern of late. What troubles you so, my friend? Are you still the brash young man who sang to the maids at Pieterson's on warm summer nights such as this one shall be?"

"That fellow is still here," Joseph said pointing to his heart.

"I doubt that this is true, but I promise I will assist you in any way that I can, for I wish only that your heart may not be so burdened."

Joseph stood up by the table and took a deep breath. "I am considering a bid for the purchase of my brother's house servant," he blurted out.

"I would assume that you speak of Sarah, for I would not know what you would need of little Ruth," Augustine said softly.

"Yes, I speak of Sarah, and well you know that Ruth is not a servant," Joseph replied.

Augustine cleared his throat.

"I have wondered how you have survived so long without obtaining an indentured woman or a good slave, for a man may do without a wife, but not a woman. If you pick the right time, you can purchase a Negro for a fair price before all the good ones are grabbed by English agents and promptly shipped off to the Virginia Colony."

"Augustine, I have no use for a woman picked from the ships that arrive. I would make my bid for Sarah," Joseph interrupted.

"Your sister-in-law will throw her pot at you when she hears you want to purchase her Sarah; and I can well understand her wishing to do so.

"I myself felt as if I had cut off my arm when I let her go and only agreed to the arrangement because I was convinced that Mistress Tennake would be wailing every night to her husband to take her back to her mother and father in Holland. So, I cut off my arm, but gained a fist full of Waldron Dutchies to hold in my good hand," Augustine said merrily.

"You were generous from the beginning," Joseph said quietly.

"You will never get Sarah," Augustine said with sudden flat somberness.

Joseph answered with renewed confidence. "Times are changing, Augustine, and Resolved is not one to hide his head in the sand. He sees that the English may, at any day, be upon us and he vows not to live in a city under an English governor. Already he makes his plan for that day as he swears he'll never be caught with his breeches down as he was in Brazil."

Augustine glanced at the documents on his table. "We are not dead in the water yet," he responded.

"No, not as yet. Please God, we will never face such treachery, though my brother is leaving nothing to chance. He has applied to purchase more lots in the village of New Haarlem. Although I know that if he continues to stretch himself this way and falls dead, there will be no money to take care of his widow since every piece of property he owns would have to be sold off to pay his debts. He is in need of funds, and I am in need of a housemaid and a cook. You see, it would be a proper barter."

"Ah," Augustine said, "it sounds to me that you have already worked out your plan most carefully. Perhaps you could catch this fish, if he were not already such a sly old shark!"

Joseph breathed a sigh.

"I plan to cautiously approach my sister-in-law, first. I will tell her, once again, that I feel I have been a burden to her long enough.

God knows this is a truth, Augustine. I should be about my own person, and since I have been unable to find a suitable wife, I am forced to find a good servant to run my house.

"I will remind her that if her husband finds himself in need financially, he may well be forced to sell his slave to the highest bidder, and it would be better for Sarah if she came into my service rather than go to the hands of strangers. Believe me; my words will put an understanding spirit within her."

Augustine's eyes twinkled brightly. "Come now, Joseph. I have noticed that Mistress Tennake hardly speaks to you anymore. However, I must say that such a situation would interest me. It will be amusing to watch as you crawl upon your belly before your sister-in-law. I say, beware of the pot," Augustine chuckled.

Joseph smiled wanly.

"Before I make my offer for Sarah, I have questions only you could answer since you were Sarah's first owner."

"Ah, now comes the root of this discourse."

"I have hesitated many times to approach you, Augustine, because as you know, I am not a man to intrude into one's private affairs as I cannot tolerate such; but now I feel I must ask questions regarding the girl's past. I hope you will not reproach me for my curiosity about her," Joseph said politely.

Augustine drank down half a tankard with one swallow. He belched loudly. "Pray speak! You leave my head wandering in circles! Ask what you wish," he said with the wave of his arm.

"Yes, I come to —" Joseph began.

"I was not Sarah's first owner as you seem to believe," Augustine interrupted. "My uncle was her first master, but pray do go on."

"Your uncle?" Joseph half whispered to himself.

"Yes." stated Augustine, tersely.

"Augustine, Sarah has told me that she is half white," Joseph blurted out. "She has said that she learned this from the Negro, Dorothy. Do you know if this be a truth?"

Augustine placed his drink upon the table, folded his hands together, and sat up straight in his chair much with the same air of contemplated dignity that Joseph had seen the Director Stuyvesant assume while attending services at St. Nicholas.

"Sarah has told you that she has white blood flowing through her veins?" Augustine's gaze had become curiously stern.

"Yes," Joseph replied.

The elder man's full lips thinned as he spoke. "There are many babe's running all over this island that are of mixed blood. What of it?"

Joseph was taken aback by the unfamiliar frigid tone of voice. "I have no interest in the others," he responded, looking down at the clean white sand sprinkled upon the plank floor.

Augustine breathed a sigh. "I understand your needs more than you would ever know, Joseph; so I will tell you the story of Sarah's lineage whilst the tale be for your ears only. I will tell you once, and we will then never speak of it again, for should you ask me I will deny this conversation. I offer you this truth as a gift of our friendship."

Joseph nodded and was silent.

"My uncle bought a Negro woman who he called Judah, from a Dutch slaver that had arrived off our shores direct from the African coast. She was only a young girl of fourteen or fifteen when he made his bid for her. He took her to his wife with all good and pure intentions as a gift, though I am sure that many tongues curled as his cart passed them with this maiden cargo.

"The African woman was a fine looking Negro and made a good servant for her mistress. As you observe, Sarah is dark, but has the look of a dark Dutchman, and there is not one of the old folk who did not believe that my uncle was her father and young Judah her mother. This is the tale that you would be told had you bribed old Peter Hayes with enough rum," Augustine paused and winked at Joseph.

"And would I have received value for the rum?" Joseph asked.

"You would have wasted a good drink, I fear."

"I did not recall that your uncle was married," Joseph said thoughtfully.

"Yes, my uncle was married." Augustine settled back in his chair. "My aunt was a strange creature, a tall, restless, wild-eyed woman, whom he found while visiting a friend on his plantation in the Islands. My uncle fell deeply in love with her and they married within a month's time. Once in New Amsterdam, she would disappear alone into the fields or woods for hours, despite the warnings of the elders.

"When first they married, they lived in Holland, in a small manor house outside of Rotterdam, and upon such absences, I have been told that my uncle would search for her into the dark hours. When finally he came upon her, she would emerge laughing, just as a small child might after a game of hide and seek. But my uncle had great patience with his wife, seeming to adore her.

"When he brought my Aunt Annetie to this country and we met again, she must have been a woman of thirty-five. I had not seen her since childhood for I had been in Brazil, joining my uncle here to make my fortune in this glorious land. And happy was I to have the assistance of my prosperous well-favored uncle.

"I found his wife to be as strange as I remembered her, although she hid her true nature from our neighbors, praise God, and was the perfect flower of a hostess in the eyes of all. However, her darkness was soon to cover us all.

"Late one Sunday afternoon, after having been gone for a very long time during which my uncle believed her to be resting within their bedchamber, she appeared at the edge of the woods, screaming violently.

"We all ran to meet her fearing that the savages had done her ill. Seeing her torn dress and her body covered with dirt, we imagined that this must be the truth of it; but when our party of kinsmen and servants reached her, she pulled my poor distraught uncle to herself and cried out that it was Nathan, the Negro, and not the savages who had violated her and beat her with his fists.

"Of course, my uncle was enraged. He vowed to all that he would have his revenge upon Nathan who lived in a cabin near to the river's edge. He swore that he would cut off the man's head with his own sword. Nathan, who at the time was not more than twenty-five years of age, was a freed man, a chimney sweep who also laid fine brick. He was, as I recall, timid as a lamb, although he had the chest and loins of a lion."

Augustine paused, and took a large swallow of beer.

"My uncle, seeing the condition of his wife, needed no urging from her to get his musket, his sword, and, together with his field hand, Jacob, proceed to hunt down this man. Within the hour Nathan was shot dead, his head cut off and his body left to rot in the field. All were warned against mentioning this incident to anyone.

"As for myself, I recalled my aunt's crazed wit and wondered who had been the beast of prey. My aunt was sorely damaged and her condition soon apparent to all. She, who had never been able to conceive, was now with child. She saw no one, save her slaves, during her confinement.

After the customary months had passed, she gave birth to a daughter who, although not as black as the Afrikaner my uncle had purchased, seemingly was the product of her tradgedy. The traumatic event must have been far too great for my aunt's wicked soul because three days after the birth, she poisoned herself."

Augustine drew in his breath and looked over at Joseph.

"This child was Sarah?" Joseph asked.

"Yes," Augustine replied. "Sarah is the child of Annetie Herrman".

Joseph put his hand to his forehead. The tale was one he could never have imagined. *Sarah was born of a white woman!"*

"There is more," Augustine said.

"The infant was given to my uncle's Negro cook, who had acted as midwife to my aunt. Cook came to raise Sarah as her own while my uncle sternly instructed her to keep her silence regarding the child's birth, or she would feel his blade.

"Uncle returned to Holland and not a white soul in New Netherlands knows that Sarah is not the child of my uncle's folly with his African slave girl, Judah.

"Few slaves knew our family secret, although I believe that Sarah knows, as I have reproached her severely for going to my Aunt Annetie's marker." Joseph had begun to pace the length of the room. "Augustine, how could you keep Sarah in bondage knowing full well that any child born to a Christian white woman must be free?" Joseph's voice was but a whisper.

Augustine smiled. "I am no fool, Joseph. I know you crave Sarah. If you take her to mistress, I would breathe easy knowing that she's in the care of a trusted friend." He grew silent and waited for Joseph's response.

Joseph had indeed heard the story that Augustine's uncle sired Sarah and he had come to Augustine for solid confirmation of this rumor. He believed that he would have an ally in his cause. But, Sarah had a white mother! Could Sarah not make a claim in the courts to freedom? For only those children born of Negro mothers must remain slaves.

Joseph's eyes pleaded with Augustine. "How can you keep your own cousin as a slave? Does your heart and soul not cry out to you for justice for this woman? You are kin to one another," he said.

"I do not lose sleep over the matter. Sarah has never been beaten, and I have always seen to her good care."

Joseph's face reddened as he thought of his brother's recent harsh treatment of Sarah. "But, she is kin to you," Joseph groaned.

"I am sorry, Joseph, but Sarah is a slave, the property of your own brother. Her father and her mother, as well as my tormented uncle, are all resting now, so there is no one to give testimony, save myself, and I will never do so.

"Do not look at me with those sad eyes of a young lover, Joseph. You are not the first or the last good Christian to fall to the sweet charm of a Negro wench. Take her quietly to your bed, and be done with these moral religious chains that bind you. Keep your wits about you. If you manage to purchase her from your brother, in good time you can give her freedom. That would be your right!" Augustine exclaimed.

"I would go away with her, Augustine, and have her to wife, as I cannot live as a fornicator. I will sin no more with Sarah. These were not my intentions as I came to you and I will not do so now that I know the truth."

Augustine narrowed his eyes.

"You have lost all your wits!" He paused, and then slowly asked, "You will not betray me with this mindless talk?"

"Nay, Augustine. I would never bring you the suffering that the truth would cause; but I beg you to speak for this woman's true rights. What harm can be done now that your kin are all dead?"

"I have my own reputation to consider," Augustine replied. "There will come a day when I might be fortunate enough to marry and I will not place such a black mark against my own unborn children.

"Do what is best for you, Joseph, but leave me apart from it all. If the woman is freed, she will still be one half Negro. Would you take to wife one of mixed blood and sire such children to inherit your good Dutch Bible? What good house would invite you to dine at their table with Sarah at your side as wife? Take heed, consider all before you make a bad stand," Augustine warned.

Joseph nodded and stood up, walking toward the door. Augustine followed.

At the entrance Joseph paused and turned toward the master of the house.

"Thank you for the fine brew and the talk," he said. Augustine nodded, placing a firm hand upon the younger man's shoulder.

Joseph wanted to say more, but turned away and passed through the front door onto the noisy Broadway. The heavy ornate door closed softly behind him.

Outside, he stood at the top of the stoop facing the Company orchard. He sighed deeply. He would consider everything he had just learned. All he needed was time enough to find a way to make Sarah his wife.

Inside, Augustine collapsed into a chair knowing he had shared but half a truth. His heart pounded as he recalled the last correspondence received from his uncle written only days before his soul pass on to the Almighty. In it he had confessed that his beloved wife had been the granddaughter of a Negro woman. He knew this when he married her. His uncle asked God to forgive him, for he had come to believe that poor Nathan had been unjustly accused. Sarah might well have been his child.

Sighing, Augustine closed his eyes. Long ago he had burned that letter.

EIGHTEEN

Resolved stood on New Amsterdam's wharf and watched as four well-gunned English frigates sailed toward his town. News of enemy approach had spread swiftly after farmers along the shoreline of Long Island had sighted the vessels; and now he and half the city stood near the tip of the Island of Manhattan frozen in terror.

The English royal brother of King Charlie had finally sent his soldiers to collect his gift.

As Resolved gazed out over the water, he felt the familiar presence of another by his side and turned around to meet the concerned deep blue eyes of his old friend, Augustine Hermann.

"It appears Richard Nicolls has come to claim his master's trophy," Augustine said quietly.

Resolved nodded in disgusted agreement. "I have been commanded to row out to his vessel and greet the English King's messenger come the morrow."

Augustine astutely observed the man who had once called New Netherlands, "a sweet pie ready to be sliced and eaten by any good Dutchman with a hearty appetite." He knew what was in Resolved's heart because the same rock pressed hard against his own.

"How considerate of our leader to send you on such a glorious mission," Augustine observed sarcastically.

"Augustine, I have been at death's doorway before, and you know me to be a man that did not run from the Spanish or the English, but I grow weary of the bloodshed upon bloodshed that does not leave us."

Augustine leaned closer. "Men are capable of nothing save their greed; but we also have had our share, have we not, my friend? I thought you would be down here with the rest. I have been looking all over for Joseph. Have you seen him?" he asked.

"Nay, I have not. We barely see him nowadays, yet my wife says that her brother-in-law nips at her heels like an unyielding wild goose. As for our greed, I know not what you speak of. I have worked honestly for nearly ten years for the position I hold in this colony, and now it is to be taken away before the light of another day."

"You do me injury, Resolved; I mean you no insult. I do not know what quarrel Tennake has with Joseph. But, perhaps your good wife is overcome with family since her brother has come to live among us. I am sure that she welcomed Johnannes with open arms, but his wife may have become a larger burden than she is big."

Resolved calmed himself.

"Forgive my bad temperament, old friend. You have an astute eye. My poor Tennake has much to bear. Her newly arrived sister-in-law, Betty, gives her little comfort. Methinks that Tennake holds her sharp words of retaliation with the spirit of the most glorious of God's holy angels." Resolved continued to watch the ships closing in upon them.

"Your wife is a fine woman," Augustine replied soothingly.

"Ah, Augustine, we've known that the English had a mind to plant their feet into our soil for many years, though knowledge of a wolf's presence does not make his fangs less sharp when tearing away the flesh."

Augustine touched Resolved's shoulder. "I feel as you, but we are at their mercy. We have barely two thousand colonists here, most of whom are women, children and slaves.

"We have received little fresh supply of gun powder from our uncaring Dutch government, and if we could find five hundred able men amongst us we would be fortunate, though they would be made to fight the enemy with sticks."

Resolved threw his hands into the air, speaking heatedly, almost in desperation:

"Methinks that the whole of Holland has made a grave mistake in letting this colony go the way of the English.

Our Director's hand could have fallen off his arm for all of the letters he has written home in the past begging for assistance."

Augustine nodded in agreement.

"Resolved, you and I know the heart of our leader has bled much these past weeks. The man neither eats nor sleeps since he received word last July that this invasion force was at Boston. He persists in keeping the news from his beloved children, so that he might give them another good day in the Dutch New Netherlands.

"What strength it must have taken to go about his duties at our horse race as if all were still golden; but I fear that history will treat him poorly and the blame for the failure of the colony shall fall upon his shoulders."

Resolved let out an audible sigh and continued loudly so that those standing nearby would hear.

"Peter Stuyvesant has done his best to shield the impending treachery from his children. 'Tis the high and mighty in Fatherland who have washed their hands of us all and who should be made accountable for what becomes of our babes."

Augustine turned toward the approaching ships. "Perhaps Pete Stuyvesant will be relieved to have this burden taken from him and happy to be left in peace to read his Bible and tend his garden," he commented thoughtfully.

"If the garden patch is still his to attend," Resolved replied.

Augustine smiled as the sunlight flickered playfully across the blade of his sword. "I doubt that the English will slaughter all her good Dutch, for who will be left for them to tax?"

Resolved hardly heard Augustine's words. "Pete did his best," he continued. "Our government should have treated King Charlie more kindly when he was tossed off his throne, but what good would have come of our open hearts. I always said you cannot trust any of them and Winthrop proved to be just another snake in the grass. Did he not?"

"A serpent of the worst kind," Augustine responded vaguely.

"To think that our Director gave Mr. Winthrop our hospitality and secured his ship's passage to London," Resolved growled, smashing his fist into the open palm of his other hand.

"Still, one cannot fail to be amused," Augustine persisted. "I myself ate with Winthrop whilst he was in New Amsterdam. He was a meek man who professed friendship as he stuffed our large oysters into his mouth. In truth, the wolf's sharp teeth clung to another of King Charlie's grants: a pretty parchment that claims all the shore land from Connecticut to the Delaware belongs to the English King. So much for the Treaty of Hartford."

"To hell with the English!" A woman in the crowd shouted. Soon many were echoing her words.

Resolved shook his head as he looked over the angry mob around them, and shouted,

"We can no longer weep for our misfortune. Listen to me! We must assemble our wits; cast a watchful eye upon the enemy and board up our windows. Before we lament, let us see what terms the English Captain will offer. You all know that I am no coward, but neither am I foolhardy. It is better to submit to the enemy and live to fight another time."

"'Tis best!" Augustine agreed, facing the crowd.

The frightened unhappy colonists continued to grumble while Resolved turned to leave the wharf.

"I must leave you now, Augustine, to look upon the welfare of my family and advise them of my orders; although no one living on this island can be blind to what is at hand. God save us all. What a terrible life have I brought upon my good wife and children."

"Go to your wife, Resolved. We will talk again upon the eve."

As Resolved proceeded hastily through the crowds toward the Broadway, he was stopped many times by fearful friends and neighbors who questioned him for further information regarding the advancing enemy. At each encounter Resolved assured them that he knew no more than they and begged them to return to their homes and await further orders.

He walked up the hill and neared the Fort, where the Dominie was attempting to clear the street of his nervous flock. But few would listen to his words. Resolved left the minister behind, soon passing a garrison of the Company's soldiers which had begun to brutishly disperse a mob.

Finally, he left the commotion behind and arrived at his house where he found his Tenny sitting very still atop the first step of their stoop with her hands folded into her apron. Her eyes were red and swollen from tears which she tried to wipe away as she saw her husband approach.

Despair has already overcome her, he thought. He was ashamed to see her thus and thanked God that her father and mother were dead, so they would never know to what ruin he had brought their daughter.

He told himself that he should have remained a widower, or better still, never married at all because had he remained a single man as his brother had, both his wives would now be safe in the arms of Fatherland. His ambitions would see them all in their graves. He ran up the steps, taking two at a time to get to her.

"Come now, wife," he said sternly. "Does the seasoned woman who defied the heathen wild men whilst still a bride, now weep at the mere thought of a Christian English fleet? You must be a staunch mother in front of your children now, as you have been in the past!" He wiped her eyes with his thumb as he spoke.

Tennake stared at the porch steps. "Methinks that you have mistook my sentiment. I have no fear of the Englishmen!" she said bitterly.

Resolved stood to his full height. He looked down at her in amazement and hoped that the babe that grew within her did not cause her grief.

"You are in pain? Does the child come before his time?" he asked nervously.

"No, husband," she said faintly.

"Has a dark angel visited you while you slept last night?"

Tenny began to sob. "Our dark angel has flown away from us," she said.

"Woman, of what do you speak? I have little patience left today!"

She held out her arm, opening her hand to reveal a crushed piece of parchment. "Read," she commanded.

Resolved wrinkled his brow in confusion as he took what looked to be a letter. He groaned as he began to read.

The communication was from his brother, Joseph:

"I have conveyed to you my house on Broadway and all my possessions therein, save a few books that I could not leave behind.

"In exchange for said property, I am taking Sarah. We are leaving by boat during the night with the help of native friends who will convey us safely far into the North Country and then to the land of the Erie Indians, the great plains of the west where Jim Becker took his family last year. Do not be concerned for us as I have taken enough good wampum, and all that I have saved over the last nine years.

I have no idea what pursuit I will undertake, but feel confident that I am well prepared to make another life for Sarah, who at my side shall be my greatest asset. Most regretfully, I will never see you again, but I realize now that we would not be able to live there in peace. It is difficult enough living among the Dutch, but life would be impossible for Sarah and me when the English come, because they are twice as hard on the Negroes as are the Dutch.

The lot of land I purchased in New Haarlem, I convey to young Will as a gift for his wedding to Mistress Stoutenburgh. May they, and all of you, live long and safe."

"Damn him," Resolved cursed. Although tears were now forcing themselves into his eyes also, he quickly recovered himself. "He would choose to depart at such a time," he said angrily.

Tennake sighed, stood up, and smoothed her apron over her small rounded belly.

"I will miss my Sarah sorely," she said trying to steady her voice. "As for your brother, you need not curse him for he has damned himself, I fear." She walked back into their house with her husband.

"God spare me from my kin who thinks only with his heart," he said under his breath.

"Did you speak to me, father?" Aeltie asked demurely looking up from her needlepoint, seemingly unaware of any impending danger.

"No, child, 'tis the mutterings of your old father," he said.

Tennake looked at the three children in the room. "Aeltie," she said tenderly, "take Ruth and Cornelia out yonder. Methinks I can use some of the squash from our garden for our meal." Aeltie obediently put down her work and gathered up her sisters to do as she was bid.

As they left, Tennake turned to Resolved.

"You mistake Joseph's sentiment as well as mine. I, too, thought that your brother was driven by lust, but had his feelings for our Sarah not been so strong, he would have composed himself and remained with us here. Joseph was never a warrior, and the wilderness does not suit him.

"I am most certain that he would have preferred to live near his family and the comfort of his church, but his torment must have become so great that he could not so much as enter God's holy house within these last weeks. Although he should never have taken Sarah from us, what a terrible burden he must have carried within his heart."

Her husband shook his head. "I will never understand his feelings. Why could the comely Deborah VandenBergh not please him? Mistress VandenBergh is accomplished in verse, as is my brother. She is a pious goodly woman and would have made a good suitable wife for him."

"The fault of Joseph's folly must rest upon my shoulders, Tennake. After all the trouble Sarah caused us, it was in my heart to sell her to one of the farmers along the South River; but you and Augustine would have despaired and my own heart would have been heavy. However, there was no time to be wasted on domestic matters with the country in turmoil from the English and the recent Indian disputes up north.

"I put it off and hoped that good order would prevail until I had returned from Fort Orange. When I returned and saw my brother's feelings had not changed, I had decided, despite the pain that it would cause, that Sarah must be put out of our house."

The color drained from Tennake's face.

"I take back to my breast what I have thus spoken to you," she said. "Methinks that I would wish that the angels have protected Sarah from the unhappy life that you planned to give her."

Resolved put his hands on her shoulders. "A husband must do what he feels is right."

"Yes, and this is what Joseph has done, is it not?" Tennake asked tearfully.

"He should have come to me. I am the eldest," Resolved said softly.

"And you would have cursed him and bellowed your displeasure."

Seeing the sadness in her husband's face, her voice softened as she continued.

"I cannot fault you alone for all that has happened, for if my servant had wished to remain with me, she would have asked my protection. If she would give herself to your brother and risk the grasp of Satan rather than place her trust in the hands of her master or her mistress, then we are both to blame.

"I especially have failed Sarah and our good family, because I should have seen the hurt that bloomed in front of me. I must ask the Lord Almighty's forgiveness for turning my back upon this responsibility and ignoring my duty as mistress of this house!" Tears began to stream down her cheeks once again.

Resolved put his arms around his wife and pulled her close. "Methinks that we should rebuke each other no further. They are gone. Let us pray to Jesus Christ for their salvation and may the Almighty protect them from hostile savages."

Tennake composed herself. "I will pray for them both every day for the rest of my life," she said.

"Did you see Rebecca?" Resolved asked.

"Rebecca was to home and gone again the hour before you returned."

"I did not see her," Resolved said.

"She hath told me that four English ships sit in our harbor." Tennake looked into Resolved's eyes. "She went to find her brothers."

"It is good that the English come," Resolved replied. "I am sick of waiting for them."

"What will become of us now that they have come?"

"Come the morrow, I will go to the enemy and learn the answer to your questions, sweet wife," Resolved answered, forcing a laugh.

"Why must you be the one to go?" Tennake's voice was little more than a whisper.

"I have gone to far more dangerous waters."

Tennake straightened her cap. "If I were to lose you, I, too, would be lost, for I would then be under the care of my brother and Betty who would make my life a worse plight than any my Sarah will ever encounter with the savages of the wilderness."

"Come, wife. Here are your vegetables," he said as Aeltie returned with a basket. "Tonight I wish you to prepare a feast for us all."

Tennake looked into her basket of beans and squash. *"A last supper,"* she murmured under her breath as she took the basket from her daughter and returned to the protective walls of her kitchen.

The next morning, at seven o'clock, Resolved Waldron rowed out to ask Colonel Richard Nicholls to declare his intentions. A tall, distinguished looking man with kindly eyes, Nicholls had welcomed Resolved aboard his ship. But his words were sharp and to the point.

"My intentions are that all of the Manhattans, forts, towns, and other such places of Dutch strength, surrender to our English King, whose right and title to these parts of North America was assured when John Cabot claimed this land for England in the year of Our Lord 1497."

Nicolls handed the sealed document containing conditions of surrender to Resolved.

"And the terms of such a surrender?" Resolved asked boldly.

"If a peaceful surrender is made, not one of you will die in your city. All will be spared the blade and allowed to keep their wealth. I have been instructed by James, Duke of York and Albany, to treat your people with generosity and all kindness. You may keep your language and your religion; but of course, all freed men will be expected to take the oath of allegiance to His Royal Majesty, King Charles II."

Resolved bowed low to Nicolls. "I will convey your King's terms to His Honor, our Director General, Peter Stuyvesant, in all haste."

Resolved departed the English ship and rowed back to the shore where the Director and his Burgomasters awaited Nicolls' dispatch. When Stuyvesant read the Englishman's message he was enraged and tore the document to shreds, stuffing the parchment into his mouth, cursing Nicolls, the Duke of York, and finally the English King himself.

"They can carry me to my grave before I give up my colony to those thieves," Stuyvesant shouted out to the horrified crowd that was now convinced that their leader had condemned them all to death by not accepting the terms. The enraged Director General turned on his one good heel and returned to his house, where he said he would pray upon the matter.

Later that afternoon, Tennake and the children were sitting about their table when Resolved walked through the door.

"What say the English?" Tennake asked anxiously.

"The terms are most liberal," Resolved replied dully.

Tennake stiffened. "Do the English give us our lives, whilst we are to be their slaves?"

"No, we may keep our property, our inheritance rights and we will be allowed direct trade with Holland for six months. Happily, we shall not be forced to accept the Pope's rights."

"So, we are to be happy, singing slaves."

William jumped up from his seat. "They have no right to us," he shouted. "We should fight, not lay down like a pack of restless dogs."

"We women can also fight," Rebecca cried out passionately. "Barent and I can handle a pistol as well as you or William."

"And I," Aeltie added, wanting to be included.

Resolved smiled proudly at his children. "Your staunch hearts warm my own soul," he said affectionately.

William observed his father curiously. "You feel the terms are liberal, but our Director wishes to make a fight of it?"

"Will, a petition for peaceful surrender has already been circulating among our people," Resolved replied gently.

"I will not sign such a document," William said stubbornly.

"Son, your courage is to be admired, but a fight would mean ruin for all of us. There are no less than three hundred and fifty armed soldiers aboard those vessels awaiting Nicolls' orders, and ten thousand more to be had should the man bid them come.

"Would you risk the lives of your mother and little sisters and brother? Is Dutch rule worth the dishonor of your sisters? If you choose not to sign the petition, I will not hold it against you, since you are nearly a man now and about to take a wife, but I will not hear talk of a fight again in my house. Perhaps we will all live to fight the English again, but for now we must accept what is inevitable."

"What will become of us all?" Tennake wondered.

"After the English come, we will no longer live in New Amsterdam. I will sign the document for the English King, but by God, I will not look across the street at an English plantation for the rest of my days, and I will not be lorded over," Resolved said in a commanding voice.

"New Haarlem?" Tennake asked.

Resolved gave her a warm smile of assurance.

"Yes, we will all go to New Haarlem just as soon as I sell our property here. Still, unlike Pete Stuyvesant, I would rather leave this place alive than be carried away stiff. If I were a man alone, then perhaps I should see it all differently. But I am not alone, thank God."

Tennake smiled.

"The village of Haarlem and the lands there about are very beautiful and seem especially sweet near to the hook of the river."

"I will stay in New Amsterdam," William said plainly. "The English will not force me out of our town."

Resolved faced his wife and looked knowingly, but did not mention the lot of land at New Haarlem that he would hold in his keeping for his son.

"If you wish to remain," Resolved stated, "I am sure you will not be alone since enough good Dutch families shall be of your same persuasion; and many have intermarried with the English, so an English King makes no difference to them."

"Were I a man, I would stay in New Amsterdam myself," Rebecca pouted.

"I would stay with you, Rebecca," six-year-old Cornelia declared.

"Though some may stay," Resolved reflected, "many will sell their properties and leave. Augustine has told me he will depart to his beloved St. Augustine's manor house on the river in Cecil County, Maryland. He will furnish his house with a wife, and while he has not told me her name, he has invited us all to the marriage feast to be held as soon as the maid accepts his proposal."

"Proposal," Tennake whispered to herself.

"I shall miss Augustine's merry wit," Resolved lamented.

Tennake soberly nodded her agreement. "Augustine is blessed to keep his wit during times such as these," she said. "If he is able, shall he sell all his properties in New Amsterdam?"

"No, we shall see Augustine again. Do not fret, wife."

Tennake stretched her arms across the table. She held Resolved's hand and that of their lovely gentle Aeltie. "We shall thank God for the good family and friends that we have, and pray to Him to send us more excellent neighbors. And we shall ask His protection and mercy for ourselves as well as those who have chosen to leave us."

Tears filled Aeltie's eyes. "Keep heart, daughter," Tennake said, pulling herself straight on her stool. "New Amsterdam is not so great a journey from New Haarlem. We shall come back to visit when we are permitted."

Tennake looked around the table at her fine family and felt a sense of peace wash over her. She had come to realize that this house was but a house, whilst home was now firmly rooted within her breast.

On September 7, 1664, the white flag was raised over the Old Dutch Fort. New York was born.

ACKNOWLEDGEMENTS

To begin, and most importantly, I'd like to thank my husband, Andrew, for his understanding support.

I remember Ivan Waldron, a kind gentleman, my father's cousin, who, without knowing it sowed the first seeds of inspiration many years ago.

Thanks to my daughter, Julie, a great technical right arm, and to my sister Joy, always in my corner.

I extend special thanks to Helen K. Hosier, for direction and editorial skills, but primarily for her belief in a unique story and my abilities as a writer to give it justice.

Heartfelt appreciation to Carol Kern and all those helpful hands at the Western Pocono Library, Broadheadsville, PA, and to the research folks at the Albany Institute of History & Art, Albany, New York, as well as The New York State Library, and the First Church, also at Albany.

Thanks, Florence Sullivan, Sue Mishler, Alison Rapin Plant and Shirley Eschbach for reading and encouraging me to continue.

Finally, I express my most sincere gratitude to Mr. Dick Ross, whose creative eye wrapped it all up - adding a shimmering luster to the lives of many forgotten souls.

-Gloria Waldron Hukle

About the Author....

Gloria Waldron Hukle, a native of New York State, is an eleventh generation American in the line of the Dutch Waldron family upon which the novel, MANHATTAN - SEEDS OF THE BIG APPLE is based.

She and her husband, a retired nuclear engineer, share their country home in Upstate New York with their two, seven year old sister dogs, Lou (Louise) and Bertie (Bertha).

A student of history, Gloria is at work on three more novels. Her goal is to bring awareness to a long forgotten segment in time, and to spotlight scores of brave unknown pioneers, the first immigrants, who contributed to laying down the true foundation of America long before the Revolutionary War.

Made in the USA
Middletown, DE
18 November 2017